Professional Writing for Lawyers

Professional Writing for Lawyers

SKILLS AND RESPONSIBILITIES

Margaret Z. Johns

CAROLINA ACADEMIC PRESS
Durham, North Carolina

ISBN 0-89089-804-9
LCCN 98-86436

CAROLINA ACADEMIC PRESS
700 Kent Street
Durham, North Carolina 27701
Telephone (919) 489-7486
Fax (919) 493-5668
www.cap-press.com

Printed in the United States of America

Contents

Acknowledgments

Many people deserve recognition for their contributions to this book, including many thoughtful and talented legal writing scholars. I've tried to acknowledge my debts to them in the footnotes and apologize for this violation of the rules of readable writing.

Let me also thank the teachers, teaching assistants, and students who have used these materials over the years and provided so many suggestions and insights. In this group, I am especially grateful to my friends Toni Bernhard and Lois Sherman. My research assistants, Nicole Isger and Bill Smith, helped with everything from content to proofreading. Their perspective as students and teaching assistants was especially valuable in helping me understand my audience. I also wish to thank Saralee Buck for reading the manuscript.

But above all I'm grateful to Dick Wydick, my teacher, colleague, and friend. He is simply the best.

Margaret Z. Johns
Davis, California
April, 1998

Professional
Writing
for
Lawyers

Chapter 1

Office Memorandum

Lawyers are writers. In your career, you will probably write more than a novelist.[1] In this book, you'll be cast in the role of a new associate learning many basic legal writing tasks. To understand the requirements of each project, you'll need first to understand the professional responsibilities that apply. In this chapter, we'll begin with the responsibilities that arise when a client asks you to predict how the law will resolve a problem. We'll then turn to some suggestions for efficient legal research. Finally, this chapter will introduce you to the legal document new associates most frequently write, the office memorandum.

Professional Responsibilities in Providing Legal Opinions

While some jurisdictions follow slightly different rules, many jurisdictions have adopted the American Bar Association's Model Rules of Professional Conduct as the minimum standards for the practice of law.[2] The ABA believes that the Model Rules "have

---

1. William L. Prosser, *English as She Is Wrote,* 7 J. LEGAL EDUC. 155–56 (1954).

2. In 1983, the American Bar Association adopted the MODEL RULES OF PROFESSIONAL CONDUCT [hereinafter MODEL RULES] which supplanted the MODEL CODE OF PROFESSIONAL RESPONSIBILITY adopted in 1970. The MODEL RULES have been amended nine times since their adoption, most recently in 1997. References in this chapter are to the current MODEL RULES. While the MODEL RULES have been adopted in most states, the CODE remains the law in several states including New York and Virginia. And some states have also promulgated their own standards including the CAL. R. PROF. CONDUCT.

proven to reflect, in the main, an effective approach to the resolution of many ethical issues that could serve the profession well into the next century."[3] For this reason, the Model Rules serve as a convenient starting point for learning professional responsibilities.

However, the Model Rules only begin the inquiry. First, because the Model Rules focus on disciplinary standards, they do not explore the aspirations of the profession which should also inform your ethical education. Second, since the adoption of the Model Rules in 1983, the American Law Institute has been developing the *Restatement (Third) of the Law Governing Lawyers* which reflects the thinking of prominent scholars, judges, and practitioners who have devoted a decade to the project.

The proposed *Restatement* goes beyond the Model Rules to address issues outside the context of disciplinary proceedings. The *Restatement* sets out the law governing lawyers' obligations and rights in eight categories including: the lawyer-client relationship; financial and property relationships between lawyers and clients; lawyer civil liability; confidential client information; representing clients in general; representing clients in litigation; and conflicts of interest. Much of this work is completed. As of May, 1997, the ALI had approved five of the proposed chapters.[4] Charles W. Wolfram, the Chief Reporter for the project, anticipates that a final vote on the remaining chapters will occur in 1999.[5]

We will turn to both these sources, the Model Rules and the *Restatement*, to introduce the fundamental rules governing a lawyer's professional responsibilities. But as you develop your own ethical compass, avoid the temptation to view professional responsibilities as narrowly defined rules for avoiding discipline and malpractice liability. To supplement these minimal standards, we'll also consider courtesy codes and professional guidelines voluntarily adopted by many bar associations to encourage the highest ethical standards in the practice of law.

Turning to our first assignment, a lawyer's responsibilities in providing a legal opinion derive from three fundamental duties: the

---

3. 13 ABA/BNA Law. Man. Prof. Conduct 140 (May 28, 1997).
4. *Id.* at 141.
5. *Id.*

duty of competence; the duty to the client as an advisor and advocate; and the duty to our justice system as an officer of the court. This section will briefly explain these duties.

Duty of competence

In performing every legal task, a lawyer has the duty of competence. According to the Model Rules, a lawyer must provide competent representation which "requires the legal knowledge, skill, thoroughness, and preparation reasonably necessary for the representation."[6] This obligation is mirrored in the *Restatement* which requires the lawyer to "act with reasonable competence and diligence."[7] As the *Restatement* comments explain, the lawyer must have "the appropriate knowledge, skills, time and professional qualifications" and must diligently perform the required services "including appropriate factual research, legal analysis, and exercise of professional judgment."[8]

A sobering ruling on this obligation was issued by the California Supreme Court when it held that an attorney's failure to research could lead to malpractice liability even if the research would not have produced an answer to the client's question.[9] In *Smith v. Lewis,* the attorney failed to perform even minimal research on an unsettled point of law. Specifically, a wife's divorce lawyer neglected to research her rights to her husband's pension. If the lawyer had researched the issue, he would have found no clear answer. The court held that even though the lawyer might have handled the case in exactly the same way if he had researched the issue, the attorney was still liable for malpractice. The court explained that an attorney owes the client a well-informed judgment, not an ignorant guess. Thus, if the law is clear and the attorney fails to research it, the attorney is liable. And the attorney is equally liable if the law is unresolved because "an attorney is expected to perform sufficient research to enable him to make an informed and intelligent

---

6. MODEL RULES, *supra* note 2, Rule 1.1.
7. RESTATEMENT (THIRD) OF THE LAW GOVERNING LAWYERS § 28(b) (Proposed Final Draft No. 1, 1996) [hereinafter RESTATEMENT].
8. *Id.* cmt. d.
9. Smith v. Lewis, 13 Cal. 3d 349, 530 P.2d 589, 118 Cal. Rptr. 621 (1975).

judgment."[10] The duty of competence requires lawyers to thoroughly research every problem. Inexperience is no excuse; a lawyer must either become competent in the law or arrange to work with someone who is competent.[11]

Duty to the client as an advisor and an advocate

In providing a legal opinion, a lawyer has duties to the client as both an advisor and an advocate. As an advisor, a lawyer is required to keep the client informed and to help the client make informed decisions.[12] To ensure that the client is well informed, the lawyer must objectively evaluate the legal problem and explain the results to the client. Biased research and a slanted analysis may please the client temporarily but will ultimately mislead the client and prove to be a disservice. Thus, in providing a legal opinion, you must provide an accurate and unvarnished assessment.

In addition to being an advisor who must occasionally deliver unwelcome news, the lawyer is also an advocate who should zealously advance the client's interests.[13] Zealous advocacy demands creativity and sometimes requires "a good faith argument for an extension, modification or reversal of existing law."[14] After all, the law is ambiguous, dynamic, and evolving.[15] A timid lawyer is a poor advocate. As experienced practitioners know, "[l]awyers are accused of taking advantage of 'loopholes' and 'technicalities' to win. Persons who make this charge are unaware, or do not understand, that the lawyer is hired to win, and if he does not exercise every legitimate effort in his client's behalf, then he is betraying a sacred trust."[16] Thus, while legal analysis must be objective to fulfill the lawyer's responsibilities as an advisor, it should also be creative to fulfill the lawyer's responsibilities as an advocate.

---

10. Smith, 13 Cal. 3d at 360, 530 P.2d at 596, 118 Cal. Rptr. at 628.
11. *See* MODEL CODE OF PROFESSIONAL RESPONSIBILITY Canon 6; EC 6-1 through EC 6-5; DR 6-101 (1983).
12. MODEL RULES, *supra* note 2, Preamble and Rule 1.4.
13. MODEL RULES, *supra* note 2, Preamble.
14. MODEL RULES, *supra* note 2, Rule 3.1.
15. MODEL RULES, *supra* note 2, Rule 3.1 cmt. 1.
16. William J. Rochelle, Jr. & Harvey O. Payne, *The Struggle for Public Understanding*, 25 TEX. B.J. 109, 159 (1962).

Duty to the justice system as an officer of the court

The lawyer's role as an advocate is tempered by the lawyer's responsibility to the legal system.[17] Because lawyers have the privilege of access to the courts, we have an obligation to exercise this power responsibly. Frivolous arguments waste the court's time and the parties' resources; they have no place in the ethical practice of law.[18] As one court explained: "An attorney does not have the duty to do all and whatever he can that may enable him to win his client's cause or to further his client's interest. His duty and efforts in these respects, although they should be prompted by his 'entire devotion' to the interest of his client, must be within and not without the bounds of the law."[19]

Legal Research Strategies

While a thorough discussion of legal resources and research techniques is beyond the scope of this book, this section will offer some tips for minimizing the confusion that accompanies most new research projects. Specifically, before charging off to the library, take a moment to plan your attack. And as you research the problem, be sure you take careful notes of your progress.

Plan your research

In the law library, you'll discover books of every imaginable kind from statutory codes to sociological treatises to foreign-language law reviews. Legal research is often fascinating, but it can be frustrating. To minimize frustration, you need a research plan. Many different approaches will work. As your research skills develop, you'll learn to approach problems from several different directions. But at first you may find yourself struggling to get started and spinning your wheels once you begin. After hours in the library, you may not know whether you've found what you're supposed to find or even whether you've read what you intended to read in the

---

17. MODEL RULES, *supra* note 2, Preamble.
18. MODEL RULES, *supra* note 2, Rule 3.1.
19. *In re* Wines, 370 S.W.2d 328, 333 (Mo. 1963).

books you've stacked on the library table for some now-forgotten reason. In law school, inefficiency is frustrating; in practice, it is frustrating and expensive. Your client cannot afford to spend unlimited funds for research on a $1000 problem. If a deadline is looming, you may not have any time to waste. While some wheel spinning is inevitable and, indeed, part of the creative process, an efficient plan will help keep you on track. This section will present one basic and dependable approach.

First, spend some time thinking about the issue presented by the client's problem. Figure out which general area of law will apply. Do the facts seem to raise a contract problem? a tort problem? a property problem? Perhaps you are not sure. For example, assume your problem involves a guest who slipped and fell on an uneven walkway at a rented house. This sounds like a tort problem. But it could also raise contract and real property questions as to whether the tenant or the landlord is responsible for repairs. Be open to multiple possibilities in identifying the applicable areas of law.

Second, figure out which jurisdiction will govern. Is it a state law problem or a federal problem? If the parties are from different states, which state law applies? Your research should start with the jurisdiction which governs the problem. The law from other jurisdictions will usually be important only if the controlling jurisdiction has no law on the question. By focusing on the controlling jurisdiction first, you can dramatically narrow your research.

Now start your research with a secondary source covering the area presented by your problem. Secondary sources include encyclopedias, periodicals, texts, and treatises. They are not law themselves and have no binding effect. However, they will provide background information and an overview of how your issue fits into the overall scheme of things. In other words: "Reading about the 'big picture' first will help you understand how the details fit together, when you later read the primary authority. It may also alert you to legally significant facts that you missed in your initial analysis."[20] And secondary sources will lead you to the primary authorities (constitutional provisions, statutes, and cases) which apply to your problem.

---

20. CHRISTINA L. KUNZ ET AL., THE PROCESS OF LEGAL RESEARCH 9 (2d ed. 1989).

Since the library is packed with secondary sources, you may be wondering which one to use. Encyclopedias are often helpful. *American Jurisprudence 2d (Am. Jur. 2d)*, published by Lawyers' Co-Operative/Bancroft-Whitney Co., is a widely-used encyclopedia covering the entire United States. Another useful resource is *American Law Reports (A.L.R.)*, also published by Lawyers' Co-Operative/Bancroft-Whitney Co., which reports significant opinions with extensive annotations. These annotations summarize all the cases in the United States addressing the same issue as the reported case. Hornbooks can also provide a helpful general overview. For example, for tort problems, *The Law of Torts*[21] is always a good starting point. Law review articles can also provide a general overview and lead you to primary authorities.

In addition to these national resources, individual states may also have their own encyclopedias and treatises. For example, *Summary of California Law*[22] provides an excellent and up-to-date review of the current civil law. Alternatively, *California Jurisprudence 3d (Cal. Jur. 3d)* is also widely used by California practitioners. Practice books covering different legal fields are also helpful starting points. For example, in California, the University of California and the California Bar Association publish an extensive set of continuing education books covering everything from agricultural law to zoning practice.

When you find your issue in the secondary authority, read the pages specifically on your point and also skim a few sections on either side for related analysis and background. Review the table of contents to see how your issue fits into the larger legal context. Make a list of the primary authorities (statutes and cases) cited in the discussion of your issue and of the words and phrases used in connection with your issue. From this starting point, you'll be able to focus your research on the most promising primary sources and also to find additional authorities using your list of words and phrases. While your starting point is a secondary authority, remember that primary authorities embody the law that will govern your case. Your goal is to use the secondary authority for background and to locate the relevant primary authorities.

---

21. W. PAGE KEETON ET AL., PROSSER AND KEETON ON THE LAW OF TORTS (5th ed. 1984).
22. BERNARD E. WITKIN, SUMMARY OF CALIFORNIA LAW (9th ed. 1990).

As you begin to understand the problem, you can decide whether it presents more than one legal issue to explore. If it does, you can refine your research plan by mapping out the order of research. Don't try to research everything at once, or you'll become confused and frustrated. Figure out which issue should be analyzed first. Complete your research on that issue before you move on to the second issue.

For example, in a tort case, one issue may be the defendant's liability, another may be the measure of damages, and a third may be the applicable statute of limitations. The logical starting point is the question of liability because the measure of damages and the statute of limitations will depend on its resolution. To keep on track, you may find it helpful to create separate manila folders for each issue. As you research the first issue, if you happen upon authorities on the other issues, make a note of the citations and slip them into the appropriate folder. When you've completed your liability research, you'll have some good leads on the other issues without having been sidetracked or derailed.

When you've isolated the issue to research first and done some background reading, you're ready to study the primary sources. If a statute governs your problem, the secondary sources will have provided its citation. Now you can look up the statute which is your critical primary authority. Carefully read the text of the statute itself, making sure that you have the most recent version. Always check the pocket part and legislative services to ensure that your research is current. Then read through the annotations to find promising cases, digest entries, law review articles, and attorney general's opinions. If the annotations are extensive, be selective. Focus first on cases, since they are primary authorities. If you find a staggering number of cases on point, you can trim the list by focusing on recent cases, cases from the highest appellate court in your jurisdiction, and factually-related cases. Remember to shepardize the statute and check the advance sheets to find the latest cases.

From the secondary source or from the statutory annotations, you will eventually be led to cases considering your issue. Start with the most recent case on your issue decided by the highest appellate court in your jurisdiction. Read other recent cases which are factually close to your case. These recent cases will collect and summarize older authorities on the same point. Remember that broad legal principles are slippery and undependable, so you should try to find the cases which are the most factually analogous to your case. The law usually turns on the facts; the more similar the facts of the cases are to your problem, the more reliable your research will be. Update your research using *Shepard's Citations* and current advance sheets.

The statutes and the cases will refer you to other primary and secondary sources. The question becomes: Where can I stop? Unfortunately, there's no clear answer, but some guidelines may help you. First, ask yourself if you've found the most recent *prim*ary authority in the governing jurisdiction on your issue. This is the minimum. If you've started with a secondary source, followed its direction to the most recent statute or case, and updated that statute or case, your answer should be yes. If your answer is no, your research is incomplete. Keep going until you've found the most recent primary authority on your issue.

Second, ask yourself if you've read the important authorities. All authorities are not created equal. If the unread authorities are less persuasive than the authorities you've already found, then you may defer reading them. For example, if the unread authorities are from other jurisdictions and you've found recent authorities in the controlling jurisdiction, you can postpone reading the out-of-state authorities. In other words, if you have a recent California Supreme Court decision resolving an issue governed by California law, you can safely put off reading a Wyoming trial court decision on the same legal issue. Similarly, if the unread authorities are secondary authorities and you've found persuasive primary authorities, you can defer reading the secondary authorities. Don't worry about Joe Blow's law review note on an issue that has been resolved recently by your state legislature. Finally, if the unread authorities are old and you've found persuasive recent authorities, you can often defer reading the older authorities.

Above all, keep things in perspective. This is a learning process, not a marathon. You'll be working with this problem for several weeks, so you'll have time to perfect your research later. For now, try to find the most important authorities for each side of your problem. As you work with the problem over time, your understanding will develop and you'll see how to best expand your research. "Research, thinking, and writing are not really separable activities. They are all part of the single process of creation."[23]

---

23. RICHARD K. NEUMANN, JR., LEGAL REASONING AND LEGAL WRITING 117 (2d ed. 1994).

Take careful notes

Good research notes will save you hours of time. While you need discipline to take good notes during a research frenzy, you'll surely regret it later if you neglect to keep a careful record of your progress. So do yourself a favor and follow these suggestions:

Statutes

When you find a statute on point, get out a fresh sheet of paper. Write down the complete citation in proper *Bluebook* form.[24] Because statutory language is critical, an edited or paraphrased version is risky. Tape a photocopy of the text of the statute onto your paper. Now explain why you think the statute applies to your problem. Perhaps this sounds silly and unnecessary, but legal insights disappear with annoying frequency, so jot down why you think the statute applies. Go step by step through the language of the statute to see if all the requirements are met. Identify problems in the application of the statute and any possible ambiguities.

Next, take notes on the annotations to the statute. First, make a note of the annotation numbers that pertain to your issue. Then list the citations to the cases and other authorities you want to read. For the cases, include a word or two summarizing the facts so that

---

24. "THE BLUEBOOK" is the set of rules for legal citations established in THE BLUEBOOK: A UNIFORM SYSTEM OF CITATION (16th ed. 1996). It is technical and frustrating. If you are familiar with THE BLUEBOOK, you probably hate it. If you are unfamiliar with it, you will probably learn to hate it. We all do. Its tyranny has been challenged by THE UNIVERSITY OF CHICAGO MANUAL OF LEGAL CITATION (1989) published by The Lawyers Co-Operative Publishing Company and others. Nicknamed the MAROON BOOK for its maroon cover, this slender guide offers a simpler set of rules. I'm rooting for the Chicago upstarts. But for now THE BLUEBOOK prevails. As one commentator observed: "For many highly-placed aficionados of the Bluebook, deviations from its rules mark the writer as an inept lawyer. To preserve your credibility, you should adhere to the Bluebook until you gain enough prestige to challenge it." KAREN K. PORTER ET AL., INTRODUCTION TO LEGAL WRITING AND ORAL ADVOCACY 7 (1989). In this book, my research assistants and I have tried to follow THE BLUEBOOK. But, THE BLUEBOOK has two different sets of rules—one for law review articles and one for practice documents. We generally used the law review rules for the text of this book and footnotes; we have used the Practitioners' Notes for the sample documents. And we've probably made a few mistakes. If you spot any errors, we apologize and would be grateful for corrections.

you will be able to focus on the most promising cases. Be sure to note the dates of the cases and the courts deciding them. You can save lots of time by focusing first on the most recent decisions of the highest court in the governing jurisdiction.

Finally, take notes on your steps in updating the statute. It's bad enough to have to do it once; it's unbearable to have to do it all over again because you can't remember for sure whether you did it properly the first time. Be sure to make a note of the date you updated the statute so that you will know where to begin updating your research as the case progresses.

Cases

When you find a case on point, get out a fresh sheet of paper. Write down the complete citation in proper *Bluebook* form, including parallel citations, the name of the court, and the date of decision. Brief the case. Include the facts of the case, the procedural context, the issue, the holding, and the rationale supporting the decision. This brief will be the basis of your office memorandum which will be the basis of your opinion letter and could become the basis of your complaint and trial court briefs. Time spent carefully briefing the case now will both assure that your analysis is complete and save time on all future assignments. If a quotation is important to your understanding of the case, quote it and make a note of the page number where it appears. Explain how you think the case applies to your problem. Are the facts similar or distinguishable? Are the policy arguments applicable? Jot down the relevant headnote numbers and digest entries. You'll use the headnote numbers to shepardize the case and the digest entries to find related cases in the digests.

Now take notes of your steps in updating the case. To shepardize a case efficiently you should identify the headnote number which bears on your issue and find the citations pertaining to that headnote. Again, by keeping notes of the steps you followed in updating your research, you will save time updating in the future. And be sure to note the date you updated the case so that you will know where to being updating your research as the case progresses.

Caution: Photocopying is not a substitute for analysis. While it may be tempting to copy cases instead of reading them, your research will suffer. If you don't read the cases as you go, you'll end up with a mountain of photocopied cases that still have to be read, analyzed, and updated. Save time by reading, analyzing, and updating each case you find on point.

Legal Research Synthesis

Once you've collected the applicable authorities, you need to sit down and think about the problem. What's the most important authority? Why? What's the next most important authority? How do the authorities fit together? How do they apply to your case? What is the most logical order for presenting them? As Henry Weihofen explained:

> The novice, after doing his research, may be eager to get at his writing, without first digesting, organizing and thinking through the implications of his material. But time spent in thinking, before you even start to prepare an outline, is time well spent. It may be the most worth-while of all the time spent on the project. There is no more pathetic illusion than the trusting conviction that ideas will come if we just start writing.[25]

As you think about the problem, try to group the disparate and conflicting authorities into main themes. First, state in a sentence or two the most promising argument for your client. Try expressing that argument as a rule of law. Now try summarizing the policy reasons for the rule. Would the policy be furthered by applying the rule to your case? Does the rule represent the current trend of the law? Do the authorities support this argument? What are the most persuasive supporting authorities?

For example, assume your client was beaten and robbed in her apartment. As far as you know, no prior crimes occurred in your client's apartment building. You've been asked to research whether the landlord is liable for negligence because the inadequate security in the building facilitated the crime. Your research discloses that the current trend is to hold landlords liable for foreseeable crimes which could have been prevented by reasonable security precautions. The imposition of liability is based on the special landlord-tenant relationship. It serves the goal of compensating the injured

---

25. HENRY WEIHOFEN, LEGAL WRITING STYLE 135 (2d ed. 1980).

victim, spreading the risk of loss, and encouraging reasonable safety precautions. The *Restatement (Second) of Torts* and several recent cases support this view.

Now try it from your opponent's point of view. Summarize your opponent's best argument in a sentence or two. Try expressing that argument as a rule of law and summarizing the policy reasons for the rule. Would the policies be furthered by applying the rule in your case? Does the rule reflect the current trend of the law? What are the most persuasive authorities your opponent could marshal to support the argument?

Returning to our landlord liability problem, your research discloses that the highest court in the governing jurisdiction has only imposed liability on landlords for third-party crimes where a prior crime has occurred on the premises. The cases explain that landlords cannot guard against all possible crimes and that the burden of providing additional security drives up the cost of rental property. The most recent decision in this line of cases was handed down last year. Thus, your opponent has a strong argument that despite the trend toward imposing liability, the law of the governing jurisdiction supports the landlord.

Through this thinking process, you'll develop themes to organize your analysis and put the subject in focus. If you fail to provide this structure, your poor reader will be hopelessly confused and needlessly inconvenienced. Unfortunately, as Henry Weihofen explains, this happens all too often in legal writing:

> A particularly bad and particularly common form of writing without seeing the subject in perspective is that which takes us through the facts of a series of cases without telling us what they are intended to prove or what the writer's own conclusion is. Case after case is briefed for us, and the court's holding summarized, but each case is left standing alone, without any thread of argument connecting it to the others. There is no thread because the writer has apparently not yet made up his own mind. He is really writing notes to himself, which eventually he will cogitate over and discuss. But this he should do before he writes the first word.[26]

So before you write the first word, identify the threads that tie the authorities together and the arguments the parties can weave

---

26. *Id.* at 136.

from these threads. For example, returning to our landlord-tenant problem, two lines of cases emerge: (1) those refusing to impose liability unless a prior crime has been committed on the premises; and (2) those imposing liability for foreseeable crimes. You can now group the seemingly conflicting authorities under these coherent themes.

Once you've identified the themes, think about how you might be able to harmonize them. For example, if the cases imposing liability involved residential property and the cases rejecting liability involved commercial property, you might refine the analysis by focusing on this factual distinction. Perhaps the special relationship between a landlord and a residential tenant supports the imposition of liability since residential tenants are vulnerable and unlikely to provide their own security. The cases refusing to impose liability could be distinguished because of the different relationship between a commercial landlord and tenant, where the tenant has more bargaining power and the ability to arrange for additional security precautions. Using this approach you could argue that the court is not bound by the cases refusing to impose liability on commercial landlords and should instead follow the recent trend in other jurisdictions imposing liability on residential landlords.

On the other hand, the law is sometimes just plain contradictory. If you can't harmonize the authorities, you can at least identify the conflicting approaches and group the similar cases together. In this way, the conflict itself becomes a useful organizing tool. Once you've sorted the authorities into their respective camps, try to figure out which approach the court will follow. What's the trend? What's the better policy? The answers to these questions will help you refine your analysis.

Office Memorandum

After you've thought about the authorities and lines of argument, you're ready to begin work on a memorandum of law discussing your client's problem. In this book, we'll approach writing as a somewhat fluid process of thinking, planning, drafting, rethinking, rewriting, editing, polishing, and proofreading. Often as you work through these steps, you'll spot a hole in your research or analysis. That's part of the process. You shouldn't expect to figure out every last detail before you start writing. As you rethink and rewrite the draft, you'll find that your analysis improves as your understanding of the problem develops. The process of putting your ideas down on paper will help you think them through more clearly.

As Richard Neumann explains, many students see the first draft as the most important step in writing a document, but it is actually the least important step. Thinking, organizing, and revision are much more important. "Your only goal during the first draft is get things down on the page so that you can start rewriting. The first draft has no other value. Regardless of how many faults it has, the first draft accomplishes its entire purpose merely by coming into existence."[27]

Thus, your goal for this assignment is simply to bring that first draft of an office memo into existence. The following sections will consider the purpose of and audience for an office memo and then explain its form and content.

Purpose of an office memorandum

The purpose of a memorandum is to objectively present and analyze the authorities governing a legal issue. Its goal is to predict how the law will resolve the problem. Your supervising attorney will rely on the memorandum to evaluate the case and advise your client. The memo will also preserve your research for future reference. For example, if your client decides to file a complaint based on your advice, the memo will be the starting point for determining what the complaint must allege to state a cause of action. And the memo may also be used in the future for analyzing similar legal problems.

Given the purpose of the memo, you can appreciate the importance of an accurate and balanced analysis. People will make important decisions based on your work, and they need to understand both the strengths and weaknesses of their position. But, as Charles Calleros explains, "an office memorandum is not entirely neutral; in most cases, it anticipates advocacy on behalf of a client."[28] For this reason, you should try to figure out ways to overcome weaknesses

---

27. NEUMANN, *supra* note 23, at 58.
28. CHARLES R. CALLEROS, LEGAL METHOD AND WRITING 157 (2d ed. 1994).

in the case and to maximize strengths.[29] In short, your analysis should be objective, but your attitude should be helpful.

Audience for an office memorandum

Your primary audience is your supervising attorney. Take a moment to picture your reader. While you don't know much about this hypothetical reader, several universal truths hold for all supervising attorneys. First, your reader will be extremely busy—a morning court appearance, an afternoon deposition, eight phone calls to return, a car in the shop for repairs, dry cleaning to retrieve on the way home, an appellate brief to file on Friday, a birthday present to buy for a friend. Second, your reader will be interrupted at least once while reading your memo by an urgent phone call, another associate who needs guidance, or a secretary who needs signatures. Third, your reader has a dozen equally complex and important things to worry about. Your reader asked a question and longs for a concise yet complete analysis of the issue. Your reader does not want an esoteric, lyrical musing on the philosophical underpinnings of economic theory in civil litigation, as fascinating as that might be. Your reader wants an answer—or the closest thing to an answer that honesty allows.

Form and content of an office memorandum

While different offices adopt slightly different formats for office memoranda, most are fairly standardized. Lawyers are comfortable with the conventional forms. By following the conventions, you will help your reader follow your analysis. This section will present the form of a standard office memorandum which includes: (1) a heading; (2) a question presented; (3) a brief answer; (4) a statement of facts; (5) a discussion; and (6) a conclusion. At the end of this chapter you'll find an outline template, a sample outline, and a sample memo. You may wish to skim them now to get a general idea of the form and content of a memo.

Heading

The heading should include the name of the intended reader, the name of the writer, the name of the file (including the client's name),

---

29. *Id.* at 158.

the subject of the memo, and the date the memo is completed. In the subject line, briefly describe the legal issue. As the client's file grows, this description will help you quickly locate the right memo. Also, most law firms keep libraries of memoranda to save costly duplication of research. Your description of the legal issue will help you and your colleagues find the memo when faced with a similar problem in the future. For example:

To: Senior Partner
From: New Associate
File: Smith v. Brown
Re: Residential landlord's liability for third-party crime
Date: June 12, 1998

Notice how the re line includes key factual information, not just legal concepts. Specifically, the inclusion of the word "residential" will alert future researchers that this memo may be of limited value in evaluating a commercial landlord's liability. The reader won't have to read the whole memo to realize that it's not going to be on point.

Question Presented

Your question should identify the issue you will discuss by tying the legal issue to the key facts. It should be sufficiently complete to make sense standing alone and should orient your reader to the problem. Simply from reading the question presented, your reader should understand the critical legal issue and the key facts. To organize your question effectively, start with the most general information and proceed to the more specific detail. Start with the general legal area, proceed to the precise legal issue, and then to the key facts. Keep it to a readable length so that your reader can understand the question by reading it just once. For example:

Question Presented

In a negligence action, will a tavern that sponsored a soft-ball team be held vicariously liable for injuries to a spectator who was hit by a baseball thrown by a player during a game?

Be selective in deciding which facts to include. Include the facts that are legally important; omit unnecessary detail. Generally, names, dates, amounts, locations, citations, and other specifics should be omitted. If numerous specific facts are necessary, you may wish to include them in a preliminary statement so that your question does not become unwieldy. For example:

Question Presented

Our client, a local tavern, sponsored an amateur baseball team. As sponsor, the client paid league fees, provided team shirts, and hosted a banquet at the end of the season. A spectator injured during one of the games has sued our client for the injuries.

In a negligence action, is a tavern vicariously liable for injuries to a spectator who was hit by a baseball thrown by a player during a game sponsored by the tavern?

Sometimes subquestions are useful to break a problem down. If you decide to use subquestions, make sure that they don't become overly intricate and confusing. Remember that your question presented should provide a useful overview of the problem. Also, you must have at least two subquestions. After all, a single subquestion is simply a refinement of the primary question and usually indicates that the primary question needs revision. You should only use subquestions when distinct issues will be considered. For example:

Question Presented

In a negligence action, is a tavern vicariously liable for injuries to a spectator who was hit by a baseball thrown by a player during a game sponsored by the tavern?

a. Will vicarious liability be imposed on the sponsor where the players made all decisions relating to management and control of the team such as selecting players, designating positions, and determining game strategy?

b. Will vicarious liability be imposed on the sponsor where the player unforeseeably violated the rules of the game by throwing the baseball out of the ballpark in anger?

The question presented serves as a lens to put your memorandum in focus. Don't be discouraged if you're not happy with your first draft. Try it again after you've finished drafting your memorandum. The key issue and facts may be much better defined at that point. As your understanding of the problem becomes clearer, your question presented will sharpen.

Brief Answer

You should provide a direct answer to each question and a brief explanation (5–10 sentences) of the reasons for your conclusions. While the brief answer will appear in your memorandum immediately after the question presented, it should probably be written after you have thought the problem through and clarified your analysis in the discussion section.

To organize your answer effectively, you should keep in mind that your reader is not familiar with the legal analysis. So break your reader in gently. Start with the general rule of law applicable to your problem and then narrow it to the specifics of your case. If your case falls within an exception to a general rule, start with the general rule and then present the exception. A good approach is (1) to set out the applicable point of law in a sentence or two and (2) to apply it to the facts of your case in the next few sentences. Remember to provide a balanced, objective view of the problem. Your brief answer should provide a quick overview of the arguments for both sides. For example:

Question Presented

In a loss of consortium action, is an unmarried cohabitant entitled to recover for paralyzing injuries to her cohabitant where the couple had lived together for five years before the accident, was sexually exclusive, shared financial resources and obligations, and was raising their two children in a family relationship?

Brief Answer

Probably not. Generally, the courts have refused to allow loss of consortium actions to unmarried cohabitants on the ground that only married people have a cause of action. In an isolated decision, one appellate court has allowed an action where the couple established a "stable and significant relationship." The plaintiff will argue that this stable and significant standard should be applied in our case because the cases are factually similar. However, the district court in our district has refused to recognize the stable and significant standard and has insisted that marriage is a prerequisite to a loss of consortium action. Thus, the plaintiff will probably not be able to recover for loss of consortium in this case.

If you have broken your question down into subquestions, answer each question and subquestion. For example:

Question Presented

In a negligence action, is a tavern vicariously liable for injuries to a spectator who was hit by a baseball thrown by a player during a game sponsored by the tavern?

a. Will vicarious liability be imposed on the sponsor where the players made all decisions relating to management and control of the team such as selecting players, designating positions, and determining game strategy?

b. Will vicarious liability be imposed on the sponsor where the player violated the rules of the game by throwing the baseball out of the ballpark in anger?

Brief Answer

No, the sponsor will probably not be held vicariously liable for the spectator's injuries. Generally, vicarious liability is only imposed where the principal had control over the agent and where the agent's misconduct was foreseeable. We can argue that the sponsor is not vicariously liable because it exercised no control over the team and because the misconduct of the ballplayer was unforeseeable.

a. Probably not. The two cases considering a sponsor's liability both indicate that vicarious liability will be imposed only where the sponsor exercised control over the team. Here the sponsor did not exercise control over the team and should not be held liable. The plaintiff may argue, however, that the sponsor had the right to control the team because of its financial control and that this right to control (even though not exercised) is a sufficient basis for vicarious liability.

b. Probably not. Generally, vicarious liability will only be imposed for foreseeable misconduct of the sponsor's agent. Case law supports the view that spontaneous acts of violence are unforeseeable. We can argue that the sponsor had no reason to foresee that a player would injure somebody off the field by throwing a baseball in violation of the rules of the game. The plaintiff can argue that the sponsor could foresee injuries occurring in the normal course of the game, including injuries caused by a frustrated player losing his temper. In my opinion, the plaintiff is not likely to prevail on this issue.

Notice that the examples do not include citations because they are not very informative and readers skip over them. A citation should only be included in the brief answer when it is essential to the answer.

Your question presented and brief answer should provide a concise overview of the problem by identifying the legal issues, the key facts, and the major arguments each side will raise. To see if you've accomplished these goals, ask yourself whether a reader unfamiliar with the problem would basically grasp the situation by reading only your question presented and brief answer. If you can fit them both on the first page, bravo!

Statement of facts

For several reasons, you should always include a statement of facts in memos. First, the analysis only has merit to the extent it is tied to the facts. Second, your reader may not be familiar with the facts or may have forgotten them. Third, facts change as you learn more about the case and the analysis may need revision as the facts develop. Unless you specify the facts on which you relied, you won't know when you need to revise your analysis.

Keep in mind that the purpose of a memorandum is to provide an objective evaluation of a problem. For this reason, be scrupulously accurate in your statement of facts. Include the facts that hurt you as well as the facts that help you. Also, be careful not to inflate your facts or diminish your opponent's facts. Signal gaps in your knowledge; don't lull yourself or your reader into thinking that your case is stronger than it really is. If you have yet to verify some of the information, don't present what you hope to discover without letting your reader know the status of your investigation.

To help your reader understand and retain the facts, you need to organize them carefully. Use chronological order and the past tense. If the facts are complex, you may wish to organize them topically and use topic headings. For example, one common scheme in personal injury cases is to include facts about the accident under one heading and facts about the resulting injuries under another heading. Similarly, in contract cases, a statement of facts may include a section about the contract formation, a section about the contract dispute, and a section about the resulting damages. Within each topic, use chronological order.

Be selective and considerate of your reader. After all, reading legal memos is tough enough without being burdened with extraneous factual details or bored by a dull presentation. In selecting the facts to include, remember the point of your memorandum is to address a specific issue. Trim out the irrelevant facts. For example, if your memo is about liability, you can omit details about damages. Once you've identified the facts bearing on your issue, make the facts interesting. Law is a staple of television drama because it involves people with problems and conflicts. Don't beat the life out of your case with a ponderous style.

Discussion

The discussion is the heart of the memo where you present the relevant authorities and apply them to your client's problem. Bearing in mind your obligations as an advisor and an advocate, you should strive to be thorough, objective, and, when necessary, creative. Your memo should include all the information necessary to evaluate the strengths and weaknesses of the parties' arguments.

As you know, legal analysis is often unavoidably contradictory and difficult. To keep your reader from getting lost, outline your discussion carefully. Identify the themes and arguments each side will make; identify the authorities for each argument; consider the strengths and weaknesses of each authority. You can start with either point of view. Just be sure that you don't give your reader an overly optimistic picture of the likelihood of your success. If your question presented has subsections for different issues, the discussion should follow the same pattern. For example, the question presented for the baseball case identified two issues: (1) the sponsor's control of the team; and (2) the foreseeability of the player's misconduct. These issues should be presented in the same order in separate sections of the discussion.

After completing your outline, you will be able to write your discussion section without losing your way. To keep your reader on track, provide a road map and signposts along the way. If more than one issue will be discussed, put each issue in a separate section flagged by a topic heading. Begin each section with an introductory paragraph providing an overview for your reader. Sometimes background information is necessary if the subject area is novel or unfamiliar to your reader. Your introductory paragraph should acquaint your reader with the thesis of the section, identifying the arguments the parties will make and their probable resolution. You're not writing a mystery; your analysis will be much easier to follow if you tell the reader where you're going.

Once you've drafted the introductory paragraph, you're ready to explain how the parties will use the authorities to support their arguments. Generally, present the strongest authority first. Chronological order may also be effective, but remember that your reader is interested in evaluating the client's problem under current law. As you introduce each authority, state in a topic sentence the specific role that the authority will play in the analysis of the problem. For example, you may wish to introduce your strongest authority in this way:

> To state an action for interference with prospective business advantage, we will rely primarily on a recent federal case allowing recovery even though the prospective advantage had not yet matured into an enforceable contract. *Huey, Duey and Louis, Inc. v. Scrouge McDuck*, 346 F. Supp. 789 (N. D. Cal. 1998).

If you are switching to the authorities against you, let your reader know that you are changing directions:

> On the other hand, the defendants will rely on an older California case refusing to allow recovery for interference with prospective advantage unless it amounted to interference with existing and enforceable contracts. *Popeye v. Brutus*, 32 Cal. 2d 123, 455 P.2d 76, 325 Cal. Rptr. 819 (1977).

And if you are presenting your authorities in chronological order, you may wish to introduce an authority as follows:

> The earliest case allowing a bystander to recover for negligent infliction of emotional distress is *Jones v. Smith*, 114 Cal. App. 385, 12 P. 38 (1918).

As these examples illustrate, the reader is alerted to the significance of the case by the introductory sentence. Note also that the citations appear at the end of the sentence to avoid interrupting the flow with a string of numbers.

After introducing each authority, you should present and apply each authority to your case and anticipate counterarguments. The following specific suggestions should help you present and apply the authorities:

Statutes

If a statute is central to your problem, it will usually be the starting point for your analysis. Introduce the statute and summarize it in readable language. Then quote specific language your reader may need, remembering that every word of a statute has significance. After this presentation of the statute, explain how it pertains to your problem. Don't just leave the statute hanging there for your reader to ponder. Explain what you think it means to your problem. How does the language of the statute support your client's case? How does the language of the statute support your opponent's case? How does the underlying policy or legislative history of the statute support your client's case? How does the underlying policy or legislative history of the statute support your opponent's case? After explaining the application of the statute based on its text, turn to the cases interpreting and applying the statute. Remember, a memo should be objective, so you must anticipate and explain the arguments your opponent is likely to make as well as the arguments you plan to make.

Example

To determine whether Southwood is immune from punitive damages because it is a health care provider, we need to analyze Cal. Code of Civ. Proc. § 425.13. Section 425.13 protects health care providers from punitive damages, but the protection is limited to certain licensed persons and facilities. For our purposes, the key category is "any clinic, health dispensary, or health facility, licensed pursuant to Division 2 . . . of the Health and Safety Code." Southwood fails to qualify under this category because it is licensed as a group home, not a "clinic, health dispensary or health facility." Since Southwood does not have the required license, it is not protected by § 425.13 from punitive damages.

In response, Southwood may claim to be a health facility because as a group home it arranges for health services to be provided to the children at its facility and because it is licensed under Division 2 of the Health and Safety Code. But Section 425.13 barring punitive damages does not extend to all facilities licensed under Division 2. Rather, although many different kinds of facilities are licensed under Division 2, only three specific facilities—clinics, health dispensaries, and health facilities—are protected by § 425.13. Southwood is not licensed under any of these qualifying categories; Southwood is only licensed as a "group home" which is a separate licensing category. Since Southwood is not licensed as a "clinic, health dispensary, or health facility," it falls outside the scope of the statutory protection.

Finding Southwood outside the scope of the statute is consistent with the Legislature's goal of protecting certain licensed health care providers, but not other potential defendants. This legislative intent is explained in *Bell v. Sharp Cabrillo Hospital*, 212 Cal. App. 3d 1034, 1052 (1995). According to the *Bell* court, the first goal of the Medical Injury Compensation Reform Act (MICRA) was to erect a framework to assure medical quality affording governmental oversight of the education, licensing and discipline of physicians and health care providers. Furthering this goal, § 425.13 protects only those who have subjected themselves to the necessary governmental oversight of the Department of Health Services. Here, Southwood is a group home regulated by the Department of Social Services, not a health care provider subject to oversight by the Department of Health Services. Under the *Bell* approach, Southwood is outside the scope of § 425.13.

As the example illustrates, when a statute controls the outcome, its language is critical to your analysis. After you have presented the language of the statute itself and considered its application to your issue, you should then turn to the cases. Notice how the legal authorities are directly applied to the case at issue, leading the reader through the analysis step by step. The writer does not leave a big chunk of undigested authority for the reader to mull over; the application to the pending problem is explicit. The above discussion would continue by reviewing the other relevant cases and applying them to the problem.

Cases

When a case is relevant to your problem, summarize it for your reader. For each case, you should include the facts, procedural context, holding, and rationale. In explaining the court's rationale, include the policy reasons advanced by the court to support the result. If the court's language is crucial, quote it. But generally avoid lengthy quotations; everyone skips single-spaced quotations because they are "visually oppressive."[30] Be honest, don't you? If you need to quote more than 50 words (or three lines) from a decision, indent the quotation and tie it into your discussion. The sentence before the quotation should set it up, and the sentence following the quotation should weave it back into your discussion.

After presenting a case, start a new paragraph explaining its application to your client's problem. Point out how the case is factually similar to your problem and how it is different. Evaluate the significance of these similarities and differences. Is your case similar enough to the case that fairness requires the same result? Or is it different in an important way so that the prior case should be distinguished? Consider whether the policies underlying the decision

---

30. HELENE S. SHAPO ET AL., WRITING AND ANALYSIS IN THE LAW 326 (3d ed. 1995).

would be furthered or frustrated by applying it to your case. Explain whether the case is likely to be followed or distinguished and why. When relying on dictum, say so.

A useful organization for case analysis is IRAC: issue; rule; application; conclusion:

Example: IRAC Formula

Introduce the issue and state your position affirmatively. Your introduction should tell the reader your conclusion.	Fisher alleged that Larsen defamed her during the school board election campaign, causing her to lose the election. As damages, Fisher claimed the salary she would have received if elected. We can argue that the trial court should find this claim too speculative.
State the rule you want the court to apply and present authority for your argument.	An early case which found loss of elective salary too speculative to be compensable is *Southwestern Publishing Co. v. Horsey*, 230 F.2d 319 (9th Cir. 1956). In *Southwestern*, the plaintiff lost a judicial election contest. The plaintiff sued the successful candidate for defamation, claiming loss of the judicial salary as damages. The court affirmed summary judgment for the defendant, holding that loss of an elective salary was not compensable because it was too uncertain and speculative. The court pointed out that a thousand factors might influence an election, including media coverage, political party support, group endorsements, volunteer efforts, finances, political trends, and issues debated. The court concluded: "The net result of such an exploration into the uncertainties of an election could only lead to confusion." *Id.* at 323.
Explain the application of the authority to the facts of your case and why the authority should be followed.	In this case, as in *Southwestern*, many factors may have affected the election. For example, Fisher voted to grant amnesty following the teachers' illegal strike and Larsen condemned the amnesty vote;

Fisher voted against the integration plan and Larsen supported the plan; Fisher was endorsed by the teachers' union and Larsen was endorsed by all living ex-school board presidents. Although none of these factors related to the alleged defamation, all of them could have affected the outcome of the election. Since all of these factors, and many others, could have influenced the election, the impact of the alleged defamation cannot be determined.

Restate your conclusion. Thus, we can argue that the trial court should conclude that Fisher's claimed loss of salary was too speculative to be compensable.

After you've presented an authority, anticipate the possible counter-arguments. How is the case on which you rely distinguishable? Are the facts different? Are different policies involved? Have legal standards changed over time? What will your opponent have to say about the authority?

You can handle the contrary authorities with the same IRAC formula. Present the best argument your opponent can make. After you explain your opponent's side, set out the counter-arguments you can make to overcome these unwelcome authorities. But remember your duty to provide an objective analysis; don't underestimate the unwelcome authorities.

While many teachers agree that IRAC is a useful organizational tool, they caution that it must be applied flexibly.[31] It is merely a framework for setting out your legal analysis; it is no substitute for legal analysis. Make sure your discussion of the authorities does not simply go through the IRAC motions. As you present each decision, consider its factual subtleties, expand on the conflicting policy arguments, and pay attention to historical and social context.

---

31. *Point/Counterpoint: Use of IRAC-type Formulas—Desirable or Dangerous,* 10 THE SECOND DRAFT 1 (1995).

If you're feeling overwhelmed, don't panic. You'll be working with this problem for several weeks so what you do now will save time later and what you can't get done now can be completed later. Focus on the substance and organization of the discussion. String citations are not helpful. A good memo will provide a thorough analysis of important authorities rather than a superficial job with numerous authorities. For those authorities that support a point you've already made, a parenthetical explanation may be helpful. For example:

> See also *Odie v. Garfield*, 123 F.3d 432 (9th Cir. 1996) (the court reversed summary judgment for the defendant in an action for intentional infliction of emotional distress where the defendant repeatedly harassed the plaintiff by threats of physical violence).

But for now, do a thorough job with the key authorities; you can add more when you rewrite the memo. As you work on the problem over time you'll find that you'll see the strengths and weaknesses of the arguments more clearly and be able to improve your analysis.

Conclusion

Briefly summarize your analysis and set out your recommendations. Don't rehash your whole memo; just synthesize the main points and provide some specific recommendations. Your conclusion will parallel your brief answer but can be more refined since your reader will have had the benefit of your analysis. Offer to take the next step for your supervisor. For example, if the client needs to be advised of the results of the research, offer to draft a client letter. Busy lawyers love helpful associates.

Outline Template for an Office Memorandum

I. Heading

II. Question presented

III. Brief answer

IV. Statement of facts

V. Discussion

    A. The first issue

        1. Introduce the issue; identify the lines of argument.

        2. Discuss the most important authority on the issue.

            a. Present the authority.

                If the most important authority is a statute, provide the statutory language and explain the legislative purpose. If the most important authority is a case, present its facts, procedure, holding, and rationale.

            b. Apply the authority to your case.

                If the most important authority is a statute, explain how the statute applies to the facts of your case and whether its application will further the legislative purpose. If the most important authority is a case, explain how it applies to the facts of your case and whether its application will further the policies reflected in the court's rationale. Consider any distinguishing facts.

            c. Consider counter arguments.

        3. Discuss the next most important authority.

            Repeat steps a–c above.

        4. Continue until you have presented and applied the relevant authorities.

        5. Synthesize the analysis.

    B. The second issue

        Repeat steps 1–5 above.

VI. Conclusion

Sample Outline

I. Heading

II. Question presented

III. Brief answer

IV. Statement of facts

V. Discussion

    A. Introduction of Issue: Landlord's liability for crime against tenant; overview of the two lines of argument

    B. Most recent Supreme Court case holds no liability without prior crime

        1. *Ann M. v. Pacific Plaza Shopping Center* (1993)

        Most recent California Supreme Court decision alleging negligent failure to provide security guards; requires high degree of foreseeability which "rarely, if ever, can be proven in the absence of prior similar incidents of violent crime on the landowner's premises."

        2. Defendant will argue this case controls and precludes liability in our case; defendant will assert that the *Ann M.* prior crime requirement should be extended to all landowner third-party liability cases.

        3. Rebuttal: *Ann M.* is distinguishable because it involved commercial property and the precaution of hiring security guards was very expensive. Our case involves residential property and inexpensive precaution of deadbolt locks. Thus, the danger is higher and the burden is lower so liability should be imposed.

    C. Cases supporting residential landlords' liability without prior crime

        1. *Kwaitkowski v. Superior Trading Co.* (1981)

        This earlier appellate decision imposed liability on a residential landlord for failure to provide deadbolt locks; it stated that foreseeability of crime depends on totality of the circumstances, not determined solely by occurrence of prior crime on the premises.

a. We can argue that this case should be followed. It recognizes the need to protect vulnerable residential tenants and imposes minimal burdens for their safety; it suggests liability may be found without prior crime.

b. Defendant will argue that this case is distinguishable from our case. In fact, although the court pointed to other factors as well, there was a prior crime on the premises. Defendant will also argue that the dicta about the totality of the circumstances approach was implicitly overruled by *Ann M.*

2. Other jurisdictions have imposed liability in similar cases

Three sister-state decisions have imposed liability on residential landlords for failing to provide adequate door locks: *Shea v. Preservation Chicago, Inc.*, (Ill. 1990); *Paterson v. Deeb*, (Fla. 1985); and *Arroyo v. Fourteen Estusia Corp.*, (N.Y. 1992).

a. We can argue that these cases represent the emerging view for residential landlord liability and should be followed at least with respect to the minimal security precautions at issue in our case.

b. Defendant will argue these cases are irrelevant in view of the *Ann M.* requirement of a prior crime on the premises.

D. Synthesis of arguments

VI. Conclusion

Sample Office Memorandum

To: Horace Rumpole
From: Philida Trant
File: Janet Washington, No. 123.45
Re: Residential Landlord's Liability for Intruder's
       Assault on Tenant
Date: June 1, 1998

Question Presented

In a negligence action, is a residential landlord liable for personal injuries suffered by a tenant from an assault by a criminal intruder where the landlord failed to provide deadbolt locks and improved lighting in the common areas after the tenant requested these precautions because of frequent crimes in the neighborhood?

Brief Answer

Possibly yes, but a recent California Supreme Court decision will be difficult to overcome. Generally the law imposes only limited duties to protect others from third party crime, but the landlord-tenant relationship gives rise to this duty where crime is foreseeable. The most recent California Supreme Court decision on this issue concluded that there must be a high degree of foreseeability and that this requirement "rarely, if ever, can be proven in the absence of prior similar incidents of violent crime on the landowner's premises." Since there were no prior crimes at our client's apartment, this requirement may preclude liability.

We can argue that the Supreme Court decision is distinguishable because it involved commercial, not residential, property. An earlier California appellate decision, as well as decisions from our sister states, held that residential landlords are required to provide at least minimal protection against foreseeable crime including deadbolt locks and good lighting. We can also argue that crime was foreseeable because of the high neighborhood crime rate and our client's warning to her landlord.

Statement of Facts

From May, 1997, to October 13, 1997, Janet Washington rented an apartment in Sacramento from Daniel Grassly. During that time numerous burglaries, assaults, and robberies occurred in her neighborhood. Although no crimes occurred in her building, Janet was afraid because her building had cheap locks and poor lighting in the common areas. Janet complained to Grassly that the building was unsafe. She asked him to install deadbolt locks and to provide adequate lighting in the common areas. Grassly did not make these improvements.

On October 12, 1997, Janet was assaulted and robbed in her apartment. The intruder had hidden in the dark hallway and forced the cheap, button lock to gain entry. Janet moved out the next day.

Discussion

Our client Janet Washington has asked whether her landlord is liable for injuries she suffered when she was assaulted and robbed in her apartment. As the following discussion will show, while several recent cases around the United States have extended liability to landlords for failing to provide adequate security to protect against foreseeable crimes, the most recent California Supreme Court decision refused to find crime foreseeable unless a prior crime occurred on the premises. Since no prior crime occurred in our client's apartment building, the defendant will argue that crime was not foreseeable and that therefore our client cannot state a cause of action. While this decision will be difficult to overcome, we can argue that it should be distinguished since it involved the provision of security guards at a shopping mall. We can argue that given the special need to protect vulnerable residential tenants from crime in their dwellings, landlords should be required to provide at least minimal security precautions including deadbolt locks and adequate lighting. For residential property, we can argue that foreseeability can be established based on the totality of the circumstances, including the high neighborhood crime rate and our client's warnings to her landlord.

The most recent California Supreme Court decision refusing to find a landlord liable for third-party crime is *Ann M. v. Pacific Plaza Shopping Center*, 6 Cal. 4th 666, 863 P.2d 207, 25 Cal. Rptr. 2d 137 (1993). In *Ann M.*, an employee of a photo processing service was raped at her workplace by an intruder who was never apprehended. She contended that the landlord was liable for failing to provide security guards to patrol the premises. The trial court granted the defendant's motion for summary judgment and the Supreme Court affirmed.

As the court explained, the burden of providing security guards was high and therefore the required showing of foreseeability of crime was also high. The court stressed that since the social costs of hiring a security service were significant, a high degree of foreseeability is required to impose liability. As the court stated, this high degree of foreseeability "rarely, if ever, can be proven in the absence of prior similar incidents of violent crime on the landowner's premises." *Id.* at 679, 863 P. 2d at 215, 25 Cal. Rptr. at 145. According to the court, this showing is required so that landlords are not unfairly burdened with the responsibility of becoming insurers of the public safety.

The defendant will argue that the *Ann M.* decision precludes imposition of liability in our case since no prior crimes occurred on the premises. Under this view, liability cannot be imposed without a high degree of foreseeability which can only be satisfied by showing prior similar incidents of prior crime. This approach is necessary, the defendant will argue, to prevent imposition of an unfair burden on landlords making them, in effect, the insurers of their tenants' safety.

In my opinion, we have some strong arguments to distinguish *Ann M.* First, the *Ann M.* case involved commercial rather than residential property. We can argue that while commercial tenants may be expected to take precautions for their own security and may have bargaining power to work out security terms in their leases, residential tenants are generally not expected to provide their own security and lack significant bargaining power in lease negotiations.

More importantly, we can distinguish *Ann M.* based on the security precaution at issue. In *Ann M.*, the precaution at issue was the hiring of private security guards to patrol the premises. The *Ann M.* court stressed the significant monetary and social costs this precaution would impose on the landowner. For this reason, the court required a high degree of foreseeability before imposing this precaution. On the other hand, the *Ann M.* court recognized that where "the harm can be prevented by simple means, a lesser degree of foreseeability may be required." *Id.* at 679, 863 P. 2d at 215, 25 Cal. Rptr. at 145. This lesser showing of foreseeability should be the standard in our case since the precautions at issue are simple and inexpensive—the provision of deadbolt locks and adequate lighting in the common areas. Given the minimal burden these precautions impose, a lesser showing of foreseeability is adequate to protect the landlord from unfair burdens while providing vulnerable residential tenants with at least the most basic features of reasonable security.

Since the *Ann M.* case is factually distinguishable, we can argue that the court should follow the approach of cases imposing liability on residential landlords who fail to provide minimally adequate security to their tenants. While only one California case has addressed this issue, we can buttress our argument with sister-state decisions imposing liability on residential landlords. This discussion will now turn to the authorities supporting this argument.

The California case that supports our argument for a lower standard of foreseeability in residential security cases is *Kwaitkowski v. Superior Trading Co.*, 123 Cal. App. 3d 324, 176 Cal. Rptr. 494 (1981). In *Kwaitkowski*, the court found that a tenant stated a negligence action against her landlord for injuries she suffered when she was assaulted, robbed, and raped in the dimly-lit lobby of her apartment building. The building was located in a high-crime area, and the landlord knew of similar crimes in the building a few months earlier. Moreover, tenants had complained to the landlord about the inadequate security. Despite these facts making crime foreseeable, the landlord failed to repair a defective front-door lock. The trial court sustained the defendant's demurrer, and the appellate court reversed. It held that a negligence action arose from the landlord's failure to take reasonable precautions against foreseeable crime. The court ruled that the landlord should be required to provide reasonably adequate security as a cost of doing business and could spread that risk to the tenants by modest rent increases.

We can argue that the *Kwaitkowski* case should be followed in our case. As in *Kwaitkowski*, the building was located in a high crime area and the cheap locks were inadequate to provide security. The goal of requiring adequate security in residential dwellings would thus be furthered by imposing liability in our case. Also, since a deadbolt lock is inexpensive, the burden on the landlord would be minimal and the cost could be passed on to the tenants through a modest rent increase. Moreover, in both cases, the tenants' complaints put the landlord on notice of the risk of crime and the inadequacy of the security. Thus, we can argue our case presents questions of fact as to the foreseeability of the crime and the reasonableness of the existing security. Since we can allege facts creating jury questions on these issues, the complaint should be allowed.

The defendant will argue that *Kwaitkowski* is distinguishable because in *Kwaitkowski* prior crimes had occurred in the building which made future crime foreseeable. The defendant will argue that absent a prior crime in the building, crime is not foreseeable as a matter of law, just as the supreme court concluded in *Ann M.* We can counter by pointing out that the *Kwaitkowski* court considered the totality of the circumstances in determining whether crime was foreseeable and that one fact alone was not determinative. Moreover, the high degree of foreseeability required in *Ann M.* should not be imposed in cases like our case and *Kwaitkowski* where minimal burdens would be imposed on the landlord. We will argue that foreseeability presents a question of fact for the jury in our case and that the case cannot be determined as a matter of law simply because no prior crime occurred on the premises.

To reinforce our argument that foreseeability may be established without a prior crime, we can present several sister-state decisions. Specifically, an Illinois court refused to dismiss a tenant's claim based on the defendant's argument that no prior crimes had occurred on the premises, *Shea v. Preservation Chicago, Inc.*, 565 N.E.2d 20 (Ill. 1990). In *Shea*, the tenant alleged the landlord failed to repair an interior door and safety lock. The court held that a reasonable landlord would have realized that this created the risk of unauthorized entry and criminal attacks by third persons even though no prior crimes were alleged. See also *Paterson v. Deeb*, 474 So. 2d 1210 (Fla. 1985) (the tenant alleged absence of proper door locks, high neighborhood crime rate, and warnings to landlord; the court held crime foreseeable even without prior crimes on the premises) and *Arroyo v. Fourteen Estusia Corp.*, 588 N.Y.S.2d 572 (N.Y. 1992) (the tenant alleged door locks in disrepair; the court held damaged locks made crime foreseeable even absent prior crimes). See Tracy A. Bateman and Susan Thomas, *Landlord's Liability for Failure to Protect Tenant from Criminal Acts of Third Person*, 43 ALR5th 207 (1996).

Although these out-of-state cases are, of course, persuasive only, we can use them to argue that the trend is to impose liability on residential landlords for failing to provide minimal security precautions even though no prior crimes had occurred on the premises. We can stress that this view is consistent with the California law since the *Ann M.* decision expressly recognized that a lesser showing of foreseeability may be appropriate where the precautions at issue are simple and inexpensive. Moreover, the *Kwaitkowski* decision endorsed a totality of the circumstances test for residential landlords who fail to provide adequate door locks. The defendant will counter that *Ann M.* held that, as a matter of law, foreseeability always requires a prior crime on the premises.

From this review of the current case law, I conclude that we may be able to state a cause of action for negligence based on the foreseeability of crime from the totality of the circumstances. While the defendant has some strong arguments that California law requires a prior crime on the premises, the leading case is distinguishable on the facts. Moreover, our cause of action is supported by the policy of requiring residential landlords to provide at least minimal security to protect vulnerable tenants from violent crime.

Conclusion

In my opinion, we may be able to state a negligence cause of action on behalf of Janet Washington. If you would like, I'll draft a letter to Ms. Washington and advise her of the results of my research. Perhaps you would like me to arrange for her to come in for a conference so that we can discuss her options.

If she wishes to proceed with an action against Mr. Grassly, I'd like the opportunity to draft a complaint to precisely allege the occurrence of prior crimes near to the apartment. I'll see what I can come up with concerning the crime rates generally and specifically near the apartment. We should also allege as specifically as possible the warning Ms. Washington gave her landlord about the risk of crime. From these facts the court may find a question of fact is presented as to whether crime was foreseeable.

Chapter 2

Client Letter

Your supervising attorney was pleased with your excellent analysis and has asked you to draft a client letter. From an ethical perspective, the client letter reflects the central responsibilities of the attorney-client relationship. This chapter will first introduce some fundamental rules governing this relationship, including the lawyer's ethical obligation to explain the law in plain English so that clients can make informed decisions. We'll then turn to the client letter itself, considering its purpose, audience, content, tone, and style.

Professional Responsibilities in Advising Clients

This section will consider the lawyer's duty to keep the client informed, to explain the law in plain English, to discuss all relevant considerations, to give candid advice, and to preserve client confidences.

Duty to keep the client informed

The lawyer has an obligation to keep the client informed. This obligation is reflected both in the Model Rules of Professional Conduct and the *Restatement (Third) of the Law Governing Lawyers*.[1] According to the Model Rules, "A lawyer shall keep a client reason-

---

1. MODEL RULES OF PROFESSIONAL CONDUCT Rule 1.4 (1997) [hereinafter MODEL RULES]; RESTATEMENT (THIRD) OF THE LAW GOVERNING LAWYERS § 31 (Proposed Final Draft No. 1, 1996) [hereinafter RESTATEMENT].

ably informed about the status of a matter and promptly comply with reasonable requests for information."[2] The *Restatement* explains that a lawyer must both keep the client informed of significant developments and also provide progress reports at reasonable intervals.[3]

Duty to explain the law in plain English

In counseling clients, the lawyer must explain the law in plain English. According to the Model Rules, the lawyer is responsible for technical legal issues and tactics.[4] However, the client is responsible for "decisions concerning the objectives of representation" and must be consulted "as to the means by which they are to be pursued."[5] For the client's participation to be meaningful, the lawyer must explain matters to the client "to the extent reasonably necessary to make informed decisions regarding the representation."[6]

The *Restatement* refines this duty. According to the *Restatement*, the lawyer may need to communicate with the client "even in matters the lawyer is to decide ... because the lawyer's decision must seek the objectives of the client *as defined by the client*."[7] To define the objectives, the client must understand the available legal options. Lawyers should not assume that clients wish to press every point to the limit regardless of the cost to themselves or the consequences to others.[8]

Of course, in pursuing the client's objectives, the lawyer is constrained by the law. Both the Model Rules and the *Restatement* prohibit lawyers from counseling clients to engage in criminal or fraudulent conduct.[9] While lawyers advise clients about the law and the legal system, including the legality of past and contemplated conduct, this professional role does not entitle lawyers to violate the

---

2. Model Rules, *supra* note 1, Rule 1.4 (a).
3. Restatement, *supra* note 1, § 31 cmt. c.
4. Model Rules, *supra* note 1, Rule 1.2 cmt. 1.
5. Model Rules, *supra* note 1, Rule 1.2.
6. Model Rules, *supra* note 1, Rule 1.4.
7. Restatement, *supra* note 1, § 31 cmt. b (emphasis added).
8. Restatement, *supra* note 1, § 31 cmt. c.
9. Model Rules, *supra* note 1, Rule 1.2(d); Restatement of the Law Governing Lawyers § 151 and cmt. b thereto (Tentative Draft No. 8, 1997) [hereinafter Restatement, Tentative Draft].

criminal law or the rights of third parties.[10] A lawyer who advises or assists a client in conduct that violates the rights of a third person may be liable to that person and to the client for malpractice; a lawyer who advises or assists a client in fraudulent or criminal conduct may be disciplined; and a lawyer who advises or assists a client in criminal conduct may be prosecuted as a principal or an accomplice to the crime.[11] The legal restraints on advising clients are complicated by the uncertainties of the law. For this reason, a lawyer can properly test the scope and application of the law to the client's problem if a good faith argument can be made to support the client's position.[12]

Under these ethical guidelines, the lawyer must pursue the client's objectives within the bounds of the law. To fulfill this obligation the lawyer must consult the client and respect the client's decisions. But to make an informed decision, the client needs to understand the law. For example, how can a client make an informed decision to challenge existing precedent without understanding the merits of the legal arguments? To ensure that the client's decision is well informed, the lawyer must take the time to explain the substance of the law carefully, in plain English.

Duty to discuss all relevant considerations

Under both the Model Rules and the *Restatement*, the lawyer has the duty as an advisor to discuss both the law and all the other factors that bear on the client's situation, including "moral, economic, social, and political factors."[13] Initially, you may be uncomfortable with the notion that you should address anything but legal issues. After all, money and morality are awkward topics. But non-legal issues are often central to the client's problem and cannot be ignored.

Let's consider a couple of examples. Assume you represent an eighty-year-old client who has been injured in an automobile acci-

---

10. MODEL RULES, *supra* note 1, Rule 1.2 cmt. 6; RESTATEMENT, TENTATIVE DRAFT, *supra* note 9, § 151 and cmt. b and c thereto.
11. RESTATEMENT, TENTATIVE DRAFT, *supra* note 9, § 151 and cmt. b and c thereto.
12. RESTATEMENT, TENTATIVE DRAFT, *supra* note 9, § 151(2).
13. MODEL RULES, *supra* note 1, Rule 2.1. *See also* RESTATEMENT, TENTATIVE DRAFT, *supra* note 9, § 151(3).

dent. She needs money for medical care and in-home services. Should you explain that litigation is slow, stressful, and expensive? Should you discuss the advantages of accepting less money if settlement can be accomplished quickly? Or, assume you represent a partner in a family business. Should you advise your client to sue his brother without considering the damage this might cause to their family? In either instance, a purely technical analysis of the merits of litigation would be inadequate. The lawyer should discuss with the client all relevant factors to help the client define the objectives of the representation and evaluate the options.[14]

A recurring question is whether to pursue litigation. Just because the client has a valid cause of action does not mean that the client ought to sue. A lawyer will often serve the client well by finding quicker, more economical ways to resolve disputes. As Abraham Lincoln once said:

> Discourage litigation. Persuade your neighbors to compromise whenever you can. Point out to them how the nominal winner is often a real loser, in fees, expense and waste of time. As a peacemaker, the lawyer has a superior opportunity of being a good man. There will still be business enough.[15]

Given the cost of litigation, lawyers should explain alternative dispute resolution procedures (ADR). Indeed, recent ethics opinions have concluded that lawyers are required to explain ADR so that clients can make informed procedural decisions.[16] This duty to the client compliments the lawyer's duty as an officer of the court to avoid unnecessary litigation. As one court observed, to spare courts the burden of needless litigation, the lawyer and client should consider pre-suit mediation.[17]

In helping a client evaluate options, the lawyer should warn the client about negative consequences. People with problems some-

---

14. A very helpful book about the attorney-client relationship is David A. Binder, et al., Lawyers As Counselors: A Client-Centered Approach (1991).

15. The Collected Works of Abraham Lincoln 81–82 (R. Basler ed., 1953), *quoted in* P. Mars Scott, *Professionalism: Has the Meaning Changed,* Trial, June 1989, at 87.

16. Pa. Ethics Op. 90-125; Kan. Ethics Op. 94-1; Mich. Op. RI-255; Mich. Op. RI-262; Arthur Garwin, *Show Me the Offer,* A.B.A. J., June 1997, at 84.

17. Jackson v. Philadelphia, 858 F. Supp. 464 (E.D. Pa. 1994).

times make dreadful mistakes. If your client is planning to do something foolish or short-sighted, you should say so. Sometimes clients persist in socially irresponsible conduct. We may not be able to deter them, but we should not help them. The lawyer must withdraw from the representation if it would result in a violation of the rules of professional conduct or other law.[18] And the lawyer may withdraw from representation if the client persists in conduct the lawyer finds criminal, fraudulent, imprudent, or repugnant.[19]

According to the *Restatement,* a lawyer is not required to carry out an instruction that "the lawyer reasonably believes to be unethical or similarly objectionable."[20] The lawyer should try to dissuade the client from such conduct, but, if the client persists, the lawyer may withdraw after obtaining any required court approval.[21] An ethical lawyer would never say, " 'I helped my client do something evil but that's not a problem for me because it's not my fault that my client is evil.' "[22]

Duty of candor

In keeping the client informed, the lawyer has a duty of candor.[23] This duty often compels the lawyer to deliver bad news and propose unattractive options.[24] While the lawyer can try to soften the news to maintain the client's morale, the lawyer must be honest with the client, even when it hurts and, indeed, especially when it hurts.[25]

Avoid the temptation to give an unduly rosy opinion to cheer up your client. Clients buoyed by unrealistic expectations will make costly decisions. A client who has an overly optimistic view may reject a reasonable settlement offer, only to lose at trial after wasting thousands of dollars on unproductive attorneys' fees. You should also avoid the temptation to give an unduly pessimistic opinion to

---

18. MODEL RULES, *supra* note 1, Rule 1.16(a)(1); RESTATEMENT, *supra* note 1, § 44(2).

19. MODEL RULES, *supra* note 1, Rule 1.16(b) and cmt. 7 thereto; RESTATEMENT, *supra* note 1, § 44(3).

20. RESTATEMENT, *supra* note 1, § 32 cmt. d.

21. *Id.*

22. ROGER S. HAYDOCK ET AL., LAWYERING: PRACTICE AND PLANNING 19 (1996).

23. MODEL RULES, *supra* note 1, Rule 2.1.

24. MODEL RULES, *supra* note 1, Rule 2.1 cmt. 1.

25. *Id.*

protect yourself if things turn out poorly. A client who erroneously believes the case is weak will be discouraged from vigorously asserting enforceable legal rights. Simply put, you owe your client your honest opinion.

Duty to preserve client confidences

The lawyer has a duty to hold all client information in strictest confidence.[26] By explaining the rules of confidentiality, the client will be "encouraged to communicate fully and frankly with the lawyer even as to embarrassing or legally damaging subject matter."[27] You should make sure that your client understands that you can only help if you know the truth. If you don't know the truth you will be unable to accurately evaluate the situation. Moreover, the truth usually comes out eventually — often at the worst possible moment. If you are unprepared, you will not be able to protect your client. So encourage candid communication by assuring your client of your duty of confidentiality.

Having established this confidential relationship, the lawyer should consider the risk that written advice may lead to the inadvertent disclosure of confidential information or the waiver of the attorney-client privilege. A lawyer who has confidential client information must use reasonable care in controlling the manner in which the information is stored, retrieved, and transmitted.[28] Of course, by including the information in a client letter, you are not disclosing it to third parties. But letters revealing confidential information can be dangerous. Letters get misplaced; they get photocopied; and they end up in files which others may read. You cannot control them after they leave your office. If the information is sensitive, you may wish to discuss the matter orally with your client.

Purpose of a Client Letter

As we have seen, you must make sure that your clients are well informed about their legal affairs and equipped to make decisions

---

26. Model Rules, *supra* note 1, Preamble and Rule 1.6.
27. Model Rules, *supra* note 1, Rule 1.6 cmt. 4.
28. Restatement, *supra* note 1, § 112 cmt. d.

reflecting their values and priorities. The purpose of the client letter is to provide the necessary information and to present the available options. But you may feel that your responsibilities tug in opposite directions: you need to carefully explain your legal analysis, but you fear that putting it in writing may jeopardize confidentiality. In this section, we'll consider the pros and cons of writing a client letter.

To see why a client letter is often advisable, picture the following client conference. The lawyer is, of course, very comfortable in the office. The lawyer begins the session barricaded behind an impressive desk laden with other clients' files. Leaning back in the oversized chair, the lawyer launches into an incomprehensible barrage of legalese, interrupted by frequent phone calls. The client, on the other hand, is anxious. The client perches across the barricade, balancing a cup of coffee, and nervously wondering whether the news will be good or bad, whether the parking meter has expired, whether the car is being towed, and whether the bill for this conference will make bankruptcy inevitable. Understandably, the client doesn't understand anything the lawyer is saying.

Finally, the lawyer is distracted by some urgent matter and wants to get rid of the client. At this point the lawyer says, "There. Now I've told you the legal situation. I think we should sue, but it's your decision. What do you want to do?" The client has no grasp of the legal analysis nor the available options, but is reluctant to say so for fear of appearing stupid or indecisive. The client answers, "Well, I guess we should sue." The lawyer says, "O.K., if that's what you want." A secretary ushers the client to the elevator. The parking meter has expired; the client's car has been towed; the bill is enormous. The client is vaguely angry and definitely nervous about what's going on.

Now let's consider the client letter. By writing a letter, you can carefully explain the law in plain English and identify the options for your client to consider. Your client will then have an opportunity to read and reread the letter in familiar and calm surroundings. If appropriate, your client will be able to talk it over with family and friends.[29] After the client has had a chance to mull it over, he or she

---

29. *Caveat:* A lawyer should carefully explain the attorney-client privilege to the client. Be sure to caution your client not to accidentally waive the privilege by discussing confidential matters with family and friends.

will be ready to ask questions and weigh the available options. You can then get together, review the options, and reach a decision fitting your client's needs. In short, beginning the counseling process with a carefully drafted client letter may be the best way to ensure that your client will make informed decisions about the legal problem.

On the other hand, think carefully before you put highly sensitive or confidential information in writing. The *Restatement* defines confidential client information as information relating to the client "other than information that is generally known."[30] Consider this definition in drafting client letters. If the information is generally known, you are probably safe in putting it in the letter. But if it isn't, maybe you should omit it. For example, if you were representing a spouse in a divorce proceeding, you could safely write a letter discussing information known to both sides: the purchase price of the home, the balance in the joint savings account, the blue-book value of the cars, the civil code provisions governing repayment for educational expenses. On the other hand, you probably should not write a letter discussing your client's adulterous affair. As a rule of thumb, avoid putting lethal information in a client letter.

Simply put, the purpose of a client letter is to provide necessary information for decision making without unwittingly jeopardizing confidentiality. As you write client letters, be mindful of both these goals. Take the time to explain the law in plain English and to present options for your client to consider, but be cautious about including sensitive information that needs vigilant protection.

Audience for a Client Letter

Before you begin drafting a client letter, try to picture your client. Because your client has come to you with a legal problem, you can usually assume that the client is concerned about the situation and anxious to get your opinion. If you are a new associate, you may not have much client contact, but you should at least know whether the client is a lawyer, a business executive, or a lay person. A corporate executive will understand business jargon that you might have to define for a concert pianist. Tailor the level of explanation to your client's needs.

---

30. Restatement, *supra* note 1, § 111.

Form and Content of a Client Letter

A client letter will usually include: (a) an opening paragraph restating the client's question and summarizing your answer; (b) a review of the relevant facts; (c) an explanation of the governing law; (d) an outline of the options for your client to consider; (e) an explanation of any documents enclosed with the letter; (f) a request for additional information; and (g) a closing paragraph. If the letter is lengthy, you may wish to set off different sections of your letter with headings. If your letter is short, the sections can be flagged by topic sentences. An outline template and sample client letter are included at the end of this chapter.

Opening paragraph

Your opening paragraph should state the question your client has asked and provide your answer. Logically, your answer could either begin or end the letter. But your client is anxious to learn your conclusion. If you put it at the end, your client is likely to flip through the letter looking for the answer and may not read the body of the letter very carefully. On the other hand, if you begin with the answer, you will relieve your client's anxiety and help orient your client to the explanation of the law. If you can give an unqualified answer, hooray! However, as you must suspect by now, the law is seldom clear. It's scary, but you owe your client your honest opinion and should explain its limitations.

In stating your opinion, pay special attention to the language you use. Avoid gambling language such as "your chances are about 50/50." While this language can be helpful in face-to-face conversations, it seems cavalier in writing. Similarly, avoid introducing your opinion by stating "I feel" or "I believe." Your client wants your professional judgment, not your feelings or personal beliefs. To reassure your client that your opinion reflects careful research and analysis, use phrases like "in my opinion" or "our research shows." Finally, if you are delivering bad news, be sensitive to your reader's reaction. While you must be candid, you needn't be callous. Don't casually write: "My research shows that you will never recover the $500,000 that you've blown on this project." At a minimum you can acknowledge your client's certain disappointment: "While I realize that your investment represents a significant loss to your company, unfortunately my research reveals that the law fails to provide you with a legal remedy."

Here is an example of an opening paragraph of a client letter providing the lawyer's conclusion:

> I have researched the possibility that you may be able to re-cover from your landlord for injuries you suffered when you were assaulted and robbed in your apartment. Based on this research, in my opinion we can make a strong argument that your landlord should be held responsible. While I can't guar-antee that a court will agree with this conclusion, I think a lawsuit would probably be successful if you wish to proceed.

Review the facts

Explain to your client that the legal outcome depends on the facts and ask your client to review the facts to make sure you have under-stood them. Then set out the facts on which you rely. Invite your client to correct any errors or misunderstandings and to advise you of any additional facts. Stress your need to know negative facts so that you can address any problems they may create. In some cases, to en-courage frank communication, you may wish to remind your client that you will hold all damaging information in strict confidence.

Explain the law

Explaining the law in plain English takes time and thought. Your client does not need to understand every technicality but does need to understand the essence of the law as it applies to the problem. The explanation in the letter should therefore be a shorter and sim-pler version of the analysis set out in the office memorandum. To give your client a balanced understanding, advise your client of the arguments for both sides. Since abstract discussions of the law are confusing, explain how the law applies in terms of your client's problem. Avoid citations and legalese. If absolutely necessary, in-clude citations and legal terms with explanations and definitions.

Hitting the right level of explanation can be difficult. If you are writing to a lay person, imagine explaining the problem to an inter-ested and intelligent person who does not happen to have legal training. I usually use my mother as a guide: How would I explain the problem to Mom? Another test is to use yourself: Would I have understood this letter four months ago? And always tailor the explanation to the client; a letter to in-house corporate counsel will explain the law differently than a letter to a ballet dancer.

In practice, your letters should be as complete as possible. When advising clients about possible litigation, you should help them weigh the risks and costs against the potential recovery. You should discuss theories of liability, likelihood of success, potential recovery, comparable verdicts, probable defenses, and anticipated expenses. When you are discussing several issues in your letter, help your reader follow the analysis by breaking the explanation down into separate subsections with an introductory roadmap and headings.

Present the options

Your goal is to help your clients make informed legal decisions in their best interests. Be careful not to railroad your client into a decision that seems right to you; instead, present the options for your client's consideration and identify the pros and cons of each option. Encourage your client to consider economic, social and psychological aspects of each option. For example, a lawsuit may be well supported by legal authorities, but pursuing litigation will be stressful and expensive. Your client may wish to abandon a claim to save money and preserve peace of mind. Similarly, legal disputes often arise between people who have on-going relationships. Your client may have a strong legal action against a landlord, but should consider whether the benefits of pursuing that action are outweighed by the risk of losing the lease. The right decision depends on the individual client's situation and values.

In weighing the alternatives, it may be helpful for your client to discuss the matter with others. Legal decisions often affect other family members, friends, or business associates. Your client may wish to seek their advice or to take their perspectives into account. However, if confidential information is involved, be sure to warn your client not to waive the attorney-client privilege by sharing your letter with others.

Provide copies of documents

Make it your practice to send your client copies of anything you prepare or receive on your client's behalf to keep your client informed of the status of the case. Explain the document you are enclosing in the body of your letter. If the document is included solely for the client's information, make that clear in the letter. On the other hand, if some response is required from your client, make sure the client understands what is required and when. Any deadlines should be clearly set out and perhaps <u>underscored</u> in your letter.

Request additional information

You have already explained to your client that the legal opinion rests on the facts as you understand them, and you have asked for any additional information the client considers relevant. You may also wish to ask your client for specific additional information. You can include a list of questions either in the letter itself or as an attachment. By asking for specific information, you may trigger your client's memory of related details. Let your client know that your inquiry is open ended and that you'll welcome any details the client can provide.

Closing paragraph

In closing the letter, you should solicit your client's questions and concerns. If appropriate, invite your client to a conference. If your letter has requested additional information, explain when you need it and how it should be transmitted. Be sure to let your client know what needs to be done and what to expect. For example:

> Let's set up an appointment to talk over these alternatives and discuss any questions you have. Please call my office to set up our meeting at your convenience sometime in the next week or two. In the meantime, please be sure to mail me a copy of your lease so that I can review it before we meet. I look forward to seeing you soon.

A special caution should be included about any statute of limitations problem. In undertaking representation of a client who is considering litigation or may consider litigation in the future, you should calculate the earliest possible date that any applicable statute of limitations may expire. Err on the side of caution in calendaring this date. Advise the client of this date and its significance. As the date approaches, be sure to warn your client and take any steps necessary to protect your client's rights.

Tone and Style of a Client Letter

Your client came to you for help with a problem; you are a trusted ally. Remember that legal problems are always frustrating and often frightening, and be sensitive to your client's anxieties. Your client should always feel that you sincerely care about the problem and are determined to help. Since the tone of your letter should reflect your relationship with your client, adjust your tone to fit the specific client. For example, if your are writing to a client who is also an old friend, you will probably be less formal than if you are writing to a new client. With most clients you should be professional, supportive, and respectful.

Remember, if you are writing to a lay person, this is no time to show off your newly-acquired mastery of legalese. Use a simple, straightforward style and plain English. For example:

Don't write: I have transmitted on the aforesaid date a communication containing the said contractual proposition.

Write: I sent the offer on June 10.

If you must use a legal term, explain it in plain English in terms of your client's problem. For example, if you are discussing a statute of frauds problem:

Don't write: Clearly, the statute of frauds bars enforcement of a purchase-money option between the vendee and the vendor except in cases where it is signed by the party to be charged.

Write: The law requires some contracts to be in writing and to be signed. Contracts for the sale of houses fall into this category. In your case, you had an oral understanding with the owner of the house that he would sell it to you for $100,000. But unfortunately, since the owner never signed a written contract for this sale, you probably won't be able to legally force him to keep this promise.

Personalize your letter by focusing on concrete facts, not abstractions. To give your letters a conversational touch, you can use personal pronouns and contractions. A word of caution: Don't go overboard. Your spoken style may contain many colloquial expressions which would be inappropriate in a letter. For example:

Too stuffy: The firm is of the opinion that in most analogous instances an employer should refrain from terminating an employee until such time as the employer has effectuated the implementation of certain advisable precautionary procedures with respect to the basis for the proposed termination.

Too informal: You don't want to get nailed with a lawsuit from this jerk, so don't shaft him until we get somebody to say he screwed up.

About right: We don't think you should fire your sales manager until we've had time to investigate and verify your suspicions about him.

As you've probably learned from your casebooks, reading legal analysis can be daunting. So be considerate of your client and present the analysis in manageable chunks; use short sentences (average 25 words or less) and short paragraphs (average ¼ page or less). Provide a topic sentence for each paragraph to help your reader follow your reasoning. Omit surplus words and legalese, but don't sacrifice clarity for brevity. If your letter is too dense and abstract, your client won't understand it. Your client will more easily understand a longer letter written in plain, everyday English.

Outline Template for a Client Letter

I. Opening paragraph

Restate client's question and summarize of your answer.

II. Review the facts

Set out the facts on which your opinion is based and solicit corrections and additions.

III. Explain the law

Explain the law in plain English. Make sure your explanation is balanced and objective so that your client is well informed.

IV. Present the options

Present as many options as possible for your client's consideration. Explain the pros and cons taking into account both legal and non-legal factors.

V. Provide copies of documents

Enclose copies of any documents you have prepared or received on your client's behalf. Explain what they are and whether your client needs to respond to them. If a response is required, highlight the deadline.

VI. Request addition information

If you need additional information, ask for it and encourage your client to provide any other details about the case.

VII. Closing paragraph

Solicit your client's questions and invite your client to a conference. Let your client know what needs to be done and whether there are any deadlines. Warn your client if a statute of limitations is running and when it will expire.

Sample Client Letter

MASON, RUMPOLE & VAN OWEN
Attorneys at Law
Davis, California 95616

March 25, 1998

Ms. Janet Washington
123 Wolk Avenue
Davis, California 95616

Dear Ms. Washington:

I have researched the possibility that you may be able to recover from your landlord, Mr. Grassly, for the injuries you suffered when you were assaulted in your apartment. Based on this research, in my opinion we can make a solid argument that your landlord should be held responsible. While I can't guarantee that a court will agree with this opinion, I think a lawsuit would probably be successful if you wish to proceed.

Before I explain the law and your alternatives to you, I'd like to review my understanding of the facts. As you may know, most lawsuits are won or lost based on the facts that are presented. For this reason, I need to make sure my understanding is correct. Please feel free to correct me if I'm mistaken about anything and call me if you think of any other facts to add. I know it must be painful for you, but please try to think back on what happened and read these facts to make sure they are correct.

As I understand the facts, your building had a button lock on the door and poor lighting in the hallway. As far as you know, no crimes had occurred in the building until you were assaulted and robbed. You heard that several burglaries had occurred in the neighborhood, so you asked Mr. Grassly to put a deadbolt lock on your apartment door. Mr. Grassly refused. A few weeks later, an intruder broke into your apartment even though the door was locked. He beat you and stole your money and jewelry. You spent two days in the hospital and then moved out of your apartment.

Based on these facts, I researched the law. While I think we have a strong argument, the law is not entirely clear. Let me explain the legal problem to you. To determine whether your landlord is liable, the court will look at similar cases to see what they have decided. In similar cases, landlords have been held liable for failing to provide reasonable safety precautions to protect tenants from foreseeable crimes. We can argue that the court should follow these cases and hold Mr. Grassly liable for failing to provide a deadbolt lock which would be a reasonable precaution in your neighborhood because of the high crime rate.

However, Mr. Grassly will have an argument in his favor. In those cases where the landlords were found liable, a prior crime had occurred in the building. Because a crime had already occurred, the courts concluded that it was foreseeable to the landlord that crimes would occur in the future. In cases where no prior crimes had occurred in the building, the courts have been reluctant to find that the landlord should have foreseen a future crime. Mr. Grassly will argue that the crimes against you were not foreseeable because no prior crimes had occurred in the building. I haven't found a single case in California where a tenant has successfully sued a landlord without proving a prior crime occurred in the building. Thus, the court could find that the crime against you was not foreseeable and that therefore Mr. Grassly is not liable.

Although no cases are exactly like yours, we may be able to convince the court that the high crime rate in your neighborhood made crime in your building foreseeable. If the neighborhood crime rate made a crime in your building foreseeable, then Mr. Grassly was under a duty to take reasonable precautions. In recent years courts have had a tendency to hold landlords responsible for injuries that happen in their buildings which could have been prevented at a reasonable cost. We can argue that the cost of a deadbolt was a reasonable precaution.

As you can see, the law doesn't provide a clear answer as to whether you can successfully sue Mr. Grassly. Because there is no case exactly like your case, I cannot predict the outcome with certainty. You have several options to consider at this point. First, we can sue Mr. Grassly. In my opinion such a lawsuit might well be successful and you may recover substantial damages including your medical expenses, the value of the property that was stolen, your moving expenses, and compensation for your pain, suffering and emotional distress. However, as you can see, Mr. Grassly will have some strong arguments and we may lose in court. Moreover, even if we succeed, litigation is time-consuming and stressful. In the course of a lawsuit, you would have to repeatedly think and talk about the attack on you. This could be painful and upsetting for you. In deciding whether to proceed with a lawsuit, the emotional strain is something for you to consider.

A second alternative would be to begin negotiations with your landlord for an out-of-court settlement. Mr. Grassly might decide to avoid the expense of a lawsuit by paying a settlement. Even if he believes he would ultimately win in court, he might wish to save the time, expense, and adverse publicity of litigation. We can begin settlement negotiations at any time. If he fails to respond, we could then file a lawsuit.

A third alternative is to explore alternative dispute resolution procedures like arbitration or mediation. Alternative dispute resolution (or "ADR") is often quicker, less formal, more private, and less expensive than full-scale litigation. This alternative is only available if Mr. Grassly agrees. But you may wish to have me raise the possibility with him as a way to save unnecessary expenses and to resolve the matter as quickly and quietly as possible.

A fourth alternative is to file suit and then to begin negotiations. Filing a lawsuit should convince Mr. Grassly that we are serious about pursuing this matter and may promote early settlement discussions. We can also negotiate with Mr. Grassly about using ADR. We can always drop the lawsuit if you decide to accept an out-of-court settlement or if you decide that you no longer wish to pursue the matter.

Finally, you may decide that you are not interested in pursuing this matter in light of the uncertainly of the outcome. You may feel that you don't want to endure the expense, anxiety, and frustration of a lawsuit which may not turn out successfully. Please feel free to take this option.

I suggest that you talk these options over with your family and friends. Please give me a call if you have any questions or concerns. I'm enclosing a memo presenting my research. This memo is for me and the other lawyers to use in representing you; but if you wish to understand the law in greater detail, you may wish to read it as well.

After you've had a chance to think this over, please call and set up an appointment in the next few weeks so that I can answer any questions and help you decide which alternative you wish to pursue. I want to help you make the decision that is right for you. As we previously discussed, we need to keep in mind the statute of limitations which expires in six months. I look forward to seeing you soon.

Very truly yours,
Philida Trant

Enclosure

Chapter 3

Rewritten Office Memorandum

Justice Louis Brandeis once said, "There is no such thing as good writing. There is only good rewriting."[1] We'll learn rewriting by breaking the process down into sequenced steps. It's like hosting a dinner party. What if you serve the ice cream before you put the lasagna in the oven? The ice cream will melt before the main course is cooked. It's the same with writing; you need to focus on the substance before the finishing touches.

Although they differ on the exact number, scholars agree that the writing process involves distinct steps.[2] We'll approach it in five steps:

Prewriting:	Planning and performing the research and analysis; outlining a draft.
Completing a first draft:	Getting your ideas down on paper so that you can begin rewriting.
Rewriting:	Rewriting the draft to get your ideas across to the reader; revising the content, large-scale organization, and paragraphs.
Editing:	Reviewing the draft for sentence-level problems; applying plain English principles; polishing the tone and style.

---

1. RICHARD K. NEUMANN, JR., LEGAL REASONING AND LEGAL WRITING 59 (2d ed. 1994).
2. VEDA R. CHARROW ET AL., CLEAR & EFFECTIVE LEGAL WRITING 208 (2d ed. 1995) (three stages subdivided into eight steps in the writing process); LINDA HOLDEMAN EDWARDS, LEGAL WRITING, xxi (1996) (the four main stages of a writing task); NEUMANN, *supra* note 1, at 55 (four stages in the writing process); TOM GOLDSTEIN & JETHRO K. LIEBERMAN, THE LAWYER'S GUIDE TO WRITING WELL 42 (1989) (the ten stages of legal writing).

> **Proofreading:** Checking for grammatical errors, misspellings, and proper citation form.

In practice, the process is messier and less linear than these steps suggest, but they provide a rough roadmap and should free you from "the self-defeating quest to get it right the first time."[3] On any project, if you start the draft early and don't demand perfection, you'll have something to work with and time for details later.

When I was first practicing law, I thought that my writing process should proceed in a neat, linear progression, like this:

1   2   3   4   5   6   7   8   9   10

I became distressed when it always seemed more like this:

1   2   3 〰〰〰 8   9   10

I've learned to accept the squiggle in the middle as part of my creative process and to allow myself time to get off the track. But I've also learned to budget time for the later steps of editing and proofreading. For me, the best approach is to start with an organized plan, to expect some mid-way chaos, and to complete the project with an after-the-fact outline, a disciplined edit, and careful proofreading.

Turning to your office memo, in the prewriting stage, you evaluated the problem, researched the law, analyzed the authorities, developed the parties' arguments, and organized the analysis into an outline. In the first draft stage, you got your analysis down on paper in the format of an office memo. You've now gained some distance from the draft and are ready to rewrite it. The rewriting stage includes: (1) considering the reader's comments; (2) reconsidering the content; (3) revising the large-scale organization; and (4) reviewing each paragraph.

Rewrite Your Memorandum

Consider the reader's comments

Your memorandum will be returned to you with comments from either your instructor or your teaching assistant. These comments

---

3. GOLDSTEIN & LIEBERMAN, *supra* note 2, at 58 quoting from V. A. HOWARD & J. H. BARTON, THINKING ON PAPER 22 (1986).

give you a reader's honest reaction to your work and some suggestions for improvement. The reader's comments will help you identify problem areas and serve as the starting point for rewriting. If you have questions or wish to discuss the comments, arrange to talk to the reader. Often a few moments chatting in person can clarify comments and prevent confusion and frustration.

As you rewrite your memorandum, remember that you alone are responsible for your writing; your ability to criticize your own work is the most important skill to develop. The reader's comments are the beginning, not the end, of the rewriting process. Don't just make the revisions suggested by the comments, but rather review your writing with fresh eyes and strive to improve your work.

Reconsider the content

After three weeks of working on this problem, you have undoubtedly refined your analysis. With some distance from your first draft, you can read it with greater objectivity than when you completed it. Rethink your approach and revise your memo to reflect your current understanding:

- Are you satisfied with your analysis?
- Should you include additional authorities?
- Is relevant statutory language set out and applied to the problem?
- Are the cases presented completely (facts, procedural context, holding, and rationale)?
- Are the cases applied to the facts of your case? Did you explain the factual similarities and distinctions?
- Does the memo incorporate the policies supporting the legal analysis?
- Did you explore the arguments for both sides?
- Is your research current?
- Do you have additional information to evaluate?
- What additional information do you need?
- Is the memo thorough, objective, and clear?

When you're satisfied with the substantive analysis, review each section of the memo. The first thing your busy supervisor will ask is, "What the heck is the answer to my question?" Make sure your question presented and brief answer clearly set out the results of your research, your conclusion, and the crux of your analysis. Your reader doesn't want to have to read and analyze everything to figure out the answer, that's your job. Then check your statement of facts. Are they complete and well organized? Have you used chronological order? Would it be helpful to arrange them under topic headings? Have you omitted facts that don't bear of the precise legal issue analyzed in your memo? Finally, make sure that the conclusion wraps up the memo, identifies the next steps to take, and highlights any deadlines.

Revise the large-scale organization

Once you're satisfied with the content of your memo, you can revise its organization. Your supervisor needs a coherent presentation of the relevant legal authorities which have been applied to your client's problem. To help your reader follow the analysis, be sure your discussion opens with an introductory paragraph providing an overview and a roadmap of the arguments. Often in writing the first draft you will discover that the organization you initially planned needs some revision. That's a useful step in the writing process. Now make sure that those improvements are reflected in the introductory paragraph.

As you read through the body of the discussion section, make an outline from the topic sentences. This outline will serve two goals: (1) it will catch paragraphs that need topic sentences; and (2) it will reveal flaws in the organization. I have a few tricks for creating this outline quickly. One approach is to make a margin comment (one or two words) for each paragraph.[4] Or, if you're using a word processor, you can lift out and assemble all headings, subheadings, and topic sentences in a new document.[5] Finally, you can photocopy your draft and highlight the topic sentences with a colored marker.[6] Once you've identified the topic sentences, see if they create an outline of your analysis. If the combined topic sentences don't create an outline, try shifting them around to improve the organization. For example:

---

4. Terri LeClercq, Guide to Legal Writing Style 2 (1995).
5. Helene S. Shapo et al., Writing and Analysis in the Law 139 (3d ed. 1995).
6. Id.

- If a case on a single issue is discussed at several different places, try putting all the paragraphs about that case together.
- If a case addressing several distinct issues is discussed in one giant paragraph, try organizing your memo by issues rather than cases.
- If your organization buries the controlling supreme court ruling in a bundle of intermediate appellate decisions, out-of-state cases, and law review notes, reorganize the discussion to reflect the relative weight of the authorities.
- If your discussion is a jumble of unconnected authorities, figure out what they have in common and group the similar ones together. Try grouping all the cases on one issue together or grouping all the cases with similar facts together.
- If your discussion time-travels from new cases to old ones, consider whether chronological order would help your reader understand the development of the law. While the reader usually wants to know the current law, sometimes the law is evolving in a way that requires an historical explanation.

If you reorganize your discussion section, be sure to revise your introductory paragraph to reflect these improvements.

Now check your outline again. Did you discuss distinct issues in separate sections? Did you provide introductory and concluding paragraphs to each section? Is each section organized to reflect the arguments the parties will make in a logical order? Are the authorities included at appropriate points in your outline? Did you first present the authorities and then explain their application to the problem? Did you consider counter arguments? Did you draw conclusions and synthesize your analysis?

Review each paragraph

After revising the content and large-scale organization, your next priority is to structure your paragraphs to help the reader follow your memo. Paragraphs are not just random breaks on the page; paragraphs give your reader important messages about content. Each paragraph should be a meaningful unit which presents and develops a single, identifiable theme.

Read each paragraph as a unit, checking for coherence. Does each paragraph have a unifying theme? If you can't state the theme in one sentence, your paragraph probably needs revision. Is the theme expressed in the topic sentence? Don't make your reader figure out the unifying theme of your paragraph; state it directly in the topic sentence. After you've identified the theme and expressed it in a topic sentence, check the other sentences in the paragraph. Do the other sentences develop your theme? Each sentence should directly relate to the paragraph topic. If you find sentences which don't directly relate to the paragraph theme, take them out of your paragraph. They belong somewhere else. Your paragraph should now be a meaningful unit which develops a single topic.

The next step is to check paragraph length. Overly long paragraphs (more than one-half a page) are hard to read because they contain too much information for your reader to digest. Break them into shorter paragraphs. Short paragraphs (one to three sentences) can be choppy and disjointed. A series of short paragraphs will break the flow of your analysis. Find a unifying theme and combine these paragraphs into a more cohesive, longer paragraph.

The final step is to provide transitions between paragraphs. Ask yourself how each paragraph is connected to the preceding paragraph. If it continues to develop a theme, make sure the continuity is clear; if the paragraph changes directions, be sure to signal the departure. Here are a few transition devices for you to consider: (1) transition paragraphs; (2) transition sentences; and (3) transition words.

First, transition paragraphs can be used to bridge two themes or two lines of argument. Your reader has a better chance of following your discussion if you signal where you're going and explain why you are shifting from one point to another. A short transition paragraph provides closure to the first point and an introduction to the next point.

Second, transition sentences provide transitions between paragraphs. A sentence summarizing or echoing the theme of the preceding paragraph serves as a graceful link to the next paragraph. Transition sentences, if carefully drafted, can provide unobtrusive guidance to your reader, making your writing flow smoothly.

Third, transitional words or phrases provide concise signals, like road signs on the highway. Certain transition words indicate continuity, others indicate contrast, and still others indicate closure. Be sure you use them correctly or you'll give your reader a miscue. For example, continuity can be signaled in several ways. Enumeration, as illustrated by this passage, is one way to indicate continuity in developing a theme. It's not particularly subtle, but it does the job.

Other transitional words also indicate the continuing development of a theme. For example, if you are explaining an argument and want to restate it in different terms, your reader may think you are shifting to a different point unless you state your purpose. You can provide this signal by inserting a transitional word or phrase like "in other words," "to simplify," or "in short." Similarly, if you have been explaining an argument and want to provide an illustration, you reader may not see the connection without a signal. Try the following transitional words and phrases: "to illustrate," "for example," "for instance," and "specifically." And continuity can also be indicated by "and," "also," "in addition," "further," and "moreover."

You can also indicate continuity by a more subtle device called dovetailing. "Dovetailing is the overlap of language between two sentences that creates a bridge between those two sentences."[7] To create a dovetail, the writer takes the idea or language from the end of one sentence and repeats it near the beginning of the following sentence. For example:

> The defendant must respond to the complaint within <u>20 days</u>. <u>This time period</u> may be extended by stipulation of the parties for by the court for <u>good cause</u>. <u>Good cause</u> can be shown where the defendant has not been able to adequately investigate the allegations or <u>to secure legal representation</u>.
>
> To show inability <u>to retain a lawyer</u>, the defendant will have to produce evidence that a reasonable effort was made. Generally the defendant will submit a declaration stating that a number of lawyers were contacted and that they all declined the case.

As this example demonstrates, dovetailing is useful in connecting sentences within a paragraph as well as establishing continuity between paragraphs.

On the other hand, your paragraph may not be developing a prior theme but instead may be changing direction. Transition words and phrases can signal these shifts as well. If you fail to warn

---

7. LAUREL CURRIE OATES ET AL., LEGAL WRITING HANDBOOK 888 (1993).

your reader that you are changing direction, your reader may become confused and try to figure out a connection that doesn't exist. To flag a change of direction, you may use "but," "conversely," "despite," "however," "in contrast," and "on the other hand."

Finally, let your reader know if you are wrapping up your discussion of a point. If you don't warn your reader, your discussion may end abruptly and lack a sense of closure. You can signal concluding paragraphs with "as we have seen," "finally," "in short," "in summary," and "to conclude."

Edit Your Memorandum

After you've revised the large-scale organization and paragraphs, it's time to begin editing. This last step in the writing process unfortunately paralyzes too many writers in the earlier stages. As one commentator explained: "Nit-picking each word and idea as you write defeats the purpose of writing drafts. No writer can envision the larger organizational pattern and conclusion and simultaneously worry about dangling participles."[8] Now that you've revised the content and improved the organization, you can focus on sentence-level revisions.

We'll work on developing a readable style based on Richard Wydick's landmark book, *Plain English for Lawyers*.[9] Each time an assignment is rewritten, we'll add a few editing lessons and develop a checklist that sets efficient priorities. This week we'll begin with three editing lessons: (1) using short sentences; (2) omitting surplus words; and (3) minimizing quotations. Before editing your draft, study Chapters 1, 2 and 5 of *Plain English for Lawyers*.

Write short sentences

Legal writing is fairly dense. To help your reader understand, you should break the information up into manageable pieces by putting only one main idea in each sentence and keeping your sentences fairly short. Most scholars recommend an average sentence length

---

8. TERRI LECLERCQ, EXPERT LEGAL WRITING 33 (1995).
9. RICHARD C. WYDICK, PLAIN ENGLISH FOR LAWYERS (4th ed. 1998).

of 20–25 words.[10] After studying Chapter 5 of *Plain English for Lawyers,* review your draft to check the average sentence length. A quick way to spot problems is to draw slash marks through the periods marking the end of sentences. If the periods are about 1 1/2 lines apart, the sentence length is probably about right. But if the periods are more than two lines apart, the sentences may be too long to be readable. And if the periods pop up on every line, the sentences are probably choppy and disjointed. Revise your sentences until they average 25 words or less.

Omit surplus words

To write shorter sentences, eliminate unnecessary words. In Chapter 2 of *Plain English for Lawyers,* Richard Wydick presents four ways to cut surplus words: (1) avoid compound constructions; (2) avoid word-wasting idioms; (3) focus on the actor, the action and the object; and (4) omit redundant legal phrases. Study these lessons and then edit your draft to omit surplus words.

Use quotations sparingly

Be disciplined in using quotations. Trim them down to the essentials. As Richard Neumann explains, readers refuse to read big block quotations because they don't seem worth the trouble. "The more block quotations you use, the more quickly a reader will refuse to read any of them. And judges and supervising attorneys view large quotations as evidence of a writer's laziness."[11] So edit quotations carefully, including only key language and critical passages.

Some guidelines will help you edit quotations. First, always quote the statutory language governing your problem. Every word in a statute is important, and the precise statutory language may determine the outcome of your case. But don't just quote the statute; explain how it applies to your problem. Second, you may wish to quote a brief passage from a case when the exact language is critical or when it is exceptionally well written. But remember that the

---

10. Wydick, *supra* note 9, at 38; Shapo et al., *supra* note 5, at 165; Oates, *supra* note 7, at 604–605.
11. Neumann, *supra* note 1, at 232.

court was focusing on the specific problem before it. Your reader, on the other hand, is most interested in your analysis of your problem. Generally, your analysis will be more clear and concise if you summarize the decision and evaluate it in terms of your issues rather than quoting it at length in your discussion.

Proofread Your Memorandum

Save plenty of time to proofread because small errors can make a big impression. As one judge explained, while the reader usually understands what the writer meant to say, "there is a gnawing feeling on occasion that the obviousness of the uncorrected errors indicates that the brief, having not been read for these errors, may be equally unreliable in its substantive reasoning, or its analysis of authorities."[12] Simply put, careless errors make the writer look either ignorant or sloppy. No matter how careful you are, occasional errors are inevitable, but you should do everything possible to eliminate them.

---

12. Wilbur F. Pell, Jr., *Read Before Signing*, 66 A.B.A. J. 977 (1980).

Rewriting Checklist for an Office Memorandum

I. Rewriting

   A. Reconsider the content:

      1. Is the heading in the proper form?

      2. Does your question presented identify the legal issue starting with the general area of law and tying in the key facts?

      3. Does your brief answer respond directly to the question and provide an objective summary of the analysis?

      4. Does your statement of facts include the relevant facts in chronological order?

      5. Does your discussion include an introductory paragraph providing an overview of the analysis?

      6. Have you included all the necessary authorities?

      7. Have you thoroughly and objectively presented them? Have you included the key language from every statute? Have you included the facts, procedure, holding, and rationale of every case?

      8. Have you applied the authorities to your problem?

      9. Have you considered policy arguments?

      10. Have you anticipated counter arguments?

      11. Have you synthesized the analysis?

   B. Revise the large-scale organization:

      1. Have you included introductory and concluding paragraphs for each section?

      2. Can you outline your discussion using topic sentences?

   C. Review each paragraph:

      1. Does each paragraph have a topic sentence?

      2. Do the other sentences develop the topic?

      3. Have you checked paragraph length?

      4. Have you provided transitions?

II. Editing

    A. Edit each sentence:

        1. Have you written short sentences?

        2. Have you omitted surplus words?

    B. Use quotations sparingly:

        1. Have you avoided block quotations?

        2. Have you edited quotations carefully?

III. Proofreading

    A. Have you checked for grammatical errors?

    B. Have you checked for misspellings?

    C. Have you checked for proper citation form?

Chapter 4

Demand Letter

This week you'll draft a demand letter to the opposing party. We will assume that your client's informal attempts to resolve the problem have failed. You and your client have decided that your intervention may help to resolve the dispute. This chapter will first consider the ethical responsibilities in writing a demand letter. It will then address the letter's purpose, audience, form, and content. Finally, it will discuss the tone and style of a demand letter.

Professional Responsibilities in Writing a Demand Letter

When representing an unfortunate client with a compelling case, a lawyer is often tempted to write a hard-ball letter to bully the opponent into a quick settlement. This reaction raises four important ethical issues: (1) the obligation to communicate only through counsel for a represented party; (2) the constraints on threatening criminal action; (3) the obligation to be truthful; and (4) the requirements of professional courtesy.

Obligation to communicate through counsel

The Model Rules of Professional Conduct explain a lawyer's responsibilities in communicating with an opposing party. First, a lawyer is prohibited from communicating with an opposing party who is represented by another lawyer, "unless the lawyer has the consent of the other lawyer or is authorized by law to do so."[1] Fur-

---

1. MODEL RULES OF PROFESSIONAL CONDUCT Rule 4.2 (1997) [hereinafter MODEL RULES].

ther, in dealing with an unrepresented person, a lawyer shall make it clear that the lawyer is not disinterested.[2] Finally, a lawyer shall not give advice to an unrepresented person, other than the advice to retain a lawyer.[3]

To comply with this Rule, before you write directly to your client's opponent, be sure to ask your client if the opponent has an attorney and, if so, who that attorney is. If the opponent is represented, your demand letter should be addressed to the attorney. For purposes of this assignment, you may assume that the opponent has not yet retained a lawyer.

Constraints on threatening criminal process

When representing a plaintiff in a civil action, you may be tempted to threaten the defendant with criminal action. For example, you may be inclined to threaten to turn unscrupulous merchants over to the district attorney's consumer fraud unit, to report malpracticing lawyers to the state bar association, and to report malpracticing doctors to the state board of medical quality assurance.

Resist this temptation. According to some rules of professional conduct, using the criminal process to coerce an opponent in a civil action is a subversion of the criminal process which is designed for public protection. Moreover, threats to invoke the criminal process may deter an opponent from asserting legitimate legal rights and thereby undermine the civil process. For this reason, some states absolutely prohibit these threats. For example, in California a member of the bar is prohibited from threatening criminal, administrative, or disciplinary charges to gain an advantage in a civil dispute.[4]

While the Model Rules omitted the absolute prohibition against threatening criminal prosecution to gain an advantage in a civil case,[5] the Rules still impose significant restrictions. Specifically, three conditions must be met: (1) the criminal matter must be re-

---

2. MODEL RULES, *supra* note 1, Rule 4.3.
3. MODEL RULES, *supra* note 1, Rule 4.3 cmt.
4. CAL. R. PROF. CONDUCT Rule 7-104 (West 1996).
5. The MODEL RULES, *supra* note 1, deleted the absolute prohibition against threatening criminal process which was set forth in the prior MODEL CODE OF PROFESSIONAL RESPONSIBILITY DR 7-105 (1983).

lated to the client's civil claim; (2) the attorney must have a well-founded belief that both the civil and criminal proceedings are warranted; and (3) the attorney must not attempt to exert an improper influence over the criminal proceedings.[6]

In short, you should research the rule in your jurisdiction pertaining to threats of criminal action and comply with its requirements. Even if threats are technically allowed, consider whether this heavy-handed tactic is morally and professionally appropriate. Because this tactic is fraught with ethical peril, proceed with extreme caution.

Obligation to be truthful

The lawyer's obligation to be truthful is explained in Model Rule 4.1. First, in representing a client, a lawyer must not knowingly "make a false statement of material fact or law to a third person."[7] The comments to the Rule recognize that, in the context of negotiations, certain statements are not taken as statements of material fact.[8] The comments provide three important examples of statements which are not taken as material facts: (1) estimates of price; (2) estimates of value; and (3) intentions as to settlement of the claim.[9] Second, in addition to prohibiting affirmative misrepresentations, the Model Rule imposes a duty of disclosure "when disclosure is necessary to avoid assisting a criminal or fraudulent act by a client" unless the disclosure is otherwise prohibited.[10]

The boundaries of Rule 4.1 are blurry. What is an estimate of price or value? Certainly in negotiations a lawyer could say, "I think this is a big case." That opinion statement would not be taken by an opponent as a material fact. But what if the lawyer says, "We think it will cost $50,000 to repair the building," or "We have an estimate that it will cost $50,000 to repair the building." Are the two statements the same for purposes of negotiations?

---

6. ABA Comm. on Ethics and Professional Responsibility, Formal Op. 92-363 (1992).
7. MODEL RULES, *supra* note 1, Rule 4.1(a).
8. MODEL RULES, *supra* note 1, Rule 4.1 cmt. 2.
9. *Id.*
10. MODEL RULES, *supra* note 1, Rule 4.1(b).

Perhaps the issue is much simpler. In an article on ethics and advocacy, one lawyer explained that good ethics is good advocacy and developed a number of principles based on that premise. "First principle: Never lie.... Truthfulness is an essential component of ethical behavior. Nothing rings truer than the truth."[11] Lawyers who break the never-lie principle may face severe disciplinary consequences as a recent case illustrates.[12] In response to a letter from his opponent, a lawyer indicated that he did not anticipate obtaining a default against the opposing party. Then, without prior notice, he obtained a default order. After the default order was set aside, disciplinary proceedings ensued. The court found that his representations were designed to mask his intent to seek a default. As the court explained, the fabric of the legal profession is threatened when one lawyer lies to another lawyer. Lying damages the reputation of the profession and breeds distrust among practitioners, tempting ethical lawyers to follow suit rather than being made the fool. For this reason, the court suspended the lawyer from the practice of law.

In addition to disciplinary consequences, lawyers who lie in debt collection matters may face liability under consumer protection laws. Specifically, the United States Supreme Court held that the Fair Debt Collection Practices Act applies to attorneys who regularly, through litigation, try to collect consumer debts.[13] The Act prohibits a number of abusive debt collection practices including the use of false, deceptive, or misleading representations. To comply with the Act, attorneys should: (1) disclose that they are attempting to collect a debt and that any information will be used for that purpose; (2) not represent that they are authorized to sue unless a lawsuit has been authorized; (3) not send a dunning letter to a debtor who lives in a state where the lawyer is not admitted to practice without disclosing that fact; and (4) ensure that any demand for payment is authorized by the debtor's contract or by law.[14]

---

11. Thomas H. Blaske, *Ethics and Advocacy*, TRIAL, Nov. 1995, at 88.
12. *In re* Charles O. Porter, 320 Or. 692, 890 P.2d 1377 (1995).
13. Heintz v. Jenkins, 514 U.S. 291 (1995).
14. C. Joe, *Application of the Fair Debt Collection Practices Act to Attorneys*, A.B.A. CONSUMER & PERS. RTS. LITIG. NEWSL., Dec. 1995. *See also*, Robert A. Philipson, *The Attorney as Debt Collector*, CAL. LAW., Jan. 1998, at 67, and Christopher A. Golden, *Fair Debt Collection Practices Act: Has Attorney Liability Replaced Consumer Protection?*, FED. LAW., Jan. 1998, at 20.

Professional courtesy toward the opponent

It may seem naive to suggest that a lawyer has a duty of courtesy toward opponents. After all, lawyers are perceived as arrogant, egotistical, and ruthless. We all know the statistics and jokes reflecting public disapproval of our profession.[15] As the Los Angeles County Bar Association observed, "lawyers are said to be held in low esteem by the public—and sinking lower. Many see us as unpleasant people who put their own egos and monetary ambitions before the interests of clients or society."[16]

Contrary to public perceptions, reputable lawyers have always conducted themselves with dignity and civility. Many are striving to improve our profession by adopting standards of professional courtesy. One creed of professionalism provides that a lawyer should not be intentionally discourteous.[17] Another courtesy code expressly states: "Above all, a lawyer owes to all with whom the lawyer comes in contact, civility, professional integrity and personal dignity."[18] Similarly, the Los Angeles County Bar Association has adopted guidelines providing: "Counsel should at all times be civil and courteous in communicating with adversaries, whether in writing or orally."[19]

Helpful guidance for litigators is provided by the Guidelines for the Conduct of the Section of Litigation of the American Bar Association which were adopted in 1996. The guidelines provide:

Lawyer's Duties to Other Counsel

1. We will practice our profession with a continuing awareness that our role is to zealously advance the legitimate interests of our clients. In our dealings with others we will not reflect the ill feelings of our clients. We will treat all other counsel, parties, and witnesses in a civil and courteous manner, not only in court, but also in all other written and oral communications.

---

15. *Question*: What's the difference between a lawyer who has been run over and a skunk which has been run over? *Answer*: There are skid marks before the skunk.

16. Los Angeles County Bar Association, *Litigation Guidelines*, Preamble.

17. Louisville Bar Association, *Creed of Professionalism*.

18. Colorado Bar Association, *A Lawyer's Principles of Professionalism*.

19. Los Angeles County Bar Association, *Litigation Guidelines*, at 4.a.

2. We will not, even when called upon by a client to do so, abuse or indulge in offensive conduct directed to other counsel, parties, or witnesses. We will abstain from disparaging personal remarks or acrimony toward other counsel, parties, or witnesses.

*   *   *

4. We will not, absent good cause, attribute bad motives or improper conduct to other counsel.[20]

In setting your personal standards, consider your own reputation, the reputation of the bar, and the needs of your client. Usually, courtesy and candor will build your reputation, improve the reputation of the bar, and help you achieve your client's goals. Bear in mind that the adversary relationship may continue for a substantial time. A brazen attempt to bully opposing counsel is likely to provoke a reciprocal stance, wasting time and money in pointless posturing. If you hope to settle the case quickly, a tempered approach is more likely to succeed. An in-your-face attitude rarely engenders conciliation and cooperation. And even if the case is doomed to full-scale litigation, your relationship with the opponent will be off to a professional and courteous start.

Purposes of a Demand Letter

The purposes of the demand letter are to introduce yourself, to inform the reader of your client's position, and to persuade the reader to do something your client wants. In introducing yourself, think about the impression your letter will make. Let your opponent know that you are ethical, thorough, reasonable, firm, polite, and professional. In presenting your client's position, you should provide the relevant facts and establish that the law imposes a legal obligation on the reader. To persuade the reader to comply with your demand, explain how compliance will save the reader time, inconvenience, and expense.

---

20. A.B.A. Section of Litigation Guidelines for Conduct (1996)

Audience for a Demand Letter

The demand letter is likely to have two readers: the opposing party and the opposing party's lawyer. As you write the letter, consider both readers. For the opposing party, be sure to explain your client's position in plain English. This reader may become upset or angry at your letter, so strive for a firm yet professional tone. For the opposing lawyer, support your demand with solid legal arguments and establish yourself as a competent and courteous professional.

Form and Content of a Demand Letter

This section will consider the form and content of most demand letters which include: (a) an opening paragraph; (b) an explanation of the client's position; (c) a specific demand for responsive action; and (d) a statement of the consequences of noncompliance. An outline template and sample demand letter are included at the end of this chapter.

Opening paragraph

Your letterhead will identify you, so you can start your letter by identifying your client and the problem. For example: "I represent Cinderella who seeks the prompt return of a glass slipper she accidentally left at your palace last Saturday night." If the case is more complicated, an opening paragraph can summarize the problem.

Explain your client's position

The persuasiveness of the letter depends on your explanation of the facts and the law. Your office memo explained the legal analysis to your supervising attorney; your client letter explained the legal analysis to your client; and now your demand letter must explain the legal analysis to your opponent. Start with a brief statement of the necessary facts. Then set out the governing legal rules. Finally, explain how the law applies to the facts and supports your client's position. For example:

Cinderella left your palace in haste because she had to catch her coach. As she was leaving, her slipper fell off and she left it behind on your stairway. The slipper is a unique item which was custom made for Cinderella. The law provides that on timely demand, the finder of valuable lost property must return the property to its rightful owner. Thus, the law requires you to return the slipper to Cinderella. The law further provides that a finder who refuses to return the property will be liable for conversion, which may give rise to both actual and punitive damages. Therefore, if you were to refuse to return the slipper, the law provides a remedy which could prove very costly to you.

The level of your explanation should be tailored to your audience. If the opponent has retained counsel, you may wish to include citations to governing authorities. Citations show your thoroughness and may serve to educate opposing counsel quickly. Similarly, business people and insurance adjusters understand references to legal authorities they frequently encounter. But if your letter will be read by a lay person, citations are not helpful. For this reader, be sure you explain the law clearly and in plain English.

Obviously, you must be accurate in presenting the facts and the law. If you are mistaken, your opponent will naturally ignore your demand and conclude that you are either careless, ignorant, or dishonest. Mistakes will damage your credibility which will diminish your chances for achieving the desired outcome. On the other hand, accuracy does not require you to make unnecessary concessions or damaging admissions. Be precise, and be prudent.

Demand an appropriate response

The concluding paragraph of the letter should expressly state your demand. Show the reader that he or she is responsible for the outcome of this dispute and that compliance with the demand will serve the reader's self-interest. Your reader should be persuaded to see your demand as a chance to avoid unacceptable risks and consequences, as an opportunity rather than a threat. Set a specific deadline for your reader's compliance. Avoid giving your reader options to wiggle out of compliance with your demand. If it becomes necessary, you can always negotiate a compromise later. But since prior attempts by your client have failed, your initial demand should be specific and firm. For example: "As you can see, the law requires you to promptly return the slipper. Please deliver it to my office by June 7, 1998. We look forward to your anticipated cooperation."

You can enhance the credibility of your demand by including objective information and specific details supporting your position. For example, you can support a damage claim by including information about verdicts or settlements achieved in similar cases. Similarly, estimates of repair or replacement costs from reputable vendors can be used to support your claim: "If the slipper is not returned, my client will be forced to have a new slipper made. As this is a hand-crafted and unique item, the current estimate for replacing the slipper is about $1500.00. For your information, I have included a copy of written estimates from three different glass blowers which range from $1350.00 to $1785.00."

State the consequences of noncompliance

You may wish to reinforce your demand by identifying the consequences your opponent can anticipate if the demand is ignored. A carrot-and-stick approach may encourage the reader to informally resolve the dispute to avoid adverse consequences. Be sure to state the consequences credibly and unemotionally; you are providing information, not threatening retaliation. While the time may come for threats, your opening letter seeks a positive response which is rarely inspired by a threat. So inform the reader of the adverse consequences of noncompliance, but focus on the benefits of compliance with the demand: "To avoid the expense and inconvenience of formal legal proceedings, please return the slipper within 20 days."

Tone and Style of a Demand Letter

Your tone should be professional yet firm. Be careful to avoid sounding arrogant, obnoxious, or overly emotional. Remember, you hope to achieve cooperation, not to provoke animosity. Rather than calling your reader nasty names, assume that your reader is a person of good character who wishes to be fair and reasonable. In striving to maintain a polite tone, be sensitive to your choice of words. As Henry Weihofen observed, the phrase "although you assert that" is likely to arouse resistance since it implies that the assertion is wrong.[21] Other red-flag phrases include:

---

21. HENRY WEIHOFEN, LEGAL WRITING STYLE 175 (2d ed. 1980).

If this is the case	Your proposal is impractical
You cannot really believe	Do you actually mean
We question the wisdom of	We would have you know
You seem confused	I take issue with
We do not see fit to	It is perfectly clear (obvious)
We cannot understand	Your insinuation[22]

Finally, make your letter clear and concise by using short sentences and short paragraphs. Avoid legalese to the extent possible. Omit surplus words. Be as specific and concrete as possible. A no-nonsense, professional approach is more likely to induce a reasonable response than hollow threats and empty rhetoric. And even if your letter fails to bring about an informal settlement, it will set the tone for a courteous relationship with your opponent.

Outline Template for a Demand Letter

I. Opening paragraph

Identify your client and then describe the problem.

II. Explain your client's position

Set out the facts and the governing rules of law. Establish that the law resolves the dispute in your client's favor.

III. Demand an appropriate response

State specifically your demand and provide a deadline for the response. Provide objective support for your demand if possible.

IV. State the consequences of noncompliance

Explain the adverse consequences your opponent will suffer if the demand is not met. Show how compliance with your demand serves your opponent's self-interest.

---

22. *Id.* at 175–76.

Sample Demand Letter

RUMPOLE & VAN OWEN

January 31, 1998

Mr. Milton Grassly
2020 Res Judicata
Davis, California 95616

Dear Mr. Grassly:

I represent Janet Washington who was assaulted and robbed in your apartment building because of the lack of security precautions. Ms. Washington has retained me to represent her in a legal action against you but is willing to settle this matter out of court if you will accept her settlement proposal. Ms. Washington will accept $50,000 as a cash settlement of this matter provided payment is received by February 27, 1998.

As you know, your building had a button lock on the door and poor lighting in the hallway. Moreover, since several burglaries had occurred in the neighborhood, Ms. Washington specifically asked you to install a deadbolt lock on her apartment door. You refused this request. A few weeks later an intruder broke into Ms. Washington's apartment even though the door was locked. He beat her up and stole her money and jewelry. Ms. Washington spent two days in the hospital and then moved out of your apartment.

Based on these facts, the law provides that you are liable for Ms. Washington's injuries because the apartment lacked adequate precautions against foreseeable crime. The damages Ms. Washington is entitled to recover include medical expenses, lost wages, out-of-pocket costs for relocating, and compensation for her physical and emotional injuries. The medical expenses, lost wages, and moving expenses to date come to more than $20,000. Ms. Washington is still suffering both physically and emotionally from her injuries. She will be receiving medical care and counseling for an indefinite time.

In short, from our review of the facts and our legal research, we conclude that Ms. Washington has a very strong case. Given the public concern about crime, a jury would likely conclude that the failure to provide a deadbolt lock fell below the standard of reasonable care. Ms. Washington's physical and emotional injuries are substantial and her medical expenses are continuing. In other words, the case is strong both in terms of liability and damages.

If you wish to avoid litigation, please submit a cashier's check to me made payable to Ms. Washington and our firm within 30 days. Please understand that time is of the essence in this matter. The offer will be withdrawn as of March 1, 1998.

Very truly yours,

Philida Trant

Chapter 5

Complaint

This week you will draft a complaint. As you know, a complaint initiates a civil action and tolls the statute of limitations. To survive a motion to dismiss, a complaint must allege facts stating a cause of action, must be filed within the statute of limitations, and must not reveal facts establishing an affirmative defense. Since your client's complaint might be vulnerable, you must draft the complaint carefully, or this first step in the action may be the fatal step.

While in-depth coverage of pleading theory is left to your civil procedure course, this week's assignment will introduce you to some basic professional and practical considerations in drafting and filing complaints. Specifically, this chapter will discuss: (1) the professional responsibilities in drafting a complaint; (2) the purpose of a complaint; (3) the audience for a complaint; (4) the organization, content, and form of a complaint; (5) a few pleading strategies; and (6) filing a complaint. An outline template and sample complaint are included at the end of this chapter.

Professional Responsibilities in Drafting a Complaint

As with all court documents, the complaint must be drafted with an understanding of the lawyer's dual responsibilities to the client and to the court. This section on professional responsibilities also considers professional etiquette in handling service of process and in granting extensions of time to file responsive pleadings.

Drafting as an advocate and an officer of the court

In litigation the lawyer serves two masters: the client and the legal system. Lawyers should be zealous advocates, but within the bounds of the law. According to the Model Rules of Professional Conduct, a lawyer may not bring an action "unless there is a basis for doing so that is not frivolous, which includes a good faith argument for an extension, modification or reversal of existing law."[1] The *Restatement (Third) of the Law Governing Lawyers* defines a frivolous position as "one that a lawyer of ordinary competence would recognize as so lacking in merit that there is no substantial possibility that the tribunal would accept it."[2] As the *Restatement* explains "[f]rivolous advocacy inflicts distress, wastes time, and causes increased expense to the tribunal and adversaries and may achieve results for a client that are unjust."[3]

Federal courts police this responsibility through Rule 11 of the Federal Rules of Civil Procedure. Rule 11 provides that the lawyer's signature certifies that the lawyer has read the document and that to the best of the lawyer's knowledge, information, and belief after reasonable inquiry, the document is well-founded in fact and either warranted by existing law or by a good faith argument for the extension, modification or reversal of existing law.[4] Rule 11 further provides that, by signing the document, the lawyer certifies that it is not filed for any improper purpose such as to harass or cause unnecessary delay or expense.[5] Finally, for Rule 11 violations, the court may impose sanctions on the party or the attorney, including attorneys' fees and expenses incurred by the opponent.[6] Through this sanctioning authority, Rule 11 brings an ethical rule into practical focus: an attorney who files a frivolous action may be personally required to pay the opponent's costs. Most of us, guided by enlightened self-interest, stand ready to heed Rule 11.

---

1. MODEL RULES OF PROFESSIONAL CONDUCT Rule 3.1 (1997) [hereinafter MODEL RULES].
2. RESTATEMENT (THIRD) OF THE LAW GOVERNING LAWYERS § 170 cmt. c (Tentative Draft No. 8, 1997) [hereinafter RESTATEMENT, TENTATIVE DRAFT].
3. *Id.*
4. FED. R. CIV. P. 11.
5. *Id.*
6. *Id.*

But even though we wish to comply with Rule 11, we are vexed by the questions of how far to stretch the inferences from conflicting facts and how far to extend the interpretation of ambiguous authorities. At the pleading stage, our knowledge of the facts is often incomplete, and our legal research rarely reveals certain answers. Moreover, the lawyer owes the client zealous and creative advocacy. The lawyer is required to make legal arguments for the "fullest benefit of the client's cause" taking into account "the law's ambiguities and potential for change."[7] Faced with an ambiguity or an antiquated authority, the advocate may properly challenge existing precedent. After all, the lawyer is "not an umpire, but an advocate."[8]

An illustration of this dilemma comes from tort cases involving negligent infliction of emotional distress. Assume that under the applicable law, a witness to an accident is entitled to recover for negligently inflicted emotional distress if three factors are present: (1) the witness was near the scene of the accident; (2) the witness had a sensory and contemporaneous observation of the event; and (3) the witness was closely related to the accident victim.[9] Assume further that in all reported cases allowing recovery, the plaintiff had actually seen the accident and was either a parent or sibling of the victim.

Now assume that your client suffered serious emotional distress when her sister was badly injured in a traffic accident. Your client, who is blind, did not see the accident, but she heard it and immediately realized what had happened. The question becomes whether the law can be extended to cover your case or whether a claim would be in bad faith. Similar questions arise when the facts are varied slightly. For example, what if your client was not the victim's sister but her cousin who lived in the same household? What if your client was the victim's grandmother? What if a sister state had refused to extend recovery to identical facts? What if the controlling supreme court had indicated in dicta that it would only impose liability where the plaintiff had seen the accident? What if that decision were ten years old? What if the supreme court bench

---

7. MODEL RULES, *supra* note 1, Rule 3.1 cmt. 1.

8. ABA Comm. on Professional Ethics and Grievances, Formal Op. 280 (1949).

9. Dillon v. Legg, 68 Cal. 2d 728, 69 Cal. Rptr. 72, 441 P.2d 912 (1968).

had changed since that dicta was published? What's a poor lawyer to do?

By thinking about these variations, you begin to develop a sense of the struggle to serve both the client and the legal system. These overarching issues of professional responsibility suffuse both the substantive analysis of a client's case and the nuts-and-bolts task of drafting a complaint. Though the line between zealous creativity and bad-faith frivolity may be wavering and fuzzy, at some point a line must be drawn.

Lacking precise rules, we are left with illustrations. One case that crossed the line involved a spelling bee loser who sued the contest sponsor.[10] The plaintiff lost to a competitor who advanced to the national competition in Washington D.C. But the plaintiff's encounter with the competitor only occurred because the judges had earlier mistakenly disqualified the plaintiff for missing a word that had two acceptable spellings. Once the error was discovered, the judges held a spell-off between the plaintiff and the competitor. The plaintiff lost this match. In his complaint he alleged that the sponsors were liable for his harm since the spell-off should never have taken place, and he should have been credited with winning in the first place. In rejecting the action, the court explained that the plaintiff lost the spelling bee because he misspelled a word: "[T]wo things are missing here, causation and common sense."[11] Further, the court admonished lawyers to be cautious in "drawing the line between making new law and wasting everyone's time."[12]

Ethical lawyers draw the line as best they can between zealous advocacy and frivolous litigiousness. At first the lawyer's role as a gatekeeper seems to create a hopeless conflict between the duty to the client and the duty to the court. But, in fact, in most cases both the client's interest and court's interest are congruent. A frivolous lawsuit only wastes the client's time and money. And in these days of under-funded and over-crowded courts, lawyers must act responsibly in determining when to resort to litigation.

This responsibility brings to mind the story of a shopper who called my law firm seeking representation in a consumer action. A

---

10. McDonald v. John P. Scripps Newspaper Inc., No. B032591, April 12, 1989, Calif.
11. *Id.*
12. *Id.*

grocery store advertised a sale on twelve-ounce bags of potato chips. Although the twelve-ounce bags were available at the advertised price, our caller had selected a sixteen-ounce bag and was outraged to find that the price was not at the same unit rate as the sale price. On this basis she wanted to sue for false advertising. The firm politely followed the advice of Elihu Root who noted: "About half of the practice of a decent lawyer is telling would-be clients that they are damned fools and should stop."[13]

Professional etiquette in service of process

After the complaint has been filed, it must be served on the opponent. In the movies, a process server usually ambushes the hapless defendant in an embarrassing public forum. In practice, it would be a breach of etiquette to dispatch a process server to slap papers on the defendant under humiliating circumstances, especially if you have had contact with the defendant or defense counsel.

Consider for a moment the rule that an attorney is prohibited from directly contacting an opponent known to be represented by counsel.[14] While this rule would not bar service by a process server, it suggests that it is always best to go through counsel rather than directly to the adversary. If you know your opponent is represented by counsel, the proper approach is to request that counsel accept service on behalf of the client.

Even where the opponent is not represented by counsel, service should rarely be accomplished by a process server. Rule 4 of the Federal Rules of Civil Procedure provides a cost-saving alternative to formal service by authorizing a waiver of service. Under Rule 4, failure to waive service will usually result in sanctions for the cost of formal service. In other words, if the defendant refuses to waive service, a process server is justified and the defendant is required to pay the expense.[15]

---

13. Elihu Root was the American Secretary of State from 1905 to 1909. His sage advice is quoted in *McCandles v. Great Atlantic & Pacific Tea Co.*, 697 F.2d 198, 201–202 (7th Cir. 1983) and *Amstar v. Environtech*, 730 F.2d 1476, 1486 (Fed Cir.), cert. denied, 469 U.S. 924 (1984).

14. MODEL RULES, *supra* note 1, Rule 4.2.

15. Of course, exigent circumstances may justify and even compel a departure from this courteous and potentially time-consuming approach. If the op-

In deciding how to effect service, be mindful of the statutory time limit imposed by Rule 4(j). Under this Rule the complaint must be served within 120 days of filing or the court may dismiss the action without prejudice. A dismissal on this grounds is at least inconvenient and at worst fatal. It is inconvenient to file a second complaint and fatal if the statute of limitations has run. Always calendar a service deadline well in advance of the 120-day limit so that you will have time to move to enlarge the time for service if necessary.

Professional courtesy in allowing time to respond

Assume the complaint has been served and a response is nearly due. How should you respond if your opponent telephones a few days before the deadline and requests a thirty-day extension of time? Professional courtesy generally requires a lawyer to grant an initial, reasonable request for an extension of time. Most voluntary courtesy codes provide that the first request for an extension of time should be granted. For example, according to the American Bar Association Litigation Guidelines: "We will agree to reasonable requests for extensions of time and for waiver of procedural formalities, provided our clients' legitimate rights will not be materially or adversely affected."[16]

Acknowledging this widespread custom, courts frown on the overzealous enforcement of deadlines. For example, one court vacated a default judgment because of the lawyer's discourtesy in refusing to grant an extension of time to a busy opponent.[17] Another court vacated a default judgment where the lawyer refused to reschedule a hearing despite knowing of the adversary's physical incapacity.[18] Thus, the courts refuse to allow parties to gain unfair advantage by denying reasonable requests for time extensions.

On the other hand, delays are problematic in civil litigation; a United States Supreme Court Justice aptly described the progress of

---

ponent has been uncooperative and unavailable in the past, time constraints may dictate the use of a process server.

16. A.B.A. Section of Litigation Guidelines for Conduct (1996) Lawyers' Duties to Other Counsel no. 17 (1996) [hereinafter A.B.A. Guidelines].

17. Robinson v. Varela, 67 Cal. App. 3d 611, 136 Cal. Rptr. 783 (1977).

18. Williams v. Hertz Corp., 91 A.D. 2d 548, 457 N.Y.S.2d 23 (1982), aff'd 59 N.W.2d 893, 465 N.Y.S.2d 937, 451 N.E.2d 1265 (1983).

civil litigation as "glacial."[19] The need to expedite litigation is manifest since the legendary delay in our courts undermines public respect for the law.[20] In recognition of this problem, the Model Rules require a lawyer to expedite litigation.[21] The A.B.A. Guidelines address the problem by providing: "We will not request an extension of time solely for the purpose of unjustified delay or to obtain unfair advantage."[22]

Thus, lawyers struggle to accommodate the conflicting requirements of professional courtesy in granting extensions and expediting litigation by enforcing deadlines. As a basic rule-of-thumb, one reasonable extension of time should be granted. However, to expedite litigation, additional extensions should usually be granted only on a showing of special need or good cause.

Purposes of a Complaint

The complaint initiates the legal action, identifies the parties, sets out the factual basis of the claim, and prays for the remedies or relief the plaintiff seeks. The complaint has two formal purposes. First, the complaint formally invokes the jurisdiction of the court and establishes the basis of the plaintiff's claim. Second, the complaint stops the running of the statute of limitations. In addition to these formal purposes, the complaint serves several informal goals. Specifically, the complaint introduces you and your client to the court. The complaint should convey your competence, your preparation, and the seriousness and merit of your client's cause.

Audience for a Complaint

The complaint has two important readers: the court and opposing counsel. Both are professionals who will appreciate a well-crafted pleading. In developing your pleading strategy, be sensitive

---

19. Roadway Express, Inc. v. Piper, 447 U.S. 752, 757 n.4 (1980).
20. MODEL RULE, *supra* note 1, Rule 3.2 cmt.
21. MODEL RULE, *supra* note 1, Rule 3.2.
22. A.B.A. GUIDELINES, *supra* note 16, Lawyers' Duties to Other Counsel no. 13.

to these readers and your need to establish your credibility. As commentators have observed, courts have long memories:

> Judges can sense hokey pleadings and motions and, while they may not assess sanctions as often as they should, they will remember the near-sham papers and this undoubtedly colors the court's thinking on close call motions, evidentiary rulings, jury instructions, and other procedural matters such as scheduling.[23]

The impression you make on opposing counsel is also critical. Your complaint can demonstrate that your client is serious, you have investigated the facts, you have researched the law, you know your way to the courthouse, and you are prepared to litigate. If the complaint carries the message that you are a competent, well-prepared, and worthy adversary, it will instantly increase the value of your client's case.

Form and Content of a Complaint

Despite some variations among jurisdictions, the federal rules are a good starting point for learning the art of pleading. This section will review the organization, content, and form of a federal complaint including: (a) the caption; (b) the statement of jurisdiction; (c) the statement of the claim; (d) the demand for judgment; (e) the attorney's signature; (f) the jury demand; and (g) the additional requirements imposed by local rules. Complaints and other court documents are printed on pleading paper which has numbered lines. An outline template and sample complaint are included at the end of this chapter.

Caption

The caption of a court document sets out the name of the court, the title of the action, the file number, the names of the parties, and a description of the document.[24] When the complaint is filed in the clerk's office, it will be stamped with a docket number. All subse-

---

23. ROGER S. HAYDOCK ET AL., FUNDAMENTALS OF PRETRIAL LITIGATION 107 (3d ed. 1994).
24. FED. R. CIV. P. 10(a).

quent filings in the action will have the same caption and docket number.

Pay special attention to naming the parties. Under Rule 17 of the Federal Rules of Civil Procedure, every action must be filed in the name of the real party in interest which is controlled by the local law of the domicile, state of incorporation, or forum. Some common designations include:

- John Smith
- Sharon Jones, as guardian of the Estate of Robert Jones, a minor
- Robert Smith, as conservator of the Estate of Ellen Smith, an incompetent
- Frank Watson, as executor of the Estate of James Morley, deceased
- Barbara Meyers, as trustee in bankruptcy of the Estate of Robert Jackson, bankrupt
- R. J. Smith, a corporation
- Johnson Hospital, a not-for-profit corporation
- Robert Smith d/b/a Smith Cleaners
- Barnett and Lynch, a partnership
- Western Ranches Association, an unincorporated association[25]

If you are suing a person in more than one capacity, include all appropriate capacities in the caption.

Local rules may require additional information in the caption. For example, many courts require the state bar number of the attorney filing the action.[26] The following is a caption that complies with the local rules of the United States District Court for the Eastern District of California.[27] Note that the case number is omitted because the complaint is the first document in the case; the clerk will stamp it with the docket number when it is filed.

---

25. THOMAS A. MAUET, PRETRIAL 108 (2d ed. 1993).
26. E.D. CAL. R. 7-131.
27. E.D. CAL. R. 7-130–7-132.

Philida Trant
State Bar No. 71355
Rumpole & Van Owen
200 Main Street, Suite 1400
Capitol City, California
Telephone: 555/234-1234
Attorneys for Plaintiff Mary Smith

IN THE UNITED STATES DISTRICT COURT

EASTERN DISTRICT OF CALIFORNIA

MARY SMITH, Plaintiff,	No.
vs.	Complaint for Negligence
JOHN DAVIS, Defendant.	
_____/	

Statement of jurisdiction

Because federal district courts are courts of limited jurisdiction, the plaintiff must allege the basis of the court's jurisdiction under Rule 8 of the Federal Rules of Civil Procedure. The grounds of federal jurisdiction include diversity jurisdiction and federal question jurisdiction. The following examples meet this requirement and illustrate the simplicity and brevity which the rules contemplate.[28]

Jurisdiction—Diversity and Amount

Plaintiff is a citizen of the State of Connecticut and defendant is a corporation incorporated under the laws of the State of New York having its principal place of business in a State other than the State of Connecticut. The matter in controversy exceeds, exclusive of interest and costs, the sum of seventy-five thousand dollars. Jurisdiction therefore arises under 28 U.S.C. § 1332.[29]

---

28. FED. R. CIV. P. 84.
29. Adapted from FED. R. CIV. P. app. Form 2(a).

Jurisdiction—Federal Question arising under Statute

The action arises under the Federal Civil Rights Act, 42 U.S.C. § 1983, as hereinafter more fully appears. Jurisdiction therefore arises under 8 U.S.C. §§ 1331, 1332, and 1343.[30]

In state court actions, the jurisdictional statement is generally not required since most state trial courts are courts of general jurisdiction.

Statement of the claim

Rule 8 provides that a complaint shall contain a short and plain statement of the claim. This statement briefly alleges the facts giving rise to the cause of action and shows that the pleader is entitled to relief.[31] To satisfy this requirement, you must investigate the factual basis of the claim and research the legal theory supporting recovery. A complaint which fails to meet these requirements is subject to a motion to dismiss under Rule 12. Under Rule 10, allegations shall be made in numbered paragraphs. The contents of each paragraph shall be limited to a single set of circumstances. The Appendix of Forms found at the end of the Federal Rules of Civil Procedure contains many examples of claims and illustrates the simplicity and brevity contemplated by the rules.[32] The following example is sufficient to state a claim for negligence and properly sets out the allegations in numbered paragraphs:

[1. Allegation of jurisdiction.]

2. On June 1, 1998, on a public highway called Bolyston Street in Boston, Massachusetts, defendant negligently drove a motor vehicle into plaintiff who was then crossing the highway.

3. As a result plaintiff was thrown down and had his leg broken and was otherwise injured, was prevented from transacting his business, suffered great pain of body and mind, and incurred expenses for medical attention and hospitalization in the sum of one thousand dollars.[33]

In contrast to the above example, sometimes a complaint will be based on a series of separate events. Rule 10 requires that claims

---

30. Adapted from FED. R. CIV. P. app. Form 2(c).
31. FED. R. CIV. P. 8(a).
32. FED. R. CIV. P. 84.
33. Adapted from FED. R. CIV. P. app. Form 9.

founded on separate transactions or occurrences shall be stated in separate counts. For example, assume that a plaintiff was suing to recover on two different promissory notes. Each claim should be set out in a separate count of the complaint as illustrated by the following:

JURISDICTION

[1. Allegation of jurisdiction.]

COUNT I
(Promissory Note Dated January 2, 1997)

2. On or about January 2, 1997, defendant executed and delivered to plaintiff a promissory note a copy of which is hereto annexed as Exhibit A whereby defendant promised to pay to plaintiff or order on June 30, 1998, the sum of $25,000 with interest thereon at the rate of twelve percent, per annum.

3. Defendant owes to plaintiff the amount of said note and interest.

COUNT II
(Promissory Note Dated February 2, 1997)

4. On or about February 2, 1997, defendant executed and delivered to plaintiff a promissory note a copy of which is hereto annexed as Exhibit B whereby defendant promised to pay to plaintiff or order on July 30, 1998, the sum of $25,000 with interest thereon at the rate of twelve percent, per annum.

5. Defendant owes to plaintiff the amount of said note and interest.[34]

In this example, the jurisdictional statement is set out first, followed by the two separate counts on the two promissory notes. The separate counts are flagged with headings, including parenthetical explanations of the substance of each count. The paragraphs are numbered consecutively from the beginning of the complaint. Notice how the complaint dispenses with the need to plead the terms of the contracts by simply incorporating them by reference. Under Rule 10, documents may be attached as exhibits to complaints. If a document is attached, it is a part of the pleading for all purposes.

To ensure you have included all the necessary elements, check the jury instructions which will be given. For state law claims, use the

---

34. Adapted from FED. R. CIV. P. app. Form 3.

instructions which the state court will use. For example, in California for civil cases the court will give instructions from the *Book of Approved Jury Instructions (BAJI)*. For federal claims, use federal instructions. Some circuits including the Ninth Circuit have developed model instructions. There are also good commercial sources including *Federal Jury Practice and Instructions.*[35] The jury instructions will set out each element that the plaintiff must plead and prove to prevail. Check your complaint against them to be sure that you have alleged facts supporting every element.

While the federal rules favor simple, straight-forward allegations, additional allegations should be considered if you are alleging a novel cause of action. Specifically, on occasion you may wish to include citations to legal authorities so that the court and your opponent will be able to quickly verify the legal basis of the action.[36] Similarly, on occasion you may wish to include more factual detail than is absolutely necessary to present a more sympathetic story and reveal the strength of the case.[37] In addition, the federal rules require that certain special matters, including fraud and mistake, be pleaded with particularity.[38]

Frequently, the same underlying facts are relevant to separate claims or theories. Under Rule 10, statements in a pleading may be adopted by reference in a different part of the pleading to keep complaints to a manageable length. For example, a plaintiff in an employment discrimination case may base one count of the complaint on a federal statute and another count on state law. By incorporating allegations by reference, you can keep the complaint concise.

JURISDICTION

[1. Allegation of jurisdiction.]

STATEMENT OF FACTS

2. Facts about the employment relationship.
3. Facts about the discrimination.

---

35. EDWARD J. DEVITT & CHARLES B. BLACKMAR, FEDERAL JURY PRACTICE AND INSTRUCTIONS (4th ed. 1987).

36. CHARLES R. CALLEROS, LEGAL METHOD AND WRITING 324–326 (2d ed. 1994).

37. CALLEROS, supra note 36, at 329; MARY BARNARD RAY & BARBARA J. COX, BEYOND THE BASICS: A TEXT FOR ADVANCED LEGAL WRITING 267 (1991).

38. FED. R. CIV. P. 9.

COUNT I
(Violation of Federal Statute)

4. Plaintiff refers to and incorporates by reference the allegations of paragraphs 1 through 3 as though set forth in full at this point.

5. Allege a violation of the statute.

6. Allege damages for the statutory violation.

COUNT II
(Liability under State Common Law)

7. Plaintiff refers to and incorporates by reference the allegations of paragraphs 1 through 3 as though set forth in full at this point.

8. Allege a violation of the state common law.

9. Allege damages arising under the common law.[39]

Demand for judgment

Rule 8 also requires a demand for judgment for the relief which the plaintiff deems appropriate. Again, the Appendix of Forms illustrates the requirement:

> Wherefore plaintiff demands judgment against defendant in the sum of $135,000 and costs.[40]

The demand lists all the relief which the plaintiff deems appropriate including general damages, special damages, punitive damages, costs, attorneys' fees, interest, and equitable relief. Most lawyers also include a blanket request for "any other relief the court deems just." In most cases this demand is superfluous because Rule 54(c) provides that the final judgment should include all the relief to which the winner is entitled, even if it has not been requested in the pleadings. However, this catchall may expand the relief available on default judgments.[41]

---

39. Adapted from FED. R. CIV. P. app. Form 3.
40. FED. R. CIV. P. app. Form 9.
41. RAY & COX, *supra* note 37, at 271.

Attorney's signature

Rule 11 provides that every pleading must be signed by at least one attorney of record in his or her individual name and must disclose the attorney's address. As discussed above, this signature certifies that the attorney has read the pleading and that, to the best of his or her knowledge and belief formed after reasonable investigation, it is well grounded in fact and warranted by law, and that it is not interposed for any improper purpose. If the pleading violates this rule, the attorney is subject to sanctions. The form of the signature is:

RUMPOLE & VAN OWEN

_____

Philida Trant
Attorney for Plaintiff Mary Smith
[Address if not on first page]

Jury demand

In federal court, a party is entitled to a jury trial in certain civil cases by demanding one in compliance with Rule 7. If a jury trial is available, you and your client should carefully weigh the advantages and disadvantages of court and jury trials. If your client decides to exercise the right to a jury trial, the demand should be included in your complaint. While demanding a jury trial is not required to state a cause of action, local rules may require the demand at the earliest possible stage of the litigation. For example, one local rule provides that the complaint must state whether a jury trial is demanded.[42] Even if the demand is not required to be included in the complaint, it is good practice to do so because the time limits are short, and delay may lead to an inadvertent waiver of the right.

The demand itself is straightforward:

JURY TRIAL

The Plaintiffs hereby demand a jury trial in this matter.

RUMPOLE & VAN OWEN

_____

Philida Trant
Attorney for Plaintiff Mary Smith

---

42. E.D. CAL. R. 38-201.

Local rules requirements

In addition to setting out the basic procedural requirements for pleadings and other court documents, the Federal Rules authorize the promulgation of local rules by district and appellate courts. Fed. R. Civ. P. 83. Acting under this authority—and sometimes in excess of it—district courts have promulgated more than 5000 local rules.[43] These local rules often supplement the federal rules with specific formatting requirements. For example, one local rule provides formatting requirements which are fairly common in federal district courts:

> All documents presented for filing or lodging shall be on white, unglazed opaque paper of good quality with numbered lines in the left margin, 8 ½" × 11" in size, and shall be flat, unfolded (except where necessary for presentation of exhibits), firmly bound at the top left corner, pre-punched with two (2) holes (approximately ¼" diameter) centered 2 ¾" apart, ½" to ⅝" from the top edge of document, and shall comply with all other applicable provisions of these Rules. Matters contained thereon shall be presented by typewriting, printing, photographic or offset reproduction, or other clearly legible process, without erasures or interlining which materially defaces the document, and shall appear on one side of each sheet only. Documents shall be double-spaced except for the identification of counsel, title of the action, category headings, footnotes, quotations, exhibits and descriptions of real property. Quotations of more than fifty (50) words shall be indented. Each page shall be numbered consecutively at the bottom.[44]

In addition to these common requirements, each court may have its own individual requirements. For example, in the Eastern District of California, the attorney's California state bar number must be included on the first page of all documents.[45] In the Northern District of California, a footer describing the document must be included on all documents.[46] Other local rules impose additional pleading requirements in certain categories of cases such as RICO

---

43. COMMITTEE ON RULES OF PRAC. AND PROC. OF THE JUD. CONF. OF THE U.S., REP. OF THE LOC. RULES PROJECT 1 (April 1989).
44. E.D. CAL. R. 7-130.
45. E.D. CAL. R. 7-131.
46. N.D. CAL. R 3-4(c)(3).

actions.[47] Given the idiosyncrasies of each jurisdiction, be sure to research and comply with the local rules.

Pleading Strategies

The preceding section briefly explains the pleading standards of the Federal Rules of Civil Procedure and alerts you to supplemental requirements imposed by local rules. But compliance with the rules is just the starting point for artful pleading. The complaint is the first document filed in litigation and will make a powerful impression, for good or ill, on your opponent and on the court. In other words, the complaint is both a formal document and also a strategic tool. This section outlines some basic pleading strategies: (a) plead all appropriate theories and remedies; (b) follow the guidance of the appellate courts; (c) use form books cautiously; (d) disclose facts strategically; (e) allege uncertain facts on information and belief; and (f) make your complaint interesting.

Plead all appropriate theories and remedies

While your complaint must allege at least one valid claim for relief, it may also include different theories for recovery and different remedies. Rule 8(e)(2) specifically allows multiple claims to be pled in the alternative. Often several different theories and remedies are available to the plaintiff, and the best theory may not be identified until some discovery has been completed.

For example, a defendant may have sold a plaintiff a parcel of real property by misrepresenting its zoning status. The plaintiff may have both a contract action and a tort action and may be entitled to both damages and equitable relief. In such cases, the plaintiff will generally benefit by pleading all theories and seeking alternative remedies. In our hypothetical, the contract action is advantageous because it has a longer statute of limitations and may be easier to prove. But the tort action is advantageous because it justifies greater damages and may allow recovery if the contract action fails. Moreover, a prayer for equitable relief may give the plaintiff a priority on

---

47. S.D. CAL. R. 11.1.

the trial setting calendar and may provide a remedy if plaintiff fails to establish the legal actions.

In short, pleading different theories allows flexibility in trial strategy and may secure procedural advantages, shift burdens of proof, and afford better remedies. To obtain these advantages, research alternative theories. Novel claims can be alleged in a good faith attempt to create new law. As some commentators have observed, "In reality every existing cause of action was first brought by a plaintiff who, in retrospect, was courageous. . . . It is appropriate in some cases for a plaintiff's lawyer to endure raucous laughter from the defendant's lawyer upon reading the complaint."[48]

In pleading alternative theories, remember that pleadings can be read to the jury. As Thomas Mauet has cautioned, "[A]lternative or inconsistent pleadings may cast the party in a poor light. Hence, drafting must also be done with an eye toward the impression the pleading will have on the jurors."[49] If you have one strong theory, well supported by the evidence, and providing generous remedies, it may be best to include only that claim.

Follow the guidance of the appellate courts

In developing areas of the law, courts often reject a plaintiff's attempt to state a novel claim for relief while suggesting, in dicta, additional factual allegations which might cure the deficiency. By following these judicial hints, a plaintiff may succeed in stating a cause of action where others have failed. In other words, cases which reject complaints for insufficient allegations may be the most helpful because they provide a blueprint for drafting a successful complaint. Study these cases carefully and tailor your complaint to fit their advice.

Use form books cautiously

Practicing lawyers save time by using form books. If you stroll through the library, you will discover volumes of forms compiled for most areas of practice by many major legal publishers. While

---

48. Roger S. Haydock et al., Fundamentals of Pretrial Litigation 97 (3d ed. 1994).
49. Mauet, *supra* note 25, at 107.

these books can help get you started, use them cautiously. Make sure they are current and that you adapt the form to your case. As commentators have explained: "Major difficulties can result from selection of the wrong form, or use of a standard form that does not precisely fit the needs of a particular case."[50] The best approach is to read through several sources for helpful ideas and then to draft a complaint reflecting the unique facts of your case.

Disclose facts strategically

Experienced lawyers usually avoid being tied down to specific facts until the last possible moment. This practice provides flexibility in determining the final trial strategy and prevents embarrassment from unanticipated facts. At first, this practice may seem to lack candor and conviction, but, for several reasons, it is generally wise.

First, people make mistakes. We've all heard of studies where eyewitnesses to a car crash come up with amazingly inconsistent accounts of the accident and descriptions of the people and vehicles involved. In addition, the passage of time and the presence of self-interest may alter perceptions and color memories. Thus, even though your client is sincerely trying to tell you the truth, mistakes will be made. By avoiding commitment to specific details until they can be verified, you preserve the necessary margin for honest error.

Second, your information is incomplete. Your client will not know everything you need to know about the case. During the course of litigation, your investigation and discovery will fill in the needed facts. Until then, avoid committing yourself to a position that you may not be able to maintain. You preserve your credibility by admitting uncertainty; you damage your credibility by asserting something that you are later forced to retract. In other words, because your information may be erroneous or incomplete, avoid tying yourself down to specifics by pleading the facts generally.

On the other hand, you may have uncovered solid facts which are enormously helpful to your case. You may wish to include them in your complaint to show the court the strength of your case and to show your opponent the depth of your knowledge. This tactic is

---

50. Christina L. Kunz et al., The Process of Legal Research 220 (2d ed. 1989).

especially effective when the helpful facts are based on your opponent's own witnesses or documents and therefore difficult to dispute. As some scholars have observed: "[P]roviding additional information establishing a strong case for your client at the outset can induce settlement negotiations and may require the defendant to admit or deny information that will assist you with discovery."[51]

Allege uncertain facts on information and belief

Your complaint should be as accurate as possible. Never plead facts you know to be false unless they are accepted legal fictions, such as allegations against fictitious defendants. Pleading untrue allegations may constitute perjury and may give rise to a malicious prosecution action. At a minimum, false pleading exposes you to Rule 11 sanctions. But what should you do when, after a reasonable investigation and with the statute of limitations running, your information is still incomplete or based on hearsay? To preserve your credibility, if you and your client have no personal knowledge of a fact, you can allege it "on information and belief." For example: "Plaintiff is informed and believes, and thereon alleges that the Defendant intentionally misrepresented the structural condition of a house located at 210 Maple Street, Centerville, Columbia."

Make your complaint interesting

In many cases you can draft a complaint by copying samples in the Federal Rules Appendix of Forms or a commercial form book. But you should always improve on the standard template. Strive to tell your client's story in an interesting and sympathetic way. The court may be less inclined to dismiss your complaint if you have conveyed a real sense that the law should provide a remedy to your client. Moreover, in areas where the law is evolving, courts often require greater detail in pleading than in routine actions.

In striving to tell a good story, remember that judges are a sophisticated audience unlikely to fall for obvious emotional ploys. Since histrionics will backfire, be subtle and selective in your choice

---

51. RAY & COX, *supra* note 37, at 261.

of facts and language. Often the most powerful allegations set out shocking facts in objective language.

Filing the Complaint

Rule 3 provides that a federal action is commenced when the complaint is filed with the court clerk. The complaint must be filed in accordance with local rules. Be sure to check these rules before sending a complaint in for filing, especially if a statute of limitations problem is involved. In addition to a filing fee, the local rules may impose additional formal requirements. For example, some courts require that the document be pre-punched and that an extra copy be submitted.[52]

In addition to the complaint itself, two other documents should be prepared to submit to the clerk's office with the complaint: (1) a summons and (2) a civil cover sheet. Rule 4(a) provides that when the complaint is filed, the clerk shall issue the summons. In practice, the attorney should fill out a summons for each defendant and present it with the complaint. The clerk will then issue the summons by stamping it with the court's seal. Most federal courts also require the filing of a civil cover sheet at the time the complaint is filed. Samples of both these documents are included at the end of this chapter with the sample complaint.

Recently, some courts have begun experimenting with electronic filing over the Internet.[53] For example, the U.S. District Court for the Northern District of Ohio requires all documents in maritime asbestos cases to be filed electronically.[54] The district is processing more than 25,000 asbestos files, with about 5,000 new cases being filed annually. The clerk's office was overwhelmed. Out of "operational necessity," the Administrative Office of the U.S. Courts worked with the clerk's office to develop the electronic filing system.[55] The Honorable George W. White, Chief Judge, has pronounced the experiment a success. This system has saved about

---

52. E.D. CAL. R 7-130.
53. Joseph W. Ryan, Jr., *Filing Motions and Pleadings on the Internet: Today the Prototype, Tomorrow the Practice,* 23 LITIG. NEWS, Jan. 1998, at 3.
54. George W. White & Chris Malumphy, *Electronic Filing: Shocking Developments,* FED. LAW., June 1997, at 40–41.
55. *Id.*

$80,000 per year to the judiciary in personnel costs and has freed the court staff to provide meaningful service to the court and the litigants for the first time in years.[56] In the future, more courts will take advantage of electronic technology, so be sure to keep up with your court's system.

Outline Template for a Federal Civil Complaint

I.   Caption

The caption includes: the name of the court; the title of the action; the names of the parties; and a description of the document. Name the parties carefully and specify any capacities that apply. Comply with any local rules requiring additional information.

II.   Statement of jurisdiction

State the basis of federal jurisdiction and provide statutory authority.

III.   Identification of the parties

Identify the parties to the action and allege the capacities in which they are liable.

IV.   Statement of the claim

Provide a short and plain statement of the claim. If you have claims based on separate facts, state them separately. If you have alternative theories for recovery based on the same set of facts, first present a statement of the facts and then set out your theories in separate counts incorporating the relevant facts by reference. You may also attach documents and incorporate them by reference.

V.   Demand for judgment

List all the relief you are seeking including general damages, special damages, punitive damages, costs, attorney's fees, interest, and equitable relief. Pray for any other relief which the court deems just.

---

56. *Id.*

VI. Attorney's signature

Every document filed in court must be signed by counsel This signature subjects you to the provisions of Fed. R. Civ. P. 11.

VII. Jury demand

Demand a jury if one is desired. While the federal rules do not require the jury demand to be included in the complaint, some local rules do require it. Moreover, since the time limits for demanding a jury are short, the prudent practitioner includes the demand in the complaint.

VIII. Summons

IX. Civil cover sheet

Sample Complaint, Summons, and Civil Cover Sheet

3   Philida Trant
State Bar No. 71355

4   Rumpole & Van Owen
200 Main Street, Suite 1400

5   Capitol City, Columbia
Telephone: 555/234-1234

6   Attorneys for Plaintiff Mary Smith

7   UNITED STATES DISTRICT COURT

8   EASTERN DISTRICT OF COLUMBIA

9	MARIA GARCIA and ROBERTO GARCIA,	No.
10	Plaintiffs,	COMPLAINT
11	v.	Violation of Constitutional Rights
12	JAMES DOE, Director, Columbia Department of	Demand for Jury Trial
13	Corrections, and DR. JOHN ROE	
14	Medical Director, Columbia Department of Corrections,	
15	Defendants.	

16   ————————————————/

17   <u>Introduction</u>

18   1. This is a complaint for damages for the wrongful death

19   of Irena Garcia during her confinement at the Columbia Insti-

20   tute for Women (CIW) at New City, Columbia. During her in-

21   carceration, Ms. Garcia suffered chronic gastritis with gastric

22   stenosis (scarring) from an earlier blunt abdominal injury. As a

1 result of the defendants' deliberate indifference to Ms. Garcia's

2 serious medical needs, on October 6, 1997, Ms. Garcia died of

3 starvation.

4   Jurisdiction

5   2. This action arises under Title 42 U.S.C. §§ 1981 and

6 1983. Therefore jurisdiction is based upon 28 U.S.C. §§ 1331,

7 1332, and 1343.

8   Plaintiffs

9   3. Plaintiffs MARIA GARCIA and ROBERTO GARCIA

10 are the children of the decedent, Irena Garcia.

11   Defendants

12   4. Defendant JAMES DOE is and was at all times herein

13 mentioned the Director of the Columbia Department of Cor-

14 rections (CDC) which is responsible for supervision and man-

15 agement of CIW.

16   5. Defendant DR. JOHN ROE is and at all times mentioned

17 herein was the Medical Director of CDC and was responsible

18 for medical treatment of prisoners incarcerated at CIW.

19   6. At all times herein mentioned, the individual defendants

20 named above were employed by CDC, and were working

21 within the course and scope of their employment under color

22 of state law.

1   7. At all times mentioned herein, the defendants were each

2   the agent, servant and employee of each other, and these defen-

3   dants were acting within the course and scope of said agency

4   and employment with the knowledge and consent of said em-

5   ployer and principal.

6   Statement of Facts

7   8. On February 25, 1997, decedent Irena Garcia pled guilty

8   to forgery of four checks, the approximate value of which to-

9   taled $1,000.00. She was sentenced to serve two years in

10   prison and entered the custody of CDC and was later trans-

11   ferred to CIW.

12   9. During her confinement at CIW, the decedent suffered

13   from chronic gastritis with gastric stenosis (scarring) from an

14   earlier blunt abdominal injury.

15   10. During the decedent's confinement at CIW, defendants

16   adopted and effected a policy and custom of indifference to the

17   serious medical needs of the inmates at CIW, including Ms.

18   Garcia, which was manifested in substandard and inadequate

19   medical facilities and incompetent and inadequate medical

20   staffing.

21   11. Beginning in about April, 1997, Irena Garcia began ex-

22   periencing severe stomach pain, nausea, loss of appetite and

1 weight loss. Over the next seven weeks she lost approximately

2 35 pounds. By August 31, 1997, Ms. Garcia, who was 5' 3"

3 tall, weighed 85½ pounds; one week later she was down to

4 only 72 pounds.

5   12. During this time and continuing until October 6, 1997,

6 defendants acted with deliberate indifference to Ms. Garcia's

7 serious medical needs by failing to provide proper treatment

8 for her medical condition. Specifically, defendants failed to

9 perform a nutritional assessment or dietary counseling, failed

10 to develop a patient care plan or nursing plan, failed to pro-

11 vide psychiatric treatment, and failed to isolate Ms. Garcia

12 from the general prison community and monitor her condi-

13 tion.

14   13. The deliberate indifference to Ms. Garcia's serious med-

15 ical needs as alleged in Paragraph 12 resulted in significant

16 part from the policies and customs of defendants with respect

17 to the provision of inadequate and substandard medical facili-

18 ties at CIW and with respect to the incompetent and inade-

19 quate medical staffing at CIW.

20   14. On or about October 4, 1997, Ms. Garcia's condition

21 deteriorated dramatically: her blood pressure was 90/60, her

22 lungs were congested, and her temperature was 103° F.

1   15. On or about October 6, 1997, Ms. Garcia was taken to

2   the CIW infirmary because she could not stand up without los-

3   ing consciousness. At that time, Ms. Garcia's blood pressure

4   was 80/40. At approximately 10:30 a.m., blood tests were or-

5   dered on an emergency basis. Despite her urgent medical

6   needs, Ms. Garcia was sent away from the infirmary because

7   no bed was available.

8   16. The delay in analysis of Ms. Garcia's blood and the lack

9   of a bed in the infirmary resulted in substantial part from the

10   policy and custom of defendants with respect to provision of

11   substandard and inadequate medical facilities and with respect

12   to the provision of incompetent and inadequate medical

13   staffing.

14   17. Between approximately 12:00–12:30 p.m. on October 6,

15   1997, the physician on duty at CIW, received notice from two

16   CIW employees that Ms. Garcia was "shaking" and "looked

17   like a seizure." The physician on duty told the employees to

18   "ignore [Ms. Garcia]" and "not to make a fuss" over her.

19   18. At approximately 1:40 p.m. on that day, a bed finally

20   became available in the infirmary. At that time, Ms. Garcia

21   was brought to the infirmary in a wheelchair and was pro-

22   nounced dead.

1   19. The medical records do not indicate that any resuscita-

2 tion was attempted.

3   20. As a direct and proximate result of the defendants' con-

4 duct as herein alleged, plaintiffs suffered the loss of the com-

5 fort, companionship, love and support of Irena Garcia.

6   21. As a further direct and proximate result of the defen-

7 dants' conduct as herein alleged, plaintiffs incurred funeral and

8 related expenses in an amount according to proof at trial.

9

FIRST COUNT

10

(Eighth Amendment Violation — Policy and Custom of
Inadequate Staffing and Inadequate Medical Facilities)

11   22. Plaintiffs refer to and incorporate by reference the alle-

12 gations of paragraphs 1 through 21.

13   23. Defendants violated Ms. Garcia's eighth amendment

14 constitutional right to protection from cruel and unusual pun-

15 ishment by their policy and custom of maintaining inadequate

16 and incompetent medical staffing and substandard and inade-

17 quate medical facilities at CIW, which constituted deliberate

18 indifference to Ms. Garcia's serious medical needs.

19

SECOND COUNT

20

(Eighth Amendment Violation — Deliberate
Indifference to Serious Medical Needs)

21   24. Plaintiffs refer to and incorporate by reference the alle-

22 gations of paragraphs 1 through 21.

1   25. Defendants violated Ms. Garcia's eighth amendment

2   constitutional right to protection from cruel and unusual pun-

3   ishment by acting with deliberate indifference to her serious

4   medical needs. Specifically, defendants failed to adequately

5   monitor her condition, failed to provide a patient care plan or

6   nursing plan, failed to provide nutritional assessment or di-

7   etary counseling, failed to provide psychiatric treatment, failed

8   to promptly perform Ms. Garcia's blood analysis on October

9   6, 1997, sent her away from the infirmary on October 6, 1997,

10   when she urgently needed medical care, refused to provide

11   treatment on October 6, 1997, when she was going into appar-

12   ent seizure, and failed to provide prompt resuscitation at the

13   time of her death on October 6, 1997.

14

THIRD COUNT
(Common Law Negligence)

15

16   26. Plaintiffs refer to and incorporate by reference the alle-

17   gations of paragraphs 1 through 21.

18   27. Defendants negligently failed to provide Ms. Garcia ad-

19   equate medical care while she was incarcerated at CIW.

20   Specifically, defendants negligently failed to adequately moni-

21   tor her condition, negligently failed to provide a patient care

22   plan or nursing plan, negligently failed to provide nutritional

1 assessment or dietary counseling, negligently failed to provide

2 psychiatric treatment, negligently failed to promptly perform

3 Ms. Garcia's blood analysis on October 6, 1997, negligently

4 sent her away from the infirmary on October 6, 1997, when

5 she urgently needed medical care, negligently refused to pro-

6 vide treatment on October 6, 1997, when she was going into

7 apparent seizure, and negligently failed to provide prompt re-

8 suscitation at the time of her death on October 6, 1997.

9 Prayer

10 WHEREFORE, plaintiffs pray for judgment against defen-

11 dants and each of them as follows:

12 1. For general damages according to proof;

13 2. For special damages according to proof;

14 3. For punitive damages;

15 4. For reasonable attorney's fees pursuant to 42 U.S.C.

16 § 1988;

17 5. For costs of suit; and

18 6. For such other and further relief as the Court may deem

19 just and proper.

20 Dated: February 4, 1998   RUMPOLE & VAN OWEN

21 _____
Philida Trant

22 Attorney for Plaintiffs Maria
Garcia and Roberto Garcia

1   <u>JURY TRIAL</u>

2   The plaintiffs hereby demand a jury trial in this matter.

3   Dated: February 4, 1998   RUMPOLE & VAN OWEN

4   _____

5   Philida Trant
                                      Attorney for Plaintiffs Maria
6   Garcia and Roberto Garcia

7

8

9

10

11

12

13

14

15

16

17

18

19

20

21

22

AO 440 (Rev 1/90) Summons in a Civil Action

United States District Court

_____ DISTRICT OF _____

SUMMONS IN A CIVIL ACTION

V.

CASE NUMBER:

TO: (Name and Address of Defendant)

YOU ARE HEREBY SUMMONED and required to file with the Clerk of this Court and serve upon

PLAINTIFF'S ATTORNEY (name and address)

an answer to the complaint which is herewith served upon you, within _____ days after service of this summons upon you, exclusive of the day of service. If you fail to do so, judgment by default will be taken against you for the relief demanded in the complaint.

CLERK

DATE

BY DEPUTY CLERK

AO 440 (Rev. 1/90) Summons in a Civil Action

RETURN OF SERVICE

Service of the Summons and Complaint was made by me[1]	DATE
NAME OF SERVER (PRINT)	TITLE

Check one box below to indicate appropriate method of service

☐ Served personally upon the defendant. Place where served : _____

_____

☐ Left copies thereof at the defendant's dwelling house or usual place of abode with a person of suitable age and discretion then residing therein.
Name of person with whom the summons and complaint were left: _____

☐ Returned unexecuted: _____

_____

_____

☐ Other (specify): _____

_____

_____

STATEMENT OF SERVICE FEES

TRAVEL	SERVICES	TOTAL

DECLARATION OF SERVER

I declare under penalty of perjury under the laws of the United States of America that the foregoing information contained in the Return of Service and Statement of Service Fees is true and correct.

Executed on _____   _____
                    Date   *Signature of Server*

                                            _____
                                                        Address of Server

1) As to who may serve a summons see Rule 4 of the Federal Rules of Civil Procedure.

JS 44
(Rev. 07/89)

CIVIL COVER SHEET

The JS-44 civil cover sheet and the information contained herein neither replace nor supplement the filing and service of pleadings or other papers as required by law, except as provided by local rules of court. This form, approved by the Judicial Conference of the United States in September 1974, is required for the use of the Clerk of Court for the purpose of initiating the civil docket sheet. (SEE INSTRUCTIONS ON THE REVERSE OF THE FORM.)

I (a) PLAINTIFFS

DEFENDANTS

(b) COUNTY OF RESIDENCE OF FIRST LISTED PLAINTIFF _____
(EXCEPT IN U.S. PLAINTIFF CASES)

COUNTY OF RESIDENCE OF FIRST LISTED DEFENDANT _____
(IN U.S. PLAINTIFF CASES ONLY)
NOTE: IN LAND CONDEMNATION CASES, USE THE LOCATION OF THE
TRACT OF LAND INVOLVED

(c) ATTORNEYS (FIRM NAME, ADDRESS, AND TELEPHONE NUMBER)

ATTORNEYS (IF KNOWN)

II. BASIS OF JURISDICTION (PLACE AN × IN ONE BOX ONLY)

☐ 1 U.S. Government
Plaintiff

☐ 2 U.S. Government
Defendant

☐ 3 Federal Question
(U.S. Government Not a Party)

☐ 4 Diversity
(Indicate Citizenship of
Parties in Item III)

III. CITIZENSHIP OF PRINCIPAL PARTIES (PLACE AN × IN ONE BOX
FOR PLAINTIFF AND ONE BOX FOR DEFENDANT)
(For Diversity Cases Only)

	PTF	DEF		PTF	DEF
Citizen of This State	☐ 1	☐ 1	Incorporated or Principal Place of Business in This State	☐ 4	☐ 4
Citizen of Another State	☐ 2	☐ 2	Incorporated and Principal Place of Business in Another State	☐ 5	☐ 5
Citizen or Subject of a Foreign Country	☐ 3	☐ 3	Foreign Nation	☐ 6	☐ 6

IV. CAUSE OF ACTION (CITE THE U.S. CIVIL STATUTE UNDER WHICH YOU ARE FILING AND WRITE A BRIEF STATEMENT OF CAUSE

DO NOT CITE JURISDICTIONAL STATUTES UNLESS DIVERSITY)

V. NATURE OF SUIT (PLACE AN × IN ONE BOX ONLY)

CONTRACT	TORTS		FORFEITURE/PENALTY	BANKRUPTCY	OTHER STATUTES
☐ 110 Insurance	**PERSONAL INJURY**	**PERSONAL INJURY**	☐ 610 Agriculture	☐ 422 Appeal 28 USC 158	☐ 400 State Reapportionment
☐ 120 Marine	☐ 310 Airplane	☐ 362 Personal Injury—	☐ 620 Other Food & Drug		☐ 410 Antitrust
☐ 130 Miller Act	☐ 315 Airplane Product	Med Malpractice	☐ 625 Drug Related Seizure of	☐ 423 Withdrawal	☐ 430 Banks and Banking
☐ 140 Negotiable Instrument	Liability	☐ 365 Personal Injury—	Property 21 USC 881	28 USC 157	☐ 450 Commerce/ICC Rates/etc.
☐ 150 Recovery of Overpayment	☐ 320 Assault, Libel &	Product Liability	☐ 630 Liquor Laws	**PROPERTY RIGHTS**	☐ 460 Deportation
& Enforcement of	Slander	☐ 368 Asbestos Personal	☐ 640 R.R. & Truck		☐ 470 Racketeer Influenced and
Judgment	☐ 330 Federal Employers'	Injury Product	☐ 650 Airline Regs	☐ 820 Copyrights	Corrupt Organizations
☐ 151 Medicare Act	Liability	Liability	☐ 660 Occupational	☐ 830 Patent	☐ 810 Selective Service
☐ 152 Recovery of Defaulted	☐ 340 Marine	**PERSONAL PROPERTY**	Safety/Health	☐ 840 Trademark	☐ 850 Securities/Commodities/
Student Loans	☐ 345 Marine Product	☐ 370 Other Fraud	☐ 690 Other		Exchange
(Excl. Veterans)	Liability	☐ 371 Truth in Lending		**SOCIAL SECURITY**	☐ 875 Customer Challenge
☐ 153 Recovery of Overpayment	☐ 350 Motor Vehicle	☐ 380 Other Personal	**LABOR**	☐ 861 HIA (1395ff)	12 USC 3410
of Veteran's Benefits	☐ 355 Motor Vehicle	Property Damage	☐ 710 Fair Labor Standards	☐ 862 Black Lung (923)	☐ 891 Agricultural Acts
☐ 160 Stockholders' Suits	Product Liability	☐ 385 Property Damage	Act	☐ 863 DIWC/DIWW (405(g))	☐ 892 Economic Stabilization
☐ 190 Other Contract	☐ 360 Other Personal	Product Liability	☐ 720 Labor/Mgmt.	☐ 864 SSID Title XVI	Act
☐ 195 Contract Product Liability	Injury		Relations	☐ 865 RSI (405(g))	☐ 893 Environmental Matters
REAL PROPERTY	**CIVIL RIGHTS**	**PRISONER PETITIONS**	☐ 730 Labor/Mgmt. Reporting & Disclosure Act	**FEDERAL TAX SUITS**	☐ 894 Energy Allocation Act
☐ 210 Land Condemnation	☐ 441 Voting	☐ 510 Motions to Vacate	☐ 740 Railway Labor	☐ 870 Taxes (U.S. Plaintiff	☐ 895 Freedom of Information Act
☐ 220 Foreclosure	☐ 442 Employment	Sentence	Act	or Defendant)	☐ 900 Appeal of Fee Determination
☐ 230 Rent Lease & Ejectment	☐ 443 Housing/	Habeas Corpus:	☐ 790 Other Labor	☐ 871 IRS—Third Party	Under Equal Access to
☐ 240 Torts to Land	Accommodations	☐ 530 General	Litigation	26 USC 7609	Justice
☐ 245 Tort Product Liability	☐ 444 Welfare	☐ 535 Death Penalty	☐ 791 Empl. Ret. Inc.		☐ 950 Constitutionality of
☐ 290 All Other Real Property	☐ 440 Other Civil Rights	☐ 540 Mandamus & Other	Security Act		State Statutes
		☐ 550 Other			☐ 890 Other Statutory Actions

VI. ORIGIN (PLACE AN × IN ONE BOX ONLY)

☐ 1 Original
Proceeding

☐ 2 Removed from
State Court

☐ 3 Remanded from
Appellate Court

☐ 4 Reinstated or
Reopened

☐ 5 Transferred from
another district
(specify)

☐ 6 Multidistrict
Litigation

Appeal to District
☐ 7 Judge from
Magistrate
Judgment

VII. REQUESTED IN
COMPLAINT:

CHECK IF THIS IS A **CLASS ACTION**
☐ UNDER F.R.C.P. 23

DEMAND $

Check YES only if demanded in complaint:
JURY DEMAND: ☐ YES ☐ NO

VIII. RELATED CASE(S) (See instructions):
IF ANY

JUDGE _____ DOCKET NUMBER_____

DATE

SIGNATURE OF ATTORNEY OF RECORD

UNITED STATES DISTRICT COURT

INSTRUCTIONS FOR ATTORNEYS COMPLETING CIVIL COVER SHEET FORM JS-44

Authority For Civil Cover Sheet

The JS-44 civil cover sheet and the information contained herein neither replaces nor supplements the filings and service of pleading or other papers as required by law, except as provided by local rules of court. This form, approved by the Judicial Conference of the United States in September 1974, is required for the use of the Clerk of Court for the purpose of initiating the civil docket sheet. Consequently a civil cover sheet is submitted to the Clerk of Court for each civil complaint filed. The attorney filing a case should complete the form as follows:

I. (a) Plaintiffs - Defendants. Enter names (last, first, middle initial) of plaintiff and defendant. If the plaintiff or defendant is a government agency, use only the full name or standard abbreviations. If the plaintiff or defendant is an official within a government agency, identify first the agency and then the official, giving both name and title.

(b) County of Residence. For each civil case filed, except U.S. plaintiff cases, enter the name of the county where the first listed plaintiff resides at the time of filing. In U.S. plaintiff cases, enter the name of the county in which the first listed defendant resides at the time of filing. (NOTE: In land condemnation cases, the county of residence of the "defendant" is the location of the tract of land involved).

(c) Attorneys. Enter firm name, address, telephone number, and attorney or record. If there are several attorneys, list them on an attachment, noting in this section "(see attachment)".

II. Jurisdiction. The basis of jurisdiction is set forth under Rule 8 (a), F.R.C.P., which requires that jurisdictions be shown in pleadings. Place an "X" in one of the boxes. If there is more than one basis of jurisdiction, precedence is given in the order shown below.

United States plaintiff. (1) Jurisdiction is based on 28 U.S.C. 1345 and 1348. Suits by agencies and officers of the United States are included here.

United States defendant. (2) When the plaintiff is suing the United States, its officers or agencies, place an X in this box.

Federal question. (3) This refers to suits under 28 U.S.C. 1331, where jurisdiction arises under the Constitution of the United States, an amendment to the Constitution, an act of Congress or a treaty of the United States. In cases where the U.S. is a party, the U.S. plaintiff or defendant code takes precedence, and box 1 or 2 should be marked.

Diversity of citizenship. (4) This refers to suits under 28 U.S.C. 1332, where parties are citizens of different states. When Box 4 is checked, the citizenship of the different parties must be checked. (See Section III below; federal question actions take precedence over diversity cases.)

III. Residence (citizenship) of Principal Parties. This section of the JS-44 is to be completed if diversity of citizenship was indicated above. Mark this section for each principal party.

IV. Cause of Action. Report the civil statute directly related to the cause of action and give a brief description of the cause.

V. Nature of Suit. Place an "X" in the appropriate box. If the nature of suit cannot be determined, be sure the cause of action, in Section IV above, is sufficient to enable the deputy clerk or the statistical clerks in the Administrative Office to determine the nature of suit. If the cause fits more than one nature of suit, select the most definitive.

VI. Origin. Place an "X" in one of the seven boxes.

Original Proceedings. (1) Cases which originate in the United States district courts.

Removed from State Court. (2) Proceedings initiated in state courts may be removed to the district courts under Title 28 U.S.C., Section 1441. When the petition for removal is granted, check this box.

Remanded from Appellate Court. (3) Check this box for cases remanded to the district court for further action. Use the date of remand as the filing date.

Reinstated or Reopened. (4) Check this box for cases reinstated or reopened in the district court. Use the reopening date as the filing date.

Transferred from Another District. (5) For cases transferred under Title 28 U.S.C. Section 1404(a). Do not use this for within district transfers or multidistrict litigation transfers.

Multidistrict Litigation. (6) Check this box when a multidistrict case is transferred into the district under authority of Title 28 U.S.C. Section 1407. When this box is checked, do not check (5) above.

Appeal to District Judge from Magistrate Judgment. (7) Check this box for an appeal from a magistrate's decision.

VII. Requested in Complaint. Class Action. Place an "X" in this box if you are filing a class action under Rule 23, F.R.Cv.P.

Demand. In this space enter the dollar amount (in thousands of dollars) being demanded or indicate other demand such as a preliminary injunction.

Jury Demand. Check the appropriate box to indicate whether or not a jury is being demanded.

VIII. Related Cases. This section of the JS-44 is used to reference relating pending cases if any. If there are related pending cases, insert the docket numbers and the corresponding judge names for such cases.

Date and Attorney Signature. Date and sign the civil cover sheet.

(rev. 07/89)

GPO : 1989 - 237-312

Chapter 6

Memorandum Evaluating Responsive Pleadings

This week you'll switch roles. Your firm represents a client who has just been served with a complaint. Your senior partner wants you to evaluate the complaint to determine how to respond. As you may recall from civil procedure, you must file an answer or pre-answer motion within 20 days of service of the complaint.[1] Your memo should discuss the pros and cons of these possible responses.

The basic form of the memo will be the same as the first one you wrote. However, we'll consider some additional ethical issues. And to analyze this question, you will have to address both substantive law and also procedural strategies. This week you'll see how to integrate the procedural issue into your legal analysis.

Professional Responsibilities in Filing Responsive Pleadings

In evaluating responsive pleadings, we revisit the lawyer's duties to be a zealous advocate, to avoid frivolous pleadings, and to expedite litigation. As you learned in drafting the complaint, every document a lawyer files must be written to meet the lawyer's dual duties to the client and the court. To the client, the advocate owes zeal and creativity in advancing good faith arguments.[2] This duty inclines the lawyer to file a motion to dismiss if it has any chance of success. On

---

1. FED. R. CIV. P. 12.
2. MODEL RULES OF PROFESSIONAL CONDUCT Rule 3.1 (1997) [hereinafter MODEL RULES].

the other hand, to the court, the lawyer owes a duty to refrain from frivolous litigation.[3] According to the Model Rules of Professional Conduct, the lawyer is required "to make reasonable efforts to expedite litigation consistent with the interests of the client."[4] And the new *Restatement (Third) of the Law Governing Lawyers* prohibits practices which cause unnecessary delay.[5] The resolution of the conflict between these duties turns on the strength of the substantive arguments, the goals of the client, the reputation and politics of the judge who will hear the motion, and a myriad of other factors. While no bright-line test will resolve this conflict, be mindful of these obligations in considering your options.

In addition to the ethical rules, you should also consider the economic consequences of filing a motion. In determining how to respond to a complaint, remember that every paper you file costs money to your client, your firm, your opponent, and the court. You shouldn't squander time and resources on unjustified motions. But even if a motion is weak, a lawyer may be tempted to file it for several reasons: (1) the defendant may profit from the delay; (2) the plaintiff will be damaged by the delay; and (3) the lawyer may be enriched by the motion.

First, the defendant in a civil action will often profit from a delay in litigation. For example, assume that the defendant owes the plaintiff money. The defendant will often be able to invest the money at a rate of return above the judgment rate. The longer the litigation takes, the more money the defendant will earn. Thus, the defendant has a financial incentive to delay the litigation as long as possible. Regardless of the interest rate, the defendant will usually benefit from keeping the plaintiff's money for as long as possible, if only because the delay provides a lever to force the plaintiff to settle for a lesser amount.

Second, the plaintiff in a civil action will suffer financially from any delay. Obviously, the plaintiff cannot invest or pay bills with money the defendant keeps. To a struggling business, the lack of capital may cause a cash-flow crisis. And in more human terms, the family of an injured worker will suffer from any delay in receiving

---

3. RESTATEMENT (THIRD) OF THE LAW GOVERNING LAWYERS § 170 (Tentative Draft No. 8, 1997) [hereinafter RESTATEMENT, TENTATIVE DRAFT].
4. MODEL RULES, *supra* note 2, Rule 3.2.
5. RESTATEMENT, TENTATIVE DRAFT, *supra* note 3, § 166.

compensation for medical bills and lost earnings. A desperate plaintiff who cannot financially withstand the delay may be forced to accept a greatly discounted settlement.

Finally, a lawyer compensated on a hourly basis can generate high fees by filing every possible motion. In this regard, the lawyer's interest directly conflicts with the client's interest. Like the proverbial taxi driver with an out-of-town fare, an unscrupulous lawyer can run the meter on an unsophisticated client with virtual impunity. In recognition of this temptation, some states have adopted criminal sanctions for charging unnecessary legal fees. For example, in California, it is a misdemeanor punishable by imprisonment in the county jail for up to six months or a fine up to $2500 or both if the lawyer "willfully delays his client's suit with a view to his own gain."[6]

This unholy trio of temptations has been acknowledged in the Model Rules which state:

> Delay should not be indulged merely ... for the purpose of frustrating an opposing party's attempt to obtain rightful redress. ... The question is whether a competent lawyer acting in good faith would regard the course of action as having some substantial purpose other than delay. Realizing financial benefit or other benefit from otherwise improper delay in litigation is not a legitimate interest of the client.[7]

Similarly, the *Restatement* provides that "a lawyer may not use means that have no substantial purpose other than to embarrass, delay, or burden a third person."[8]

The costs of abuse go beyond the immediate parties. In addition to the burden on the courts, the burden to society can be significant. For example, according to The Washington Monthly, a corporate client sought counsel in an antitrust case. The lawyer advised that the case was ultimately doomed to lose but that it could last ten years if the client was willing to spend the $500,000–$1,000,000 in legal fees that the delay would entail. The client readily agreed since forcing the government to its proof would protect 10 years of profits by the antitrust violation.[9]

---

6. CAL. BUS. & PROF. CODE § 6128(b) (West 1990).
7. MODEL RULES, *supra* note 2, Rule 3.2 cmt.
8. RESTATEMENT, TENTATIVE DRAFT, *supra* note 3, § 166.
9. WASH. MONTHLY, Sept., 1979, at 10, *reprinted in* STEPHEN GILLERS & NORMAN DORSEN, REGULATION OF LAWYERS 402 (1985).

In short, consider the ethical and practical implications of moving to dismiss. A successful motion will save the parties and the court time and money by terminating the litigation at the earliest possible stage. On the other hand, a frivolous motion violates Rule 11 and causes unjustified expense and delay. And as you might expect, most motions lie in the vast gray area of uncertainty. You need to evaluate the options and explain them to your client.

Integrating Procedural Issues into an Office Memorandum

Procedurally, Rule 12 provides the defendant four options in response to a complaint: (1) answer; (2) move to strike "any redundant, immaterial, impertinent or scandalous matter;" (3) move for a more definite statement; or (4) move to dismiss. In our case, the motion to strike and the motion for a more definite statement are not appropriate. You need only consider whether to answer or to move to dismiss. As you will see, this procedural question fits into every section of the memo and provides a focus for the legal analysis.

Question Presented

The question presented should provide the procedural context and present the substantive issue using the key facts of the case. This sounds like a lot to accomplish in one sentence, and it is. But with practice you can write a well-organized question which will give your reader a synopsis of the problem in a neat package.

In organizing your question, remember to start with the most general information and then proceed to the specific details. This will introduce your reader to the larger context of the problem and then ease into the specifics. So ask yourself, what's the big picture? After you've characterized this general area of law, move to the procedural context, and then precisely identify the issue to be analyzed in terms of the facts of your case. For example:

Question Presented

In a negligence action, should the defendant landlord move to dismiss the complaint on the grounds that tenant's injury was unforeseeable as a matter of law where the tenant was attacked in her apartment but no prior crimes had occurred on the premises?

Notice how the example opens with the general legal area, negligence. The reader now knows it's a tort action for negligence, which narrows the possible substantive issues. Next the question tells the reader the procedural device being considered, a motion to dismiss. Now the reader knows where the lawsuit stands chronologically, which narrows the range of available options and establishes the applicable legal standard. After setting this context, the question then presents the precise issue of substantive law and ties it to the specific facts of the case.

By following this formula, your question will provide your reader all the necessary information in a well-organized and readable framework:

General substantive area: In a negligence action,

Procedural vehicle: should defendant employer move to dismiss

Legal theory: on the grounds that worker's compensation is the exclusive remedy

Key facts: where plaintiff suffered prenatal injuries as a result of her mother's exposure to toxic chemicals at work?

Brief Answer

Like the question presented, the brief answer should address both the substantive and the procedural issues under consideration. The brief answer should explain whether a specific procedural device is an appropriate and advisable vehicle for raising the substantive issue. For example:

Brief Answer

Yes, the defendant landlord should move to dismiss. While foreseeability of injury is generally a question of fact and thus not susceptible to a motion to dismiss, some exceptions have been recognized. In landlord-tenant cases, the foreseeability of injuries from a third-party crime has only been established where prior crimes have occurred on the premises. Where no prior crimes were alleged, two cases have upheld dismissals on the grounds that the crime was not foreseeable as a matter of law. Thus, we have a strong argument that a motion should be granted in our case since no prior crimes occurred on the premises.

The plaintiff will respond that the complaint raises a question of fact as to the foreseeability of crime by alleging a high neighborhood crime rate and tenant demands for additional security precautions. Admittedly, the allegations of foreseeability of crime in this case are much stronger than in the cases where the dismissals were upheld. In short, the court may distinguish the favorable cases and fall back on the general rule that foreseeability is a question of fact. Despite this risk of losing, a motion to dismiss would be an inexpensive and quick method for raising this issue, and it might well succeed.

Note that the brief answer sets the context by opening with the general rule of law before proceeding to the exception which the writer hopes the court will apply. Note also that the substantive issue (foreseeability of injury) is considered in the context of a specific procedural vehicle (motion to dismiss). Finally, remember to present a summary of the counterarguments so that your reader will have a realistic notion of the likelihood of prevailing. Because this brief answer includes both a substantive and a procedural issue, it can run 10–15 sentences in length.

Statement of Facts

As with the question presented and the brief answer, the statement of facts should be tailored to suit the substantive and procedural issues under consideration. Since you are discussing your response to a complaint, the court will consider only the facts alleged in the complaint. For this reason, you may wish to confine your statement of facts to the allegations of the complaint. Further, select only the relevant allegations. For example, if you are challenging the basis of liability, the facts pertaining to damages are irrelevant. Condense your statement of facts by limiting it to facts which are relevant to the motion.

Discussion

The organization of your discussion section should follow the guidelines provided in chapters 2 and 4. Remember to include an introductory paragraph identifying the parties' arguments; keep it short (3–6 sentences). Present and apply the authorities one at a time. You may organize your authorities by order of significance or chronologically, remembering that usually your reader wants to know the current state of the law. Introduce each authority with a topic sentence explaining the role that it will play in the case. Design this sentence so that the citation appears at the end. Present each authority thoroughly. When presenting a statute, remember to quote the critical statutory language and apply it to your case. When presenting a case, remember to include the facts, procedure, holding, and rationale for the decision. Explain the policy reasons for the decision. After you have presented each authority, explain its application to your problem. Anticipate and evaluate counter-arguments. Close the discussion with a paragraph synthesizing your analysis.

While the organization of the discussion remains the same, the content will have a different emphasis because the procedural issue narrows the focus. The question is not simply whether the defendant can prevail but whether the defendant can prevail by moving to dismiss. The analysis must be precise. Each authority must be evaluated both in terms of the substantive outcome and also in terms of the procedural context.

For example, assume you represent a landlord who has been sued by a tenant for injuries suffered in a third-party attack. No prior crimes had occurred in the building. You find a case with facts identical to your case where the defendant won and the court of appeal upheld the judgment. At first glance you may think, "Golly, that's great! A case in my client's favor that's right on point! I'll win my motion for sure." But on sober reflection you'll realize, "Oh, heck! That case doesn't help at all because it was decided by a jury and therefore won't convince the judge that the same issue should be resolved as a matter of law on a motion to dismiss." In other words, whether a case helps you or hurts you depends on the facts, the substantive law, and also on the procedural context of the decision.

In short, in evaluating how to proceed, remember that you need to chose the procedural vehicle which will present your argument most persuasively and most efficiently. In some cases, the argument that the complaint fails to state a claim might be more persuasively raised by a motion for summary judgment which allows the presentation of evidence than by a motion to dismiss which is limited to the face of the complaint. A weak motion to dismiss will waste the court's time, irritate the judge, run up unnecessary legal fees, and serve no useful purpose. In such cases, it would be better to answer the complaint than to move to dismiss. Think carefully about which procedural strategy will best serve your client.

Conclusion

In your conclusion you should briefly set out your recommendations. State whether you think an answer or a motion to dismiss would be advisable and give your reasons. Alert your reader to any unanswered questions or concerns. Explain what needs to be done next and when, keeping in mind that time is short. Highlight any deadlines, especially if they are imminent. Offer to take the next recommended step, drafting the answer or motion. Even if your supervising attorney decides to take a different approach, your interest and willingness will be appreciated.

Chapter 7

Motion to Dismiss

After considering your splendid analysis, your senior partner has decided that the possibility of successfully moving to dismiss the complaint outweighs the risk of losing and the expense of the motion. Your partner has now accepted your offer to prepare the motion. "Gadzooks!" you exclaim to yourself. "I only know the theory of motions. What do I do now?" Well, relax. This chapter will discuss the ethical responsibilities of motion practice and the papers necessary for your motion.

Professional Responsibilities in Motion Practice

In motion practice, a lawyer must continually grapple with the tension between the lawyer's duties as an advocate and as an officer of the court. Zealous representation must be tempered by the lawyer's duty to bring or defend an action only when "there is a basis for doing so that is not frivolous, which includes a good faith argument for an extension, modification or reversal of existing law."[1] Moreover, the lawyer has a duty of candor to the court.[2] Under the Model Rules of Professional Conduct, a lawyer must not knowingly make a false statement of fact or law to a court[3] and

---

1. MODEL RULES OF PROFESSIONAL CONDUCT Rule 3.1 (1989) [hereinafter MODEL RULES]. *See also,* RESTATEMENT (THIRD) OF THE LAW GOVERNING LAWYERS § 170 (Tentative Draft No. 8, 1997) [hereinafter RESTATEMENT, TENTATIVE DRAFT].
2. *See* MODEL RULES, *supra* note 1, Rule 3.3 and CAL. R. PROF. CONDUCT 5-102.
3. MODEL RULES, *supra* note 1, Rule 3.3(a)(1).

must disclose controlling, adverse authority which is not disclosed by opposing counsel.[4] This duty of disclosure is reaffirmed in the *Restatement (Third) of the Law Governing Lawyers* which explains that failure to disclose adverse legal authority "deprives the court of useful information and serves no interest of the client other than obtaining a result not provided for by the law."[5] This obligation to the court does not conflict with advocate's obligations to client because "the advocate's role is to present the client's cause within the framework of the law, which requires common terms of legal reference with the court and opposing counsel."[6]

The duty to disclose adverse authority is narrowly stated by both the Model Rules and the *Restatement* which limit the duty to directly adverse authority in the controlling jurisdiction.[7] In other words, if the case is distinguishable or from another jurisdiction, there is no disclosure obligation. For example, for state law questions, mandatory disclosure is required only for higher court decisions within that state.[8] Similarly, for federal questions, the duty includes only cases decided by the United States Supreme Court or the same circuit.[9]

But while you are required to disclose adverse authority, you are not required to bare your soul. The judge or the jury must be objective, but the lawyer's sworn duty is to present the client's case in its most favorable light.[10] In litigation, "[t]he lawyer... is not an umpire, but an advocate. He is under no duty to refrain from making every proper argument in support of any legal point because he is not convinced of its inherent soundness.... His personal belief in the soundness of his cause or of the authorities supporting it, is irrelevant."[11]

These admonitions may seem hopelessly conflicting. How can you be a zealous advocate while undermining your arguments with

---

4. MODEL RULES, *supra* note 1, Rule 3.3(a)(3).
5. RESTATEMENT, TENTATIVE DRAFT, *supra* note 1, § 171 cmt. c.
6. *Id.*
7. MODEL RULES, *supra* note 1, Rule 3.3(a)(3) and RESTATEMENT, TENTATIVE DRAFT, *supra* note 1, § 171 cmts. c and d.
8. RESTATEMENT, TENTATIVE DRAFT, *supra* note 1, § 171 cmt. d.
9. *Id.*
10. MODEL CODE OF PROFESSIONAL RESPONSIBILITY EC 7-3 (1983).
11. ABA Comm. on Professional Ethics and Grievances, Formal Op. 280 (1949).

adverse authorities? How can you fulfill your duty of candor while advancing arguments supported by authorities that you consider unsound? There are no easy answers to these questions. One partial answer is that the duty of candor is generally understood in a very limited sense, limited to an obligation to not make false representations of fact or law and to disclose the directly controlling authorities.[12] Beyond these basic requirements, the lawyer is permitted to urge a construction of the facts and law most favorable to the client and to challenge existing law, regardless of the lawyer's personal belief in the argument.[13] Our system assumes that once the court is presented with accurate facts and the applicable law, it will be sufficiently informed to reach a just result.

In drafting persuasive documents, the theoretical tension between the lawyer's duties to the client and the court often dissolves. For example, as to the disclosure of adverse authority, the lawyer's duties to the client and the court both compel the disclosure. As Charles Wolfram explains:

> The mandatory reach of the rule is effectively neutralized in many real-life settings because it merely parallels what prudence dictates independently. Effective advocacy of a client's legal position will most often involve full revelation of adverse authorities, together with arguments distinguishing or criticizing them. Candor here both takes the wind from an opponent's sails and instills judicial trust in the quality and completeness of presentation. If nothing else, a court's late discovery that an advocate has failed to confront an adverse authority is likely to produce the impression that the awakened precedent, because suppressed, should be regarded as particularly vicious.[14]

In other words, you can avoid discipline by adopting a narrow view of the duty of candor, but you will enhance your credibility by adopting a broader view. Put yourself in the position of a busy judge with a small staff and no time for independent research. Assume that a recent supreme court case in your jurisdiction favorably stated a legal principle in dicta. What would you think of an attorney who excused her failure to disclose this supreme court decision on the grounds that the statement was only dicta and therefore not

---

12. MODEL RULES, *supra* note 1, Rule 3.3.
13. MODEL CODE OF PROFESSIONAL RESPONSIBILITY EC 7-3, 7-4 (1983); ABA Comm. on Professional Ethics and Grievances, Formal Op. 280 (1949).
14. CHARLES W. WOLFRAM, MODERN LEGAL ETHICS 682 (1986).

technically "controlling"? Or, in a case of first impression in your circuit, what would you think of an attorney who failed to disclose that all the other circuits to consider the issue unanimously agreed on the proper rule to apply? As a judge, wouldn't you want to know about these decisions before making your ruling? Wouldn't you be suspicious of the attorney who omitted them? Good advocates generally agree that, regardless of whether a case is technically controlling, "the more unhappy a lawyer is that he found an adverse precedent, the clearer it is that he must reveal it."[15]

Because the disclosure of adverse authority is compelled by both ethical rules and persuasive advocacy, the lawyer should consider how far to extend this disclosure. Beyond controlling authority, the lawyer should also consider disclosing any other authority which the court would want to ponder in resolving the dispute. By addressing and effectively distinguishing adverse authorities, the advocate both undermines the opponent's arguments and gains the court's confidence.

In short, the lawyer's duties to the client and the court are harmonious since both compel the disclosure of adverse authority. If the adverse authority is controlling and the lawyer has no good faith argument for modifying or overruling it, then the lawyer should not file the motion. On the other hand, if the adverse authority can be distinguished or should be modified or overruled, then the lawyer should not simply ignore the authority and hope the judge won't find it. Rather the attorney should confront the authority and persuade the court to distinguish, modify, or overrule it. If the attorney omits the adverse authority, the attorney has breached both the duty of candor to the court and the duty of zealous advocacy to the client.

Audience for a Motion to Dismiss

Let's spend a few minutes picturing your primary audience, the district court judge. Regardless of differences in political and judicial philosophies, district judges have two things in common: (1) they are

---

15. Geoffrey C. Hazard, Jr. & W. William Hodes, The Law of Lawyering 3:3:206 (1990) *quoted in* Joanne Pitullia, *Playing Ostrich*, A.B.A. J., Aug. 1993, at 98.

burdened with heavy dockets and (2) they are generalists who may have no expertise in the area of law at issue in your case. Think of how you feel during finals week. What would you want to read to understand a perplexing point of law? Would you want an exhaustive analysis tracing the historical and social development of a doctrine replete with esoteric references to obscure law review articles and copious footnotes debating tangential issues? Neither does a trial court judge. You'd want a concise, readable explanation of the current law supported by the key cases on the issue. So does the judge. You'd not be offended if it were explained in simple, direct language; but you'd be infuriated if it were pompous, long-winded, and unnecessarily obscure. So would the judge. Be mindful of the pressures and time constraints imposed on the court, and write accordingly.

In presenting your arguments, remember that you are an advocate and that the judge expects you to take an adversarial position. Unlike an office memorandum which must evaluate a problem objectively, a motion should be persuasive. The legal system depends on all attorneys vigorously advocating their clients' positions. Your motion is your best and often only opportunity to convince the judge to rule in your favor. In practice, the best advocates research the district judge before filing a motion to learn the judge's background, philosophy, prior decisions on the issue, temperament, and idiosyncrasies. This information helps the advocate tailor the motion to the individual judge.

Form and Content of a Motion to Dismiss

Now we turn to the documents needed for a motion to dismiss. Specifically, you will need to draft a notice of motion, a motion, a memorandum of points and authorities in support of the motion, and a proof of service. And happily, virtually all motions in both state and federal trial courts begin with these basic documents. Thus, the documents you'll learn to draft this week will be used in all motion practice.

Notice of hearing

Under the federal rules, a moving party must notify the other side of the motion and the hearing date. To arrange a hearing date, you must check the local court rules and practices. Once you have arranged the hearing date, you must serve the notice and other documents within the court's time limits. For example, in the United States District Court of the Eastern District of California, the papers must be served and filed at least 28 days before the hearing date.

In drafting the notice and other papers for the motion, check carefully with the requirements of the local rules which may impose additional formal requirements. For example, many courts require all papers to be pre-punched at the top with a two-hole punch. Some require extra copies to be delivered to the court's chambers. Some require bar coding to assist the clerk in docketing. If your papers violate the local rules, the clerk may refuse to file them.

The notice is a simple document. After setting out the caption of the case, the notice states:

> TO PLAINTIFFS AND TO PHILIDA TRANT, THEIR ATTORNEY OF RECORD:
>
> PLEASE TAKE NOTICE that on May 10, 1998, at 10:00 a.m., or as soon thereafter as the matter may be heard, Defendants Doe and Roe will appear before the Hon. Joan Caucus, in Courtroom Six, United States Courthouse, 650 Capitol Mall, Capitol City, Columbia, and present a motion to dismiss plaintiffs' complaint. A copy of the motion, and supporting points and authorities, is attached hereto.

Motion to dismiss

Under Fed. R. Civ. P. 7(b)(1), all motions must be in made in writing. The motion must state with particularity the supporting grounds and the order sought. Under Fed. R. Civ. P. 7(b)(2), the motion must comply with the requirements of the rules for captions, signing, and other formal matters. Fed. R. Civ. P. 10(a) requires the motion to designate the type of document presented for filing (i.e., "Motion to Dismiss"). You should also check the local rules of your court for any additional requirements for the motion.

The motion usually is a brief, formal document. After setting out the caption, the motion states:

> Defendants Doe and Roe move this Court for an order dismissing the plaintiffs' complaint pursuant to Fed. R. Civ. P. 12. This motion is made on the grounds that the complaint fails to

state a claim on which relief may be granted because the allegations establish that the claim is barred by the statute of limitations, 28 U.S.C. § 1234. This motion is based upon the files, records, and proceedings in this action, the attached memorandum of points and authorities, oral and documentary evidence and argument to be presented at the hearing on the motion on May 10, 1998.

In practice many attorneys combine in one document the notice required by Fed. R. Civ. P. 6 and the motion required by Fed. R. Civ. P. 7, designating the document a "Notice of Motion and Motion." The sample included at the end of this chapter combines the notice and motion in one document.

Points and authorities

The moving party must serve and file a memorandum of points and authorities. This is the heart of the motion which sets out your argument for the court. This section will discuss the form and content of the points and authorities which should include: (a) an introduction; (b) a statement of facts; (c) an argument; and (d) a conclusion. An outline template and sample motion are included at the end of this chapter. To get a rough idea of the format, you may wish to skim the sample before reading the following discussion.

Introduction

Open with an introductory paragraph, providing an overview of the motion and supporting arguments. Proceed from general information about the case to the specific grounds for the motion. Include a description of the parties, the nature of the action, the grounds for the motion, and the specific issue tied to the facts of the case. For example:

Introduction

In this personal injury action, Plaintiff John White claims that his injuries resulted from a dangerous workplace condition on the U.S.S. Enterprise, an aircraft carrier of the United States of America. This motion to dismiss is brought under Fed. R. Civ. P. 12(b)(6) on the grounds that Plaintiff has failed to state a claim on which relief can be granted because the action arises in admiralty jurisdiction and is barred by the admiralty statute of limitations. Specifically, the statute of limitations in admiralty cases is two years. 28 U.S.C. § 1234. The complaint alleges that the accident occurred on June 6, 1996. However, the complaint was not filed until July 8, 1998, more than two years after the accident occurred. Since this admiralty action is barred by the two-year statute of limitations, it should be dismissed under Fed. R. Civ. Pro. 12(b)(6).

In the example, the reader is first introduced to the parties and the nature of the action and then presented with the procedural context. Once the court has this substantive and procedural background, the precise issue raised by the motion is presented in terms of the facts of the case. Notice that the movant's position is expressed affirmatively, not as a question. The introduction sets the stage for the rest of the memorandum. It states the thesis of the memorandum and should gently slant the court's perception of the facts. The court can now read the facts with the issue and argument in mind.

Statement of facts

After the introductory paragraph, present the statement of facts. Since the court has the issue in mind, the court can evaluate the relevance of the facts. Confine your statement to the facts that are relevant to the issue. For example, if you are moving to dismiss based on the expiration of the statute of limitation, omit facts bearing on the plaintiff's alleged injuries. In short, tailor your statement of facts to the substantive law and procedural context of the issue before the court.

After selecting the relevant facts, organize them clearly and strive to tell a good story. Usually, chronological order is best. Although a motion to dismiss is confined to the facts of the complaint, you are not confined to the plaintiff's exact language. Use language favorable to your client if you can do so without departing from the substance of the allegations. Ultimately, your goal is to have the court inclined in your favor after reading the statement of facts.

The sample points and authorities included at the end of this chapter includes a statement of facts which is focused on the issue before the court, organized chronologically, and shaded to favor the advocate's argument. Keep in mind that the facts determine what legal rules apply and also give the judge a sense of what justice requires.

Argument

In the argument section, explain to the court why it should rule in your favor. To convince the court, you need to present the authorities justifying that result and also head off the counter-arguments your opponent will advance. The argument section has two components: the point headings and the narrative argument.

Point Headings

The headings of the argument should succinctly state each point of your argument in terms of the facts of your case. These capsules of information may be all a busy judge has time to read to prepare for the hearing. Thus, the headings should provide both the structure of the argument and also a summary of its substance. Each heading should be carefully drafted to affirmatively state a legal point and the facts supporting your position. They should be brief (five lines or less) and persuasive. Obviously, these little stinkers can be challenging to create.

Some examples may help you get the idea. Assume you represent a school board member who has been sued for defamation by the incumbent she unseated in the last election. Your research reveals that the complaint should be dismissed because the statements expressed your client's political opinions which are protected by the First Amendment. In drafting your point heading, your goal is to express this legal argument in terms of the facts alleged in the complaint and in the context of a motion to dismiss.

Don't Write: The First Amendment protects free speech.

Don't Write: Political opinion is protected speech.

Don't Write: The First Amendment protects Defendant's statements of political opinion.

Don't Write: The complaint should be dismissed based on the First Amendment.

Write: The complaint should be dismissed because the First Amendment protects Defendant's political opinion expressed during an election debate that the incumbent's "spotty attendance at school board meetings was pitiful."

Notice how the first four headings failed to link the procedural context to the substantive issue in terms of the facts of the case. In contrast, the last example ties the procedural context (motion to dismiss) to the substantive issue (First Amendment protection of political opinion) in terms of the facts of the case (opinion of pitiful attendance at meetings). By tying these three layers together, the writer weaves together the argument. Notice too that if the court agrees with the statement, the relief requested will be granted.

Narrative argument

Under each point heading, you should present a carefully organized argument that is clear, concise, and persuasive. Since each point heading will make a different point of law, begin each section with an introductory paragraph. While it may seem slightly redundant, don't rely on the heading to serve as an introduction. The reader perceives them separately; launching into a discussion of the point without an introduction seems abrupt and disjointed. Your introductory paragraph should briefly introduce the legal issue and provide an overview of the discussion which will follow.

After introducing the point, present your strongest authority for the argument. If you expect the court to accept your argument, you must be thorough. *You need authority for every point of law you raise.* For even the most basic procedural points, you must cite authority.

If a statute governs your problem, the court will want to have the statutory language handy to evaluate its application. Start with a readable paraphrase to introduce the statute, and then provide the critical statutory language. Avoid lengthy block quotations of statutes; nobody wants to read them. But include enough of the statute for the court to analyze its applicability to your case. For the court's convenience, make your presentation of the statute so complete that the judge will not have to go to the library. Once you've presented the key statutory language, don't just leave it hanging there without analysis. You must carefully explain how it applies to your case and governs the result.

In presenting major cases, you should include the facts, procedure, holding, and rationale of the decision. Explain to the court why the same rule should apply in your case. Point out the factual similarities of the cases and the policy reasons supporting the result. Judges want to be fair. Your job is to give the judge reasons that support, if not compel, a ruling in your favor. After you have explained why the favorable authority should be followed, anticipate and head off possible counter-arguments. Finally, conclude your presentation and application of the authority stating your position affirmatively.

If you know of cases that your opponent will surely use, you may wish to address them in your points and authorities. As a matter of professional ethics, you are required to advise the court of any adverse controlling authority. As a matter of strategy, you would be foolish not to defuse potential bombs even if they are not technically controlling. First, of course, you want the court to trust you. Show the judge that you have considered every possible argument and that a ruling in your favor is the only possible result. Second, you want to disarm the unwelcome authorities. If you distinguish a case persuasively, the court will be skeptical when your opponent relies on it. If you anticipate the unwelcome authorities, sandwich them in the middle of your analysis since the beginning and ending positions are powerful and should be saved for your affirmative arguments.

In deciding which authorities to include, be selective. Remember the court's time constraints. Of course, you should present the controlling cases in your jurisdiction. If there is a supreme court case on point, use it; if there is a case from your district, use it. Beyond that, use recent cases that are factually similar to your case and well reasoned. A thorough presentation of a few carefully-selected cases carries more weight than a mountain of unanalyzed and unenlightening citations. Where several similar cases make the same point, you may present one or two cases fully and then present the others by giving a parenthetical explanation of the facts and the holdings.

After you have presented and applied the relevant authorities, wrap up each section with a brief conclusion. This concluding paragraph signals closure and reminds the court of the main argument. Keep it short and simple.

Conclusion

After the argument, a conclusion to the entire memorandum provides a polished ending. You may use the conclusion to emphasize a key point in the analysis. And you should highlight the reasons supporting your conclusion.[16] For example: "Because the two-year statute of limitations expired long before the plaintiff filed this action, this motion to dismiss the complaint should be granted."

---

16. Bryan A. Garner, *Issue-Framing: The Upshot of It All*, TRIAL, Apr. 1997, at 76.

Proof of service

Rule 5 of the Fed. R. Civ. P. requires that every filing with the court must be served on all other parties and that proof of that service must be submitted to the court within a reasonable time. While other methods of service are permissible, most lawyers serve documents by mail and file a proof of service when they file the documents. In practice, be sure to check the local rules for supplemental requirements. A sample proof of service follows the sample motion at the end of this chapter.

Outline Template for a Motion to Dismiss

I. Notice

II. Motion

III. Points and authorities

    A. Introduction

    Introduce the parties, describe the nature of the case, and identify the issue that the motion will resolve. Provide an overview of the motion. If more than one issue will be addressed, include a roadmap.

    B. Statement of facts

    Present a concise statement of facts in chronological order. Pare it down to the facts relevant to the motion.

    C. Argument

        1. Point heading for the first point: state the conclusion the court should reach tying the legal issue to the facts of your case.

            a. Introductory paragraph providing an overview of the argument.

            b. Present the strongest authority for your position.

            c. Apply that authority to the facts of your case.

            d. Present the next strongest authority for your position.

            e. Apply that authority to the facts of your case.

            f. Present the most dangerous unwelcome authority.

            g. Distinguish the unwelcome authority.

            h. Present and distinguish any other unwelcome authorities.

            i. Present an authority supporting the distinction you are drawing.

            j. Concluding paragraph synthesizing the analysis.

        2. Point heading for the second point: state the conclusion the court should reach tying the legal issue to the facts of your case.

        Repeat steps a–j above.

D. Conclusion

State precisely the order you are seeking and the reason it should be granted.

IV. Proof of service

Sample Notice of Motion and Motion

2   Hortense Rumpole
     State Bar No. 71355
3   DARROW & RUMPOLE
     12345 Main Street
4   Capitol City, Columbia
     Telephone: 555/897-4567
5   Counsel for Defendant Clarence Green

6   UNITED STATES DISTRICT COURT

7   EASTERN DISTRICT OF COLUMBIA

8   Thrifty Trucking, Inc.,   Defendant's Notice of Motion and
                                    Motion to Dismiss For Failure
9   Plaintiff,   to State a Claim
                                    [Fed. R. Civ. P. 12(b)(6)]
10   v.   Date: May 10, 1998
                                    Time: 10:00 a.m.
11   Clarence Green,   Courtroom: Six

12   Defendant.

13   _____/

14   TO PLAINTIFF THRIFTY TRUCKING, INC., AND TO

15   SALLY FORTH, ITS ATTORNEY OF RECORD:

16   PLEASE TAKE NOTICE that on May 10, 1998, at 10:00

17   a.m., or as soon thereafter as the matter may be heard, Defen-

18   dant Clarence Green will appear before the Hon. Joan Caucus,

19   in Courtroom Six, United States Courthouse, 650 Capitol

20   Mall, Capitol City, Columbia, and move to dismiss Plaintiff's

21   claim pursuant to Fed. R. Civ. P. 12(b)(6).

22   This motion is made on the grounds that the complaint fails

1   to state a claim on which relief may be granted because the

2   facts alleged establish that the claim is barred by the litigation

3   privilege. Col. Civ. Code § 47. A copy of the supporting points

4   and authorities is attached hereto. This motion is based upon

5   the files, records, and proceedings in this action, the attached

6   memorandum of points and authorities, oral and documentary

7   evidence and argument to be presented at the hearing on the

8   motion on May 10, 1998.

9   Dated: April 10, 1998

10   _____

                                            Hortense Rumpole

11   Attorney for Defendant

12

13

14

15

16

17

18

19

20

21

22

Sample Points and Authorities

2   Hortense Rumpole
      State Bar No. 71355
3   DARROW & RUMPOLE
      12345 Main Street
4   Capitol City, Columbia
      Telephone: 555/897-4567
5   Counsel for Defendant Clarence Green

6   UNITED STATES DISTRICT COURT

7   EASTERN DISTRICT OF COLUMBIA

8 Thrifty Trucking, Inc.,	Defendant's Points and Authorities in Support of
9 Plaintiff,	Motion to Dismiss for Failure to State a Claim
10	[Fed. R. Civ. P. 12(b)(6)]
11 v.	Date: May 10, 1998
	Time: 10:00 a.m.
12 Clarence Green,	Courtroom: Six
13 Defendant.	

14

15   Introduction

16   Plaintiff Thrifty Trucking, Inc. (Thrifty) operates a long-dis-

17   tance, hazardous chemical transport service. In 1996, a Thrifty

18   truck driver fell asleep at the wheel, ran off the road, and

19   spilled toxic chemicals into the New Columbia River. The

20   toxic spill caused substantial environmental damage. A trout

21   farmer downstream on the New Columbia who was financially

22   ruined by the toxic spill has sued Thrifty for the damages. De-

1   fendant Clarence Green (Green) represents the trout farmer in

2   that environmental damage action. Thrifty has brought this

3   defamation action against Green because Green gave a copy of

4   the complaint in the environmental action to a newspaper re-

5   porter who was investigating the toxic spill.

6   As the following discussion will show, the litigation privi-

7   lege protects the publication of public records. Col. Civ. Code

8   § 47 (West 1998). Numerous cases applying this privilege have

9   extended it to the delivery of copies of public records to the

10   press. Under this rule, Green's delivery of the environmental

11   complaint to the newspaper reporter is protected as a matter of

12   law. Since the litigation privilege is a complete defense to this

13   defamation action, the complaint should be dismissed. Fed. R.

14   Civ. P. 12(b)(6).

15   Statement of Facts

16   On January 4, 1997, Samuel Boswell brought an action

17   against Thrifty claiming that his trout farm was ruined after

18   Thrifty's truck driver spilled toxic chemicals into the New Co-

19   lumbia River upstream from the trout farm. Thrifty complaint

20   at 2. Green represents Boswell in that action. Thrifty com-

21   plaint at 2.

22   On January 5, 1997, Green held a press conference to dis-

1   cuss the Boswell lawsuit. Thrifty complaint at 3. In response to

2   questions, Green gave a copy of the Boswell complaint to the

3   reporter for the Capitol City News. Thrifty complaint at 3.

4   The next day the Capitol City News carried a lengthy article

5   about the Boswell action which allegedly defamed Thrifty.

6   Thrifty complaint at 4.

7   Thrifty has brought this diversity action against Green al-

8   leging that he defamed Thrifty by giving the complaint to the

9   reporter and is responsible for the defamatory article which

10   followed. Thrifty complaint at 2-4.

11

I

THRIFTY'S DEFAMATION ACTION SHOULD BE
DISMISSED BECAUSE THE LITIGATION PRIVILEGE
PROTECTS GREEN'S PUBLICATION OF THE TOXIC
SPILL COMPLAINT TO THE PRESS

12

13

14   The Columbia litigation privilege provides that "the publi-

15   cation of judicial proceedings is absolutely privileged." Col.

16   Civ. Code § 47 (West 1998). As the following discussion will

17   show, this privilege protects Green's delivery of the Boswell

18   complaint to the Capitol City Press reporter because that is a

19   publication of judicial proceedings. Under Fed. R. Civ. P.

20   12(b)(6), a motion to dismiss for failure to state a claim should

21   be granted where the complaint includes allegations which dis-

22   close some absolute defense or privilege. *Quiller v. Barclays*

1   *American/Credit Inc.*, 727 F.2d 1067, 1069 (5th Cir. 1984).

2   Thus, since the complaint discloses the absolute litigation priv-

3   ilege, this motion to dismiss should be granted.

4   The most recent case applying the litigation privilege to bar a

5   defamation action for delivery of judicial records to the press is

6   *Cooper v. Seneca Laboratories, Inc.*, 232 F. 3d 984 (14th Cir.

7   1997). In *Cooper*, an attorney held a press conference about the

8   wrongful termination action he had filed on behalf of his client

9   against a chemical company. In that action, the employee alleged

10   that he was fired for being a whistle-blower about the com-

11   pany's dangerous practices. The attorney distributed excerpts

12   from deposition transcripts to reporters. In a diversity action,

13   the chemical company sued the attorney for defamation for pub-

14   lishing the deposition transcripts. The trial court granted defen-

15   dant's motion to dismiss under Fed. R. Civ. P. 12(b)(6).

16   The Fourteenth Circuit affirmed the dismissal based on the

17   Columbia litigation privilege. The court held that the litigation

18   privilege of Col. Civ. Code § 47 (West 1998) is grounds for dis-

19   missal where a defamation action is based on publication of

20   official court documents. *Cooper* at 987. As the court ex-

21   plained, "The litigation privilege shields publication of judicial

22   proceedings from defamation liability to afford litigants the ut-

1   most freedom of access to the courts so that they may exercise

2   their rights without fear of being harassed by defamation ac-

3   tions." *Id.* Moreover, the litigation privilege protects the public

4   interest. According to the court, the privilege also ensures that

5   the press will have access to court records so that they may fol-

6   low court proceedings of public interest. *Id.*

7   The *Cooper* case governs the present action. Here, as in

8   *Cooper*, plaintiff has brought a diversity action for defamation

9   based on an attorney's publication to the press of official court

10   documents. Here, as in *Cooper*, the Columbia litigation privi-

11   lege absolutely protects publication of the official court docu-

12   ments. While the documents in *Cooper* were deposition tran-

13   scripts and the document in this case was the complaint, both

14   are official court documents entitled to the absolute protection

15   of the litigation privilege. Finally, as in *Cooper*, the policies un-

16   derlying the litigation privilege will be furthered by applying

17   the privilege to this case. The privilege will protect Green from

18   harassment by Thrifty for bringing the toxic spill case and will

19   provide the press access to the records in an environmental

20   case of great public interest. Therefore, as in *Cooper*, this mo-

21   tion to dismiss should be granted because the litigation privi-

22   lege absolutely bars this action.

1 Earlier cases have squarely recognized that the litigation

2 privilege protects all of the allegations of a civil complaint so

3 long as they are related to that action. *Financial Corp. of*

4 *America v. Wilburn*, 123 F.2d 234, 236 (14th Cir. 1987). In *Fi-*

5 *nancial Corp.*, the plaintiff brought a diversity action in federal

6 court claiming that allegations in a civil complaint filed in Co-

7 lumbia state court were defamatory. The district court applied

8 the Columbia litigation privilege and dismissed the action

9 under Fed. R. Civ. P. 12(b)(6) for failure to state a claim. The

10 Fourteenth Circuit affirmed. As the court stated, all the allega-

11 tions were privileged where "the plaintiff failed to identify a

12 single allegation in the complaint as unrelated to the litigation

13 it commenced." *Id.* at 236–237.

14 The *Financial Corp.* ruling governs the present action. Here,

15 as in *Financial Corp.*, the plaintiff has based its action solely

16 on the publication of allegations in the complaint. Here

17 Thrifty alleges that Green delivered the complaint to the re-

18 porter, but Thrifty has failed to identify a single allegation that

19 is unrelated to the environmental litigation. Therefore, under

20 *Financial Corp.*, the publication of the complaint is absolutely

21 protected and the defamation action fails to state a claim. This

22 motion to dismiss should therefore be granted.

1   To avoid the litigation privilege, Thrifty may argue that

2   Green's publication to the press is not privileged because it was

3   unrelated to the judicial proceeding, citing *Susan A. v. County*

4   *of Jackson*, 2 P.2d 127 (Col. 1997). In *Susan A.*, the court con-

5   sidered whether the privilege protected statements by a psy-

6   chologist to the press about his impressions of a minor who

7   had been arrested for attempted murder. The court held that

8   the privilege did not apply because neither the press nor the

9   psychologist were connected to the judicial proceeding. In de-

10   clining to extend the privilege, the court explained that the

11   privilege was designed to protect litigants from harassment

12   and assure public access to judicial proceedings. Neither of

13   those goals, according to the court, would be served by extend-

14   ing the privilege to nonlitigants for statements which were not

15   part of the judicial proceeding. *Id.* at 131.

16   The *Susan A.* case is both factually and legally distinguish-

17   able from the present action. First, the facts of this case stand

18   in stark contrast to those in *Susan A.* Unlike *Susan A.* where

19   the defamation action was brought against a third party for

20   comments which were not part of the judicial proceeding, here

21   the defamation is against the attorney for a party in a judicial

22   proceeding for publishing the complaint in that proceeding.

1   Thus, in contrast to *Susan A.*, here both the defendant in the

2   defamation action and the publication on which it is based are

3   directly connected to the Boswell toxic spill action.

4   Second, unlike *Susan A.*, here the litigation privilege must

5   be extended to further the policies underlying the litigation

6   privilege. Here, the privilege will ensure that Plaintiff Boswell

7   in the environmental litigation may pursue his claim without

8   fear that the defendant will harass his lawyer. Moreover, ex-

9   tending the privilege in this case facilitates public access to ju-

10   dicial records in a matter of great public interest. The public

11   and the press have a right to follow the official judicial pro-

12   ceedings in the toxic spill case. Extending the litigation privi-

13   lege in this case ensures that copies of official records from

14   those proceedings will be readily available.

15   In furthering the goals of the litigation privilege, this case is

16   similar to an earlier Columbia Supreme Court case applying

17   the privilege to publication of a proposed amended complaint.

18   *Abraham v. Lancaster*, 217 P.2d 123 (Col. 1956). In *Abraham*,

19   the parties were principals in an action between two compet-

20   ing hospitals. The plaintiff sought to file an amended com-

21   plaint and gave a copy of the proposed amended complaint to

22   the press which published a story about the dispute. After the

1   court refused to allow the amended complaint to be filed, a

2   hospital administrator sued for defamation based on the publi-

3   cation of the proposed amended complaint. The Columbia

4   Supreme Court held that the litigation privilege protected the

5   publication of the proposed amended complaint even though it

6   was never actually filed in the judicial proceeding. The court

7   explained that allowing the defamation action to proceed

8   would both chill the litigants' zealous pursuit of their rights in

9   the underlying dispute and also chill the public's discussion of

10   pending litigation.

11   The *Abraham* decision applies to this case. Here, as in

12   *Abraham*, the plaintiff has brought a defamation action

13   against a litigant for publication of a pleading to the press. In-

14   deed, this case is even stronger than *Abraham* because the

15   pleading at issue in this case was actually filed with the court

16   and was an official record in the judicial proceeding. As in

17   *Abraham*, allowing this defamation action to proceed would

18   chill the parties' pursuit of their rights and the public discus-

19   sion of the pending environmental litigation.

20   In short, the litigation privilege absolutely bars defamation

21   actions for publication of a judicial proceeding. In this case,

22   Green's delivery of the environmental complaint to the re-

1   porter was a publication of a judicial proceeding. Therefore,

2   the litigation privilege bars this defamation action.

3   Conclusion

4   Under Fed. R. Civ. P. 12(b)(6), a motion to dismiss must be

5   granted where the complaint discloses an affirmative defense

6   or privilege. Here Thrifty's complaint reveals that it is barred

7   by the litigation privilege since the allegedly defamatory publi-

8   cation was of a judicial proceeding. Since publication of a judi-

9   cial proceeding is absolutely privileged and since this privilege

10   appears on the face of Thrifty's complaint, Green requests that

11   the court grant this motion to dismiss.

12   Dated: April 10, 1998   Respectfully submitted,
                                     DARROW & RUMPOLE
13

14   _____

15   Hortense Rumpole,
                                     Attorneys for Defendant Green

16

17

18

19

20

21

22

Sample Proof of Service

2   Hortense Rumpole
State Bar No. 71355
3   DARROW & RUMPOLE
12345 Main Street
4   Capitol City, Columbia
Telephone: 916/752-8022
5   Counsel for Defendant Clarence Green

6   UNITED STATES DISTRICT COURT

7   EASTERN DISTRICT OF COLUMBIA

8   Thrifty Trucking, Inc.,   Defendant's Proof of Service
          Plaintiff,   by Mail
9   v.
    Clarence Green,
10   Defendant.

11   _____/

12   I, Della Street, declare:

13   1. I am, and was at the time of the service herein de-

14   scribed, over the age of 18 years and not a party to the

15   above-entitled action. My business address is 123 Main

16   Street, Capitol City, CO 92347, and I am employed in Yolo

17   County, Columbia.

18   2. I served the Defendant's Notice, Motion, and Points and

19   Authorities in Support of Motion to Dismiss for Failure to

20   State a Claim on April 10, 1998, by depositing a copy of each

21   of these papers in the United States mail at 123 Main Street,

22   Capitol City, CO 92347, in a sealed envelope, with postage

1   fully prepaid, addressed to:

2   Able Attorney, Esq.
       BAKER, BAKER & JONES
3   9586 Main Street
       Woodland, CO 92348

4   The above addressee is the attorney of record for Plaintiff

5   Thrifty Trucking, Inc., in the above-entitled action.

6   I declare under penalty of perjury under the laws of the

7   United States of America that the foregoing is true and correct

8   and that this declaration was executed on April 10, 1998, in

9   Capitol City, CO.

10

                             _____

11   Della Street

12

13

14

15

16

17

18

19

20

21

22

Chapter 8

Rewritten Office Memorandum

This week your assignment is to rewrite your memorandum on responsive pleadings. We'll review the writing process and add a few lessons for improving your writing style. Following these steps will help you create a document you'll be proud to use as a writing sample. Since most lawyers are not inclined to trust first-year law students to write appellate briefs, a well-written memo will give your prospective employers the best idea of what you can do for them this summer.

Rewrite Your Memorandum

Reconsider the content

After preparing the motion to dismiss, discussing the problem in class, and getting some distance from your memo, you'll be able to spot flaws in your first draft. Review your memo for content using the editing checklist at the end of this chapter.

- Is your memo thorough and objective?
- Have you included all the relevant authorities?
- Have you integrated the substantive and procedural law?
- Have you thoroughly presented each authority?
- Have you applied the authorities to the facts of your problem?
- Have you considered whether the policies supporting the authorities would be furthered or undermined by their application to your case?

- Have you analyzed your opponent's arguments and presented counter-arguments?
- Have you synthesized the analysis so that it is as coherent as the present state of the law allows?

Revise the large-scale organization

Once you're satisfied with the content, turn your attention to large-scale organization. Have you included introductions and conclusions where necessary? Do the topic sentences of the discussion form an outline? You may wish to review chapter 3 for suggestions on improving large-scale organization.

Review each paragraph

When you're satisfied with the outline created by your topic sentences, you're ready to work on each paragraph. Make sure that every sentence develops the paragraph topic; move or delete unrelated sentences. Now check for readable paragraph length. Break up paragraphs that are too long; combine or eliminate paragraphs that are too short.

Once the paragraphs are a readable length, check for transitions and revise them to reflect the improved organization of your memo. The transitions and topic sentences, read together, should lead your reader along and reveal your organization. For instance, if you've revised your discussion to follow hierarchical or chronological order, your transitions should reflect your new approach to help your reader see the relationship of the authorities. To illustrate, a discussion following hierarchical and chronological order might use the following transitions and topic sentences:

> Turning to the cases applying this statute, the leading Supreme Court case held that a public entity may recover punitive damages for toxic spills that contaminate public lands. *Brown v. Jones*, 255 U.S. 145 (1978).

> Most recently, a circuit court limited the availability of punitive damages holding that under *Brown* a state is only entitled to recover punitive damages where it proves malice or bad faith. *Jackson v. Smith*, 35 F.3d 987 (13th Cir. 1997).

Notice how these topic sentences reveal the organizational scheme of the discussion (hierarchical and chronological order), introducing each case in terms of its holding and placing the citation at the end to avoid distracting the reader.

After you've revised the content, large-scale organization, and paragraphs, your draft is complete and well-organized. Now you can productively focus on sentence-level problems and edit your draft.

Edit Your Memorandum

Here's your chance to turn an adequate draft into a polished writing sample. Don't be discouraged by the need for extensive editing. As Judge Posner confessed, he may go through ten to twenty drafts of an opinion: "Much of the editing is designed to simplify the product and give it a casual, colloquial, and spontaneous appearance. I admit to hypocrisy in working so hard to give the appearance of effortlessness!"[1] In addition to improving each product, editing will teach you to spot flaws in your writing and to correct them. With practice, you'll spot the problems as you write the first draft so that editing the final draft will take far less time.

As you begin editing, remember the lessons we've learned: (1) write short sentences; (2) omit surplus words; and (3) use quotations sparingly. In addition, this week we'll add three ways to improve your writing style. First, we'll learn how to spot nominalizations and replace them with base verbs. Second, we'll review the active and passive voice and consider why you should usually prefer the active voice. Finally, we'll cover some conventions of legal usage that will give your writing a professional tone.

Use base verbs

As Richard Wydick explains in *Plain English for Lawyers,* "At its core, the law is not abstract. It is part of a real world full of people who live and move and do things to other people. Car drivers *collide.* Plaintiffs *complain.* Judges *decide.* Defendants *pay.*"[2] To convey this liveliness, Wydick urges lawyers to use verbs in their

1. Tom Goldstein & Jethro K. Lieberman, The Lawyer's Guide to Writing Well 165 (1989).
2. Richard C. Wydick, Plain English for Lawyers 25 (4th ed. 1998).

purest form. When a verb is expressed as a nominalization, it is wordy and ponderous. Using base verbs will make your writing more concise and dynamic. For example:

> **Don't write:** Jane had knowledge that Spot engaged in car-chasing behavior.
>
> **Write:** Jane knew that Spot chased cars.

The following list will help you spot nominalizations:

Nominalization	Base Verb
bases an argument on	argues
gives consideration to	considers
has an intention to	intends
has knowledge of	knows
has a provision that	provides
has a tendency to	tends
has a requirement of	requires
is the owner of	owns
is in violation of	violates
it is our contention	we contend
it is our intention	we intend
is the cause of	causes
makes an argument	argues
makes a motion	moves
makes an objection	objects
makes an allegation	alleges
makes a statement	states
makes a substitution	substitutes
reaches a decision	decides
reaches a conclusion	concludes

This list should help you gain an understanding of base verbs.[3]

---

3. If you didn't automatically rewrite this sentence, review the list again.

Study Chapter 3 of *Plain English for Lawyers* before rewriting your memorandum.

Prefer the active voice

In *Plain English for Lawyers*, Richard Wydick teaches that the passive voice is weak and wordy while the active voice is forceful and lively. The key to recognizing the passive voice is to ask who is doing the action. If the person doing the action is not the subject of the sentence, the sentence is in the passive voice. Some writers confuse past tenses with the passive voice. If you ask who is doing the action and make that person the subject of your sentence, you won't get confused.

Active Voice	Passive Voice
Jody is filing the complaint.	The complaint is being filed by Jody.
Jody filed the complaint.	The complaint was filed by Jody.
Jody had filed the complaint.	The complaint had been filed by Jody.

While the active voice is usually preferable, sometimes you may wish to use the passive voice to focus on the action rather than the actor. History provides some memorable examples of this technique. For example, in his news conference about the sale of weapons to Iran, President Reagan told the nation that "mistakes were made." Similarly, a bureaucrat who has decided to eliminate the employees' free coffee may post a notice stating: "Free coffee is no longer to be made available." Here, passive voice is used to disguise responsibility for an action. The passive voice may also be used for the opposite reason, to emphasize responsibility for an action by placing the actor at the end of a sentence: "The tapes were hidden by the President of the United States."[4] In short, you may use the passive voice to obscure or to spotlight the actor's identity.

In addition to these uses for passive voice, sometimes you may use the passive voice when the identity of the actor is irrelevant,

---

4. C. Edward Good, *When the Passive Voice Is Preferred*, TRIAL, July 1996, at 98, 99.

unimportant, or unknown.[5] For instance, if you are informing a client that your complaint was filed within the applicable statute of limitations, you may write: "The complaint was filed on March 25, 1998." After all, the important thing is that the dang thing got filed, not that it was filed by Joe Blow the attorney-service runner.

As we have seen, the passive voice can be useful. But if you use it, you should have a reason for it. Usually you should prefer the active voice to make your writing clear, concise, and dynamic. Study Chapter 4 of *Plain English for Lawyers* before rewriting your memorandum.

Learn conventional legal usage

While dense legalese puts everyone off, quaint or offbeat expressions subtly undermine your credibility. You need to learn conventional legal usage to sound like you're a member of the lawyers' professional club. Here are a few tips:

Use appropriate procedural language

Be sensitive to the appropriate procedural language. For example, motions are neither sustained nor overruled nor affirmed nor reversed; motions are granted or denied. On the other hand, judgments are affirmed or reversed (not granted or denied). If you are unsure about the correct procedural terms, adopt the language of the cases that you are discussing.

Use appropriate verbs

Beginners sometimes use verbs that experienced lawyers would avoid in explaining the law. For example, a beginner might discuss how a court or statute "argues," or "feels," or "believes." Lawyers express the same notions as follows:

Courts	Statutes
analyze	apply
conclude	bar
decide	compel
declare	control

---

5. *Id.*

determine	dictate
examine	govern
explain	impose
find	limit
hold	mandate
modify	prohibit
reason	provide
rule	require
state	state

In selecting proper verbs, be especially careful when describing appellate court proceedings. Remember that an appellate court affirms or reverses the rulings of a trial court. The appellate court does not rule on the motions initially:

> **Don't write:** The court of appeal denied the motion.
>
> **Write:** The court of appeal affirmed the denial of the summary judgment motion.

Use appropriate tenses

Using the wrong tense will unsettle your reader. Use the present tense for statements of current law; use the past tense for past court action and historical facts.

> **Don't write:** The court rules that the statute of limitations was one year in medical malpractice actions.
>
> **Write:** The court ruled that the statute of limitations is one year in medical malpractice actions.

If you use the present tense, be sure that the law you are discussing is current. If the law has changed, the tense should change.

> **Don't write:** The court rules that the statute of limitations is two years in a medical malpractice action. However, a recent statute feels that the statute of limitations should be one year.
>
> **Write:** The court ruled that the statute of limitations was two years in a medical malpractice action. However, a recent amendment provides that the statute of limitations is one year.

Check for pronoun agreement

Beginners sometimes use plural pronouns to refer to a court or a legislature. Since those bodies are composed of many people, this usage is understandable. But when referring to a governmental entity, the proper pronoun is "it."

> **Don't write:** The legislature amended the statute. They felt...
>
> **Write:** The legislature amended the statute. It adopted...
>
> **Don't write:** The court felt the statute was unconstitutional. They argued...
>
> **Write:** The court held the statute unconstitutional. It reasoned...

Proofread Your Memorandum

Legal memoranda are the basic documents of practice and the most common assignments for evaluating summer associates. A polished legal memo is the surest way to demonstrate your research and writing skills. So take the time to create a document you're proud of. (I know that sentence ends with a preposition, and I like it that way.) Make sure it is complete, thoroughly analyzed, and well written. Proofread it carefully. Before you turn it in, make an extra copy to use as a writing sample.

Rewriting Checklist for an Office Memorandum

I. Rewriting

  A. Reconsider the content:

    1. Is the heading in the proper form?

    2. Does your question presented identify the legal issue starting with the general area of law and tying in the key facts?

    3. Does your brief answer respond directly to the question and provide an objective summary of the analysis?

    4. Does your statement of facts include the relevant facts in chronological order?

    5. Does your discussion include an introductory paragraph providing an overview of the analysis?

    6. Have you included all the necessary authorities?

    7. Have you thoroughly and objectively presented them? Have you included the key language from every statute? Have you included the facts, procedure, holding, and rationale of every case?

    8. Have you applied them to your problem?

    9. Have you considered policy arguments?

    10. Have you anticipated counter arguments?

    11. Have you synthesized the analysis?

  B. Revise the large-scale organization:

    1. Have you included introductory and concluding paragraphs for each section?

    2. Can you outline your discussion using topic sentences?

  C. Review each paragraph:

    1. Does each paragraph have a topic sentence?

    2. Do the other sentences develop the topic?

    3. Have you checked paragraph length?

    4. Have you provided transitions?

II. Editing

    A. Edit each sentence:

        1. Have you written short sentences?

        2. Have you omitted surplus words?

        3. Have you used base verbs?

        4. Have you preferred the active voice?

        5. Have you adopted conventional legal usage?

    B. Use quotations sparingly:

        1. Have you avoided block quotations?

        2. Have you edited quotations carefully?

III. Proofreading

    A. Have you checked for grammatical errors?

    B. Have you checked for misspellings?

    C. Have you checked for proper citation form?

Chapter 9

Rewritten Motion to Dismiss

This week you will rewrite your points and authorities following the writing process we've been developing. Since the office memo is objective and the motion is persuasive, you will be applying some different standards in this rewriting assignment. After first considering how the rewriting steps can be followed to improve your draft, we'll cover two new principles of plain English: (1) arrange your words with care; and (2) choose your words with care. Finally, this chapter will present some persuasive writing techniques to add polish to your points and authorities.

Rewrite Your Motion to Dismiss

Reconsider the content

After living with the problem for a few weeks and revising your office memo, you've probably developed a deeper understanding of the law and its application to the problem. Review your draft and revise it to strengthen the argument. First, read the introduction. Does it concisely tell the court what the motion is about and why it should rule in your favor? Next review the headings. When they are read in order (without reading the body) do they outline the steps of the argument and compel a conclusion in your favor? Now read the body of the argument. Have you included the necessary authorities, thoroughly and persuasively presented them, and applied them to the facts of your case? Have you explored the policies reflected in the authorities that support your argument? Have you covered and refuted unwelcome authorities? Revise your draft to improve its content and substantive analysis.

Revise the large-scale organization

When you've finished improving the substance of your draft, review the large-scale organization. Have you included introductory and concluding paragraphs for each section? Now make an outline from the topic sentences. Remember that a persuasive organization will open and close with strong points, sandwiching the opponent's arguments in the middle. Generally you should lead off with your best argument and best authority to get the court leaning your way before you distinguish the unwelcome authorities. Have you organized your argument so that the most favorable authorities are in the strongest positions?

Review each paragraph

After you're satisfied with the content and large-scale organization, check each paragraph. Make sure each sentence develops the topic of its paragraph. Now focus on paragraph length; break up long paragraphs and combine short ones. Finally, make sure you have provided transitions between paragraphs.

Edit Your Motion to Dismiss

As you edit this draft, apply the four plain English principles we've covered: (1) write short sentences; (2) omit surplus words; (3) use base verbs; and (4) prefer the active voice. Also remember to use quotations sparingly and to check your draft for conventional legal usage, following the suggestions you studied last week. Finally, this section introduces two new plain English principles and some persuasive writing techniques to improve the clarity and forcefulness of your motion.

Arrange your words with care

In Chapter 6 of *Plain English for Lawyers*, Richard Wydick provides rules for arranging words with care.[1] Study these rules before

---

1. RICHARD C. WYDICK, PLAIN ENGLISH FOR LAWYERS 43–56 (4th ed. 1998).

you rewrite your motion to dismiss. As you will see, your writing will be clearer if you follow the normal English word order (subject, verb, object) and keep the subject close to the verb and the verb close to the object. Paying attention to modifier placement can eliminate ambiguity and possible embarrassment. For example: "My client has discussed your proposal to fill the drainage ditch with his partners."[2] If you prefer to be understood rather than ridiculed, study Wydick's advice on modifier placement.

Choose your words with care

As Wydick explains in Chapter 7 of *Plain English for Lawyers*, concrete words grip and move your reader's mind.[3] To make your writing clear and forceful, study Chapter 7 and prefer the simple to the stuffy.[4] Cut out the needless legalisms. If you must use a term of art for precision, you should, of course, use it. But don't thoughtlessly bog your reader down in aforesaids, hereinafters, and Latin gibberish. Before you rewrite your paper, circle these common abstract words: aspect, basis, circumstance, condition, consideration, degree, facet, factor, situation, standard. When you rewrite your paper, consider replacing these words with concrete ones.

Be persuasive

This section presents several suggestions for writing a more persuasive motion: (1) be respectful; (2) be subtle; (3) be positive; (4) avoid clichés; (5) arrange your words for emphasis; (6) use concrete words to emphasize and abstract words to minimize; and (7) use parallelism.

Be respectful

Be respectful of the court, the parties, and counsel. Regardless of how your opponent behaves, conduct yourself with dignity and treat everyone with courtesy. Don't insult your opponent's arguments or intelligence. Falling into sarcasm or personal attacks will

---

2. *Id.* at 49.
3. *Id.* at 58.
4. *Id.* at 60.

hurt your cause. If your opponent behaves like a jerk, you will impress the court by remaining civil and professional. As one judge explained: "Lawyers enhance their credibility tremendously by maintaining their composure.... They are so much more dignified, and therefore so much more credible."[5]

Be subtle

Picture your audience: A seasoned lawyer sitting on a bench in an avalanche of motions. Your reader is skeptical and has no time for gimmicks. Conspicuous persuasive writing techniques will backfire. If you want the judge to become convinced instead of cranky, be careful. Control the tone of your argument. Inflammatory language should be stricken. As James W. McElhaney explained:

> Exaggerated words go hand in hand with unreasonable arguments.... Manifestly, clearly, fatal, clear beyond peradventure, logic that is fatally flawed, egregious, contumacious, mere gossamer, must necessarily fail, totally inapposite. These are the kinds of words and phrases you should cross out on the first revision of any brief. If you can't be reasonable, at least try to *sound* reasonable.[6]

Similarly, you should avoid being too informal or too stuffy. Strive for an assertive and professional tone.

Too inflammatory:	The tragic and excruciating suffering of the young father of infant children ended in an agonizing death.
Too informal:	When he finally died after a real bout with the big C his little kids were left without a dad.
Too stuffy:	The aforesaid premature demise of the patriarch of the nuclear family unit occurred on or about January 6, 1998.
Appropriate:	James Morgan died at the age of twenty-eight, following six months of chemotherapy for cancer. He is survived by his daugh-

---

5. Jon Newberry, *Bench Marks*, A.B.A. J., Nov. 1996, at 69, *quoting* the Hon. Ginger Berrigan, U.S. District Court, Louisiana.

6. James W. McElhaney, *Twelve Ways to a Bad Brief*, A.B.A. J., Dec. 1996, at 74–75.

ter Sarah, who is four years old, and his son Bobby, who is two years old.

As these examples show, often the most objective statement is the most compelling. But while the statement appears objective, it was drafted using the persuasive technique of placing key words in the last position of each sentence. This subtle persuasive device is more effective than obvious rhetorical flourishes.

A particularly obvious technique to avoid is underlining for emphasis. The words and structure of your sentence should tell the reader what is important. If your sentence is well written, you won't need to resort to underlining or to phrases like "it is important to note." Underlining is like shouting at someone to get their attention and implies that your reader is dense or distracted. In terms of persuasiveness, underlining is an admission of stylistic defeat. If you feel compelled to underline certain words, rewrite your sentence until the feeling goes away.

Be positive

As you edit your sentences for clarity and emphasis, pay special attention to negative expressions. To give your writing an assertive tone, use affirmative language. Negative forms are weak, wordy, and confusing. To understand a negative statement, a reader has to first figure out the positive statement and then negate it. And sometimes readers fail to take the second step. Even great writers sometimes put their readers to the test. Consider the following example:

> No Person shall be a Senator who shall not have attained to the Age of thirty Years, and been nine Years a Citizen of the United States, and who shall not, when elected, be an Inhabitant of that State for which he shall be chosen.[7]

James Madison can get away with it, but you should be kinder to your reader.

Often negative points can be expressed positively. For example, instead of writing "she did not remember," you can write "she forgot." Instead of writing "he failed to include," you can write "he omitted."

In checking for negative forms, remember that many words have negative meanings. These include: "deny," "except," "unless," "un-

---

7. U. S. Const. art I, §3.

likely," "until," and "without." If you use several of these words in one sentence, your reader will probably get lost. Watch out for paired negatives—"not...until," "not...unless," and "not only... but also." These formulas can be converted to affirmative statements in several ways:

Negative:	No letter should be signed until it has been proofread.
Affirmative:	Every letter should be proofread before it is signed.
Affirmative:	A letter should be signed only after it has been proofread.
Affirmative:	You should proofread all your letters before you sign them.

Wydick advises us to avoid multiple negatives.[8] In persuasive writing, take this advice a step farther: Prefer affirmative expressions unless you wish to stress the negative.

Avoid clichés

Just as hyperbole and legalese lack persuasive punch, clichés rob your writing of vigor because they are wordy and dull. Don't waste your reader's time with these faded phrases:

A bird in the hand is worth two in the bush	Add insult to injury
A picture is worth a thousand words	Beat a dead horse
Between a rock and a hard place	Birds of a feather
Blind leading the blind	Call a spade a spade
Cut off your nose to spite your face	Far be it from me
From the bottom of my heart	Height of absurdity
In for a penny, in for a pound	Kill two birds with one stone
Make a mountain out of a molehill	Last but not least
Neither rhyme nor reason	Open a can of worms

---

8. WYDICK, *supra* note 1, at 75–76.

Put your eggs in one basket   Thick as thieves

Throw the baby out with the   Truth is stranger than fiction[9]
  bath water

Sometimes you can surprise your reader by giving a cliché a fresh twist. For example, Judge Biddle of Philadelphia wrote: " 'The unwritten law' is not worth the paper it isn't written on."[10] But unless you can give it a new twist, a cliché is just a bore.

Arrange your words for emphasis

Wydick teaches us to arrange our words with care to make our writing more readable. Arranging words with care can also make our writing more persuasive. A technique to provide subtle emphasis is to place important words at the beginning or end of a sentence. Craft your sentences to take advantage of these powerful positions. Assume a plaintiffs' attorney is describing the facts supporting a nuisance complaint:

Misplaced emphasis:	The defendants own an ammonia factory which released gaseous vapors onto the plaintiffs' property on and off quite often for some time.
Persuasive emphasis:	Ammonia gas escaped frequently from the defendants' factory into the plaintiffs' home.

Notice how the second example takes advantage of both the beginning and end of the sentence to stress the message: ammonia gas in plaintiffs' home. By placement and word selection, the writer has emphasized the critical facts.

Use concrete words to emphasize and abstract words to minimize

The emphasis you achieve by word placement can be enhanced or undermined by your choice of language. As we've seen, familiar, concrete, and positive words make our writing more readable. But the advocate knows, some facts are unworthy of the same memorable clarity. If you want to create a vivid image, put concrete words in strong positions. Conversely, you can soften the impact of unwelcome facts by cloaking them in abstraction.

---

9. HENRY WIEHOFEN, LEGAL WRITING STYLE 121–122 (2d ed. 1980).
10. *Id.* at 123.

> **To emphasize:** Ammonia gas escaped frequently from the defendants' factory into the plaintiffs' home. The ammonia choked the plaintiffs and triggered asthmatic attacks.
>
> **To minimize:** On occasion some vapors and smells would drift to the adjacent property causing moderate respiratory symptoms according to the plaintiffs' allegations.

In selecting words to emphasize or minimize a point, be sensitive to their connotations. Consider the difference between "he falsely reported the figures" and "he made a clerical mistake" or between "he was famous" and "he was notorious." Compare "real estate" to "home" and "residential properties" to "neighborhood." Our rich language may give you a wide range of choices: fragrance, aroma, scent, smell, odor, stink, stench. Use this richness to make your writing more persuasive.

Use parallelism

Parallelism is the repetition of words or of the arrangement of words. Parallelism is often required for grammatical consistency and desired for rhetorical effect. Because it has power and polish, parallelism can be memorable:

> First in war, first in peace, first in the hearts of his countrymen.[11]
>
> Ask not what your country can do for you, but ask what you can do for your country.[12]

The most important kind of parallel structure is that required for grammatical consistency in a series. This kind of parallelism is not a frill, it's a necessity.[13] For example:

> **Faulty parallelism:** Several warranties are implied by law. They include: the implied warranty of marketability; whether the product is fit for a particular purpose; and the requirement that the seller act in good faith.

---

11. Henry "Light Horse Harry" Lee, in an eulogy to George Washington in the House of Representatives, December 26, 1799. GORTON CARRUTH & EUGENE EHRLICH, THE HARPER BOOK OF AMERICAN QUOTATIONS 583 (1988).

12. John F. Kennedy in his inaugural address, January 20, 1961. CARRUTH & EHRLICH, *supra* note 11, at 471.

13. WYDICK, *supra* note 1, at 48.

> **Parallelism:** Several warranties are implied by law. They include: the implied warranty of marketability; the implied warranty of fitness for a particular purpose; and the implied warranty of good faith.

Beyond the requirements of grammatical consistency, parallelism is a potent rhetorical device. In persuasive writing, you can achieve parallelism by:

1. beginning successive phrases, clauses or sentences with the same word or group of words;

2. ending successive phrases, clauses or sentences with the same word or group of words;

3. reversing the grammatical order of the same words in successive clauses; and

4. juxtaposing contrasting ideas in successive clauses.[14]

Some examples will help you see how to use parallelism. Let's consider the first possibility: beginning successive phrases, clauses or sentences with the same word or group of words. Winston Churchill used this device effectively when he wrote: "We must be united, we must be undaunted, we must be inflexible." [15]

The second kind of parallelism is ending phrases, clauses or sentences with the same word or group of words. This device is well illustrated by Abraham Lincoln's description of the government "of the people, by the people and for the people."[16]

The third kind of parallelism is created by using reverse word order. For example, Robert Ingersoll wrote: "Religion has not civilized man—man has civilized religion."[17] John F. Kennedy used both reverse word order and antithesis forcefully when he wrote: "Let us never negotiate out of fear. But let us never fear to negotiate."[18]

The fourth variety of parallelism is antithesis, the juxtaposition of opposing ideas. As the last example from Kennedy illustrates, the

---

14. LYNN B. SQUIRES ET AL., LEGAL WRITING IN A NUTSHELL 251–252 (2d ed. 1996).

15. WEIHOFEN, *supra* note 9, at 319.

16. Gettysburg Address, November 19, 1863. CARRUTH & EHRLICH, *supra* note 11, at 352.

17. WEIHOFEN, *supra* note 9, at 322.

18. *Id.*

juxtaposition of contrasting ideas may be emphasized by using the same words in a different order. And it can also be created by using the same grammatical structure to express opposing ideas using completely different words. A timeless example of this device is from Alexander Pope: "To err is human; to forgive, divine."[19] The same device was used by Mick Jagger in the immortal lines:

> You can't always get what you want,
> But if you try sometime,
> You just might find,
> You get what you need.

Proofread Your Motion to Dismiss

Every lawyer has painfully learned the necessity of careful proofreading. It happens like this: you've researched thoroughly, you've analyzed carefully, you've written persuasively, you've complied with every local rule, you've met your deadline, you've filed your brief, and, finally, you sit back to review your work with pride. And there, shrieking at you from the first page, accompanied by flashing strobe lights and blasting sirens, a glaring misspelling. Oh no! You try to calm yourself, thinking surely it's the only one. But it's not. You discover another on page three and still another on page six. After all that hard work, you can barely stand to look at your brief. It mocks you from the middle of your desk. You hate it.

How can you avoid this? Well, unfortunately, you can't. No matter how careful you are, it will happen occasionally, especially given the time pressures of practice. But you can keep these embarrassments to a minimum by proofreading systematically:

1. Use a spell-checking program. Spell-checking programs catch most obvious misspellings including inverted letters ("nad" for "and") and extra letters ("deefendant" for "defendant"). While these programs are a great help, they won't catch many other common errors. For example, they don't know that you meant to write "here" instead of "hear" or "statute" instead of "statue." And they can't determine whether in the process of cutting and pasting you've inadvertently dropped a line or misplaced a phrase.

---

19. *Id.*

In short, spell-checkers are only the starting point for proof-reading.

2. Take a break from your draft before you proofread. You need some distance from your work to be able to spot mistakes. If you proofread immediately after editing, you'll see what you meant to write rather than what you actually wrote. Schedule a false deadline so that you'll have at least a day between completing your editing and beginning your proofreading.

3. Proofread a hard copy. I don't know why, but errors show up more clearly on a hard copy than on a computer screen.

4. Proofread slowly and aloud. Reading aloud will force you to slow down so that you actually read the words on the page rather than reading into the draft the words you intended. If possible, read aloud to someone who has a duplicate copy of your draft.[20] If you can't read loudly, at least read softly to yourself.

5. Read backwards. The section of your draft which you completed last will usually have more errors than the earlier sections because you were probably more tired and more rushed when your wrote it. So begin proofreading with the sections you drafted last to focus your attention where it is most needed.[21]

6. Double check names, dates, numbers, addresses, and Latin phrases. Typing numbers and unfamiliar words is difficult, so typos are common. Give these little rascals special attention when you proofread.

7. Don't skip headings and quotations. We all dislike reading densely-typed material, so we tend to skip it. (Remember, that's why long, block quotations should be avoided.) In proofreading, be sure to read headings and quotations aloud.

Good writers make several passes at proofreading and keep at it until time runs out.[22] As a rule of thumb, I'd suggest proofreading

---

20. VEDA R. CHARROW ET AL., CLEAR AND EFFECTIVE LEGAL WRITING 217 (2d ed. 1995).

21. LAUREL CURRIE OATES ET AL., THE LEGAL WRITING HANDBOOK 244, 522 (1993).

22. TOM GOLDSTEIN & JETHRO K. LIEBERMAN, THE LAWYER'S GUIDE TO WRITING WELL 184 (1989).

each court document at least twice with a break between readings. Start writing early so that you have time at the end for this critical step. "Lawyers who assert that they are so squeezed for time that they must routinely file a document minutes after it is drafted are shortchanging their clients, irritating the judges, and deceiving themselves."[23]

Rewriting Checklist for a Motion

I. Rewriting

    A. Reconsider the content:

        1. Does your introduction provide a persuasive summary of your motion?

        2. Do your headings capture the structure and points of your argument?

        3. Have you included all necessary authorities?

        4. Have you thoroughly and persuasively presented them?

        5. Have you applied the authorities to your problem?

        6. Have you considered policy arguments?

        7. Have you anticipated counter-arguments and rebutted them?

        8. Have you synthesized your analysis?

    B. Revise the large-scale organization:

        1. Have you included introductory paragraphs?

        2. Can you outline your points and authorities using topic sentences?

        3. Is the organization persuasive?

            a. Did you open with your strongest argument?

            b. Did you sandwich unwelcome authorities in the middle?

            c. Did you end with a strong argument?

---

23. *Id.* at 165.

    4. Have you provided conclusions to each section of the argument?

  C. Review each paragraph:

    1. Does each paragraph have a topic sentence?

    2. Do the other sentences develop the topic?

    3. Have you checked paragraph length?

    4. Have you provided transitions?

II. Editing

  A. Edit each sentence:

    1. Have you written short sentences?

    2. Have you omitted surplus words?

    3. Have you used base verbs?

    4. Have you preferred the active voice?

    5. Have you adopted conventional legal usage?

    6. Have you arranged your words with care?

    7. Have you chosen your words with care?

  B. Use quotations sparingly:

    1. Have you avoided block quotations?

    2. Have you edited quotations carefully?

  C. Use persuasive writing techniques:

    1. Have you been respectful?

    2. Have you been subtle?

    3. Have you been positive?

    4. Have you avoided clichés?

    5. Have you arranged your words for emphasis?

    6. Have you used concrete words to emphasize and abstract words to minimize?

    7. Have you used parallelism?

III. Proofreading

  A. Have you checked for grammatical errors?

  B. Have you checked for misspellings?

  C. Have you checked for proper citation form?

Chapter 10

Oral Argument

This week we turn from written to oral advocacy. You will be paired with a classmate to participate in an oral argument on the motion to dismiss. This chapter first considers the lawyer's professional responsibilities in and the purpose of oral argument. It then reviews the mechanics of oral argument and provides some suggestions for preparing for and delivering an oral argument.

Professional Responsibilities in Oral Argument

To prepare for oral argument, you must first understand the rules of professional responsibility and etiquette for court hearings. Generally, the same professional responsibilities apply to written and oral advocacy. While your client is entitled to zealous advocacy, your zeal must be restrained by your responsibilities as an officer of the court. Moreover, sanctions for impermissible oral advocacy may be imposed under Fed. R. Civ. P. 11. For example, the Second Circuit held that Rule 11 sanctions were authorized where an attorney orally advocated baseless allegations.[1] Specifically, the court concluded that an attorney was properly sanctioned for statements at a hearing on a motion to dismiss which inaccurately represented another court's ruling in a related case.

Beyond avoiding sanctions, consider your role in the administration of justice. As former Chief Justice Warren E. Burger once observed, "Lawyers who know how to think but have not learned how to behave are a menace and a liability, not an asset to the ad-

---

1. O'Brien v. Alexander, 101 F.3d 1479 (2d Cir. 1996).

ministration of justice."[2] Recently, and perhaps belatedly, the bar has taken steps to improve the behavior of lawyers by adopting standards of civility and courtesy codes. In 1997, the Federal Bar Association adopted its Standards of Civility in Professional Conduct. As the preamble recognizes, "Uncivil conduct of lawyers and judges impedes the fundamental goal of resolving disputes rationally, peacefully, and efficiently. Such conduct may delay or deny justice and diminish the respect for law, which is a cornerstone of our society and our profession." The first General Principle provides: "In carrying out our professional responsibilities, we will treat all participants in the legal process . . . in a civil, professional and courteous manner, at all times and in all communications, whether oral or written."

The impropriety of personal attacks on an adversary deserves special attention. Under the Federal Bar Association Standards, "We will not bring the profession into disrepute by making unfounded accusations of impropriety or making ad hominem attacks on counsel, and, absent good cause, we will not attribute bad motives or improper conduct to other counsel."[3] This prohibition against personal attacks is expressed in the various local courtesy codes. For example, the Los Angeles County Bar Association Litigation Guidelines provide that "[n]either written submissions nor oral presentations should disparage the intelligence, ethics, morals, integrity or personal behavior of one's adversaries . . ."[4] Similarly, a provision of the Louisville Bar Association Creed of Professionalism provides that a lawyer should never intentionally embarrass opposing counsel and should avoid personal criticism of opposing counsel.[5]

Again, the professional rule and the client's interest are harmonious. Personal exchanges between lawyers will offend the court. The advocate is best advised to stick to the merits and maintain professional dignity regardless of the opponent's conduct or misconduct. The more an opponent rants, the better the poised professional looks. In this regard, one judge has explained that to present

---

2. Chief Justice Burger's address to the American Law Institute, May 1971, *quoted in* Robert C. Mueller, *Standards of Civility—A Lesson in Good Manners*, FED. LAW., Jan. 1998, at 2.
3. FED. BAR ASS'N. STANDARD 5 (1997).
4. LITIGATION GUIDELINES § 3.a (Los Angeles County Bar Ass'n).
5. CREED OF PROFESSIONALISM (Louisville Bar Ass'n).

an effective oral argument the advocate should avoid breaches of courtesy:

> If [an opponent's] remark is improper, counsel should remain calm and restrained and should not in turn commit the same error by manifesting a resentful attitude. If there is justification to resent the remarks of opposing counsel, one is usually vindicated by the fact that the court will also resent them.
>
> A calm and dignified attitude is essential throughout the argument. Whether the argument of opposing counsel is excellent or obviously ineffective and poor, the advocate should always listen with courtesy and dignity.[6]

Another judge echoed these sentiments and explained that "[i]ncivility is counterproductive."[7] According to Judge Koeltl, after he became a judge he came to appreciate the extent to which boorish lawyers harm their clients. He views incivility as a sign of weakness and an effort to obstruct the truth: "The result is that the lawyer's presentation will be received with skepticism rather than trust. The lawyer will have undermined the lawyer's own credibility and ability to persuade the court...."[8]

Thus, as we have seen before, professionalism is good advocacy. Simply put, bad manners will offend the court and destroy your credibility. Set a high standard of professionalism for all court appearances, rise above personal attacks, focus on the merits of your case, and always maintain courtesy and dignity. This standard will serve the client, the court, and the legal profession well.

Purpose of Oral Argument

In contrast to your motion which must thoroughly present your legal analysis, in oral argument your goals are to emphasize your strongest points and to answer the court's questions. You want to stimulate a dialogue so that you can identity the court's stumbling

---

6. HON. EDWARD D. RE, BRIEF WRITING AND ORAL ARGUMENT 173 (1983).
7. Hon. John. G. Koeltl, *From the Bench*, LITIG. NEWS, Spring 1997, at 3.
8. *Id.*

blocks and show the court how to resolve them. Your goal is not to deliver a smooth speech, but to help the court reach the right result.

Mechanics of Oral Argument

Most courts, both trial and appellate, follow the same general pattern for oral argument. Before court is called to order, counsel should check in with the clerk or courtroom deputy. As a matter of courtesy, present your business card with the case name and number written on the back. At the beginning of the session, attorneys are seated in the audience section of the courtroom reviewing their notes and chatting nervously. When the judge or judges enter, the courtroom deputy or clerk will call for order and all present will rise. After the judge or judges take their places on the bench, the audience should be seated and remain in order. The clerk will call the first case for argument.[9] Both counsel appearing on that case should then proceed to counsel table. The attorney with the burden of persuasion usually argues first. This means that the lawyer who filed the motion or the appeal goes first. Then the opponent responds. Finally, the first lawyer may be permitted a short rebuttal.[10] All arguments should be delivered from the podium.[11] It is a breach of etiquette to speak directly to opposing counsel during argument. Listen respectfully to your opponent.

Oral argument should be a dialogue between the court and counsel, not a monologue by counsel. Judges frequently begin by focusing counsel on the questions that are troubling them. For example, at the beginning of the argument a judge might say, "Counsel, I've read the briefs and understand your point about the statute of limitations, but I'd like you to address the possible waiver of this defense." Even judges who don't initially focus the argument will ask questions if given the opportunity. This is your one chance to address what is most important to the person who will be deciding your case. As one commentator observed, you should "[a]pproach

---

9. A docket list will usually be available listing the cases to be heard that day. The court may or may not go in the order listed.

10. The court may switch the order of argument if it has questions for the opposing party.

11. In some trial courts, argument may be made from counsel table. As a rule, judges prefer arguments from the podium because they can hear better.

these questions as golden opportunities rather than as obstacles in the path to completing your prearranged oral argument. Play the game on the turf that the judges choose."[12]

Courts vary as to the time permitted for argument and the strictness of time limits. Supreme courts usually have strictly enforced time limits. Appellate courts may or may not have strict limits, depending on the personalities of the judges. Often an appellate court will tell you in advance the amount of time allotted for argument, generally 20 to 30 minutes per side or less. Trial courts are usually fairly flexible, but expect short arguments.[13] In law and motion sessions, each side will usually have less than ten minutes to argue.

Preparation for Oral Argument

To prepare for oral argument, follow three steps. First, review the record and the authorities relating to the case. In our case that means you should review the complaint, the moving papers, and the authorities relevant to the case. Update your research by shepardizing the authorities. Pay special attention to the weaknesses in your case for you can be sure that the court will. As you review, organize documents and authorities in a folder or notebook so that you will have everything handy during your argument. Second, prepare an outline of your argument. While your argument will never come out the way you plan it, a good basic structure will provide a framework for the court and will help you keep on track. Finally, rehearse your argument a few times to fix it in your mind. The following discussion will give you suggestions to help you prepare your outline and rehearse your argument.

Outline the argument

Your outline should include: (1) an introduction; (2) a statement of facts; (3) a few key points of argument; and (4) a conclusion. Let's consider each of these parts of your outline.

---

12. Stephen Easton, *Losing Your Appeal*, FED. LAW., Nov.–Dec. 1995, at 33.

13. If you anticipate that you will need a lengthy argument in a trial court, check with the clerk to see if you need to have the matter specially set.

Introduction

The historically proper way to begin oral argument is well-established: "May it please the court, my name is Horace Rumpole, and I represent the defendant Lizzie Borden." Today many courts are less formal. You may wish to follow local practice and dispense with the salutation "May it please the court" and begin instead with "Good morning, Your Honor." But in my opinion, the traditional opening marks you as a professional and sets the proper tone for argument.

After the opening, promptly state the thesis of your argument in one sentence. Strive for an affirmative wording that will focus the court's attention on your strongest point. For example:

For the moving party: May it please the court, my name is Jimminy Cricket, and I represent the defendants, Jimmy Olson and the Daily Planet. The defendants have moved for summary judgment in this invasion of privacy action on the grounds that the First Amendment protects the defendants from liability for reporting on matters of public interest.

For the opposing party: May it please the court, my name is Pinnochio, and I represent the plaintiff, Clark Kent. The plaintiff has brought this action to protect his constitutional right of privacy and will demonstrate that summary judgment should be denied so that he may have his day in court on substantial questions of fact.

These opening statements can and should be carefully considered in advance. They will get you off to a confident, polished start and establish a theme that will lend coherence to the rest of your argument.

After stating your thesis, provide the court with a road map of the points you will address. Keep it short and simple. Discuss only two or three crucial points and avoid an intricate structure. If you will be arguing first, you can determine the order of your points in advance. If you are the responding party, you'll know the main points, but you should remain somewhat flexible since you will have a chance to learn the court's concerns during your opponent's argument. You can modify or rearrange your points to take advantage of this insight. Generally, the responding party begins by addressing the issue which the court and counsel were discussing at the conclusion of the moving party's argument. Here's an example of an introductory road map:

> May it please the court, my name is Amy McCoy, and I represent the plaintiff Vincent Rembrant in his action against the Duck Soup Art Gallery. The plaintiff seeks to amend the complaint to include new causes of action against the defendant because the plaintiff has recently discovered the true extent of the defendant's fraudulent conversion of plaintiff's art works. The motion is timely and proper because: (1) the proposed amendments all arise out of the same transactions at issue in the original complaint; (2) the statute of limitations has not run on the actions; and (3) the defendant will not be prejudiced by the amendments.

This roadmap provides a structure for both you and the court. It demonstrates to the court that you have prepared conscientiously and that you will address the issues of concern to the court. And a good first impression enhances the credibility of your argument.

Statement of facts

After the introduction, the party who argues first should state the facts for the court. The statement of facts should help the court understand the issues and include the facts necessary to support the legal arguments. Because the level of judicial familiarity with a case varies, you should be prepared to expand or condense your statement of facts to fit the court's needs. If the court is thoroughly prepared and wants to skip the statement of facts, the judge will let the advocate know.

In reviewing the facts, stick to facts that will be material to the issues before the court. For example, if the legal issue concerns the statute of limitations, an extensive discussion of liability is neither necessary nor appropriate. Be careful not to get bogged down in unnecessary factual detail. Keep your statement of facts brief; you can weave in additional details where necessary as you develop your argument. Organize the facts carefully; chronological order is generally the easiest to understand. Use objective language and a narrative style to make your statement credible and interesting. But don't forget that as an advocate you can use subtle techniques of persuasion to emphasize favorable facts. Bring the legal problem to life by helping the court see the parties as people.

The responding advocate may state the facts from the other perspective or may choose to accept the opponent's statement and save time for other points. Most experts advise the advocate to emphasize the most important facts and establish a foundation for a favorable ruling. To seize this opportunity, don't repeat undisputed background information and don't quibble over trivial details. Use your time to isolate favorable facts and focus the court's attention on your strongest points.

Points of argument

The body of the argument should follow the roadmap you provided in your introduction. Keep the number of points to a minimum and "go for the jugular,"[14] not the capillaries. Your argument will be more cohesive if you stick to two or three related points addressing the main issue presented by your motion. Avoid intricate discussions of numerous authorities; focus on the main authorities which will control the outcome of your case. Usually the outline of your points will mirror your brief. But, while the structure will generally remain the same, the argument should not simply repeat the written arguments but should supplement them.

You can supplement your written argument in several ways. If you have discovered a more recent authority, you can explain how it applies to your case. If you have not had the opportunity to respond to your opponent's closing brief, now is your chance. And if in reviewing the record you discover a point that was not adequately developed in your points and authorities, you may emphasize it in oral argument. You can also supplement your argument by elaborating on the most persuasive authorities and strongest facts of your case.

On the other hand, raising entirely new points or citing new authorities is risky because the court may lose confidence in you. After all, if the new matter is so important, you should have included it in your written argument. Thus, unless the matter is newly discovered or published after you submitted your papers, you risk losing more than you will gain by raising the point.

---

14. Myron H. Bright, *The Ten Commandments of Oral Argument*, 67 A.B.A. J. 1136, 1138 (1981).

Under each point in your outline, enter the key facts and supporting authorities. You need not and probably should not write out the entire substance of your argument. Just enter the key words and catch phrases that will trigger your memory of the point.

Conclusion

The final item in your outline is your conclusion. Planning a conclusion will enable you to end your argument on a positive and professional note. Your conclusion should first signal the court that you're wrapping it up, then summarize the theme of your argument, and ask for a ruling in your favor. Finally, you should thank the court. For example:

> In conclusion, the actions all arise out of the same facts as the original complaint, the actions are within the statute of limitations, and the plaintiff is entitled to seek damages for defendant's fraudulent conversion of plaintiff's property. The plaintiff therefore requests that the motion to amend the complaint be granted. Thank you.

Rehearse the argument

After preparing your outline, rehearse your argument. Observe the two cardinal rules of successful oral argument: don't read and don't memorize. If you read your argument, you will bore and irritate the court. As explained by Mr. Justice Jackson, the court likes to look the advocate in the eye which reading prevents. For this reason, "[i]f you have confidence to address the Court only by reading to it, you really should not argue there."[15]

And memorizing an argument is just as bad as reading. If you memorize your argument, you may fall into a sing-song or monotonous delivery. Indeed, memorizing creates the added danger of forgetting lines and becoming paralyzed with panic. According to one commentator:

> Forgotten lines are embarrassing for everyone in the courtroom. The attorney stands at the podium silent, blood draining from the face, obviously struggling to find the next word. Seconds pass, each an eternity. The more time that passes the

---

15. Robert H. Jackson, *Advocacy Before the Supreme Court: Suggestions for Effective Case Presentations*, 37 A.B.A. J. at 801, 861 (1951).

more difficult it is to rekindle the presentation. Escape, rather than persuasion, becomes the focus of the moment.[16]

On the other hand, if you learn your outline well and practice a few times, it will be fixed in your mind so that you can deliver it with spontaneity and without excessive reliance on notes. This approach also permits the flexibility needed to respond to the court's questions and return to the argument without getting flustered. And even if you momentarily forget your place, you can easily find it again by glancing at your outline to trigger your recollection of your argument.

So with this goal in mind, rehearse your argument until you can run through it smoothly. As you move from point to point, provide sign posts so the court will be able to follow along. For example, in moving from your first point to your second point, you might signal the transition by saying, "This brings me to my second point: the statute of limitations has not yet expired on this cause of action." Your argument should be shorter than the allotted time to permit questions from the bench. This rehearsal will both ensure an organized and coherent presentation and will also give you confidence and poise.

In addition to rehearsing your argument, you can also rehearse your answers to questions. You can usually anticipate the troublesome points which are likely to provoke questions. Write these questions down on note cards, shuffle them, and place them face down beside your outline. As your rehearse your argument, flip over a question card periodically to practice your answers.

Techniques of Oral Advocacy

This section will discusses some techniques of successful oral advocacy: (a) be prepared; (b) adopt the appropriate demeanor and attitude; (c) be yourself; (d) stand up, look up, and speak up; (e) watch your body language; (f) welcome questions from the bench; and (g) conclude quickly.

---

16. MICHAEL R. FONTHAM, WRITTEN AND ORAL ADVOCACY 147 (Student ed. 1985).

Be prepared

As explained above, a good oral argument depends on careful preparation. If you follow the approach of reviewing the record and the authorities, preparing an outline, and rehearsing your argument, you will be well prepared for your argument. Preparation will also help you overcome the nervousness every advocate suffers before argument.

Adopt the appropriate demeanor and attitude

Court hearings are formal occasions. You will want to think about the impression you make on the court and adopt a professional demeanor and appropriate attitude. Dress up, and shine your shoes. As Mr. Justice Jackson explained, "[Y]ou will not be stopped from arguing if you wear a race-track suit or sport a rainbow necktie. You will just create the first impression that you have strayed in at the wrong bar."[17]

In addition to creating the right impression by your appearance, you should also adopt the appropriate attitude toward the court. You should be neither overly obsequious nor overly familiar. For example, you should never compliment the court or members of the court. (I actually heard one lawyer from Los Angeles tell a San Diego Superior Court judge that he was honored to appear before the judge because the judge's fine reputation had even reached as far as Los Angeles.) This sounds like flattery and will embarrass everyone in the court room. Strive for an attitude of respectful intellectual equality. And always address members of the court as "Your Honor."

Be yourself

In oral advocacy, an infinite range of personal styles can be effective. Some advocates are animated and dramatic; some are reserved and polished; some are witty and urbane; some are halting and folksy. Any personal style can succeed as long as the style is natural and the advocate is sincere. Don't try to be something you're not. As

---

17. Jackson, *supra* note 15, at 862.

your experience grows, you'll learn to make the best of your own personal style. Be on your best formal behavior, and you'll be fine.

Stand up, look up, and speak up

When you are addressing the court, remember to stand up, look up, and speak up. Proper courtroom etiquette requires that you stand when you address the court. Don't slouch or lean on the podium. Eye contact will heighten the court's interest in your argument and enhance your credibility. Speak with authority. A timid, squeaky delivery seems tentative and weak; a strong voice projects confidence and commitment. You don't want to yell at the court, but speak so that everyone in the room can easily hear you, even those behind you in the back row of the courtroom. Courtroom acoustics are universally abysmal, but a good strong voice will be heard. When we are nervous most of us speak more quickly and at a higher pitch, so remember to slow down and lower your pitch during argument.

Watch your body language

When arguing, stand at the podium facing the court. Moving around in the well of the courtroom is inappropriate. To convey confidence, avoid clasping your hands tightly together or crossing your arms across your chest. Keep your gestures restrained: no pointing at the court or counsel, no pounding on the podium, no rocking on your heels, no fidgeting with your hair, no waiving about a pen, no jingling your car keys, no shuffling papers. Small hand gestures can be effective, such as showing the "broad" scope of argument or "weighing" alternatives.[18] When your opponent is arguing, be politely attentive. No smirks, groans, or grimaces.

Welcome questions from the bench

The fledgling advocate fears that the court will ask questions; the experienced advocate fears that it won't. As hard as it may be for

---

18. HARVARD LAW SCH. BOARD OF STUDENT ADVISERS, INTRODUCTION TO ADVOCACY: RESEARCH, WRITING, AND ARGUMENT 73 (1996).

you to believe, questions are the most important and enjoyable part of argument. Questions give you the unique and precious opportunity to understand and respond to the court's concerns. An uninterrupted argument may go smoothly, but it is less likely to influence a court's view than a conversation with the court directly addressing the court's questions.[19] As one former state supreme court justice observed:

> We talked about where a lawyer was distressed about a question, it interrupted his train of argument, and he didn't have the full appreciation that that very question the judge was asking is going to be the thing that the judge will be talking about in conference, and what counsel ought to do is jump for joy that some judge has asked a question.[20]

After your initial jump for joy at being questioned, then what? Listen carefully to the question and don't interrupt. The normal rules of social conversation do not apply in the courtroom: the judge can interrupt you with questions, but you must never interrupt the judge. If you interrupt, you will irritate the judge and may miss the point of the question. Wait until the question is completed and briefly pause to show that you are thoughtfully considering your answer. Then respond directly and unequivocally. Never put the court off by saying, "I was going to address that in the next section of my argument." If the court asks a question, the time has come to address the point. And don't give a convoluted explanation before answering. If you respond evasively, the court's questions may turn into cross-examination. When the court asks a direct question requiring a yes or no answer, answer first, then explain: "Yes, Your Honor, however..." At times you may have to disagree with the court, but this can be done politely. For example:

Court: Isn't it true that the *Smith* case goes directly against you and controls the outcome of this case?

Counsel: No, Your Honor, I read the *Smith* case somewhat differently. A key distinction between the facts of *Smith* and the facts of our case is that the insurance policy in *Smith*

---

19. FONTHAM, *supra* note 16, at 175.
20. Bright, *supra* note 14, at 1138.

had no umbrella provision whereas the policy in our case has a separately negotiated provision for umbrella coverage. For this reason, the *Smith* case is distinguishable and does not control the outcome of this case.

When you've answered the question and the judge looks satisfied, return to your argument. Don't wait for the court to prompt you, just proceed. If the court has a follow-up question, it will let you know. Don't put the burden on the court to move the argument along, that's your job. For example, after distinguishing the *Smith* case in the preceding example, counsel might continue: "While the *Smith* case is distinguishable, the *Mahoney* case is directly on point. In *Mahoney*..."

You may be afraid you'll get a question that you don't know how to answer. Generally, the well-prepared advocate has anticipated most questions. For example, if the court asks a question about the procedural status or facts of the case, adequate preparation will provide the answers. Similarly, the court will often ask questions about legal authorities and arguments. Again, the well-prepared advocate has usually anticipated these questions. You'll know the relevant authorities, how to use those that help you, and how to distinguish those that harm your case. Finally, the court will sometimes ask questions concerning policy considerations and the equities of the case. Judges want to effect simple justice. Be prepared to explain how a ruling in your favor furthers public policy and achieves a just result.

Occasionally, you might be thrown an impossible question. Don't panic. If you can't answer the question because it's confusing, try your best to respond or politely ask for clarification. If you can't answer a question because you're having a temporary memory lapse, you should admit it and ask the court for help. For example, if the court asks you about a specific case and you've momentarily forgotten its facts, simply apologize for the lapse and ask the court to refresh your recollection or for a moment to check your file. If you can't answer a question because it's off the wall and irrelevant, candidly admit that you haven't considered the case from that perspective and offer to submit a supplemental brief. Don't try to come up with an answer on the spot. Answering a question like this may trap you into a prolonged discussion of something you haven't carefully analyzed and may get you into trouble.

While the court is asking questions, don't worry about losing time for the other points you planned to make. The court knows what it needs to clarify, and that's what you need to address. The experienced advocate will gladly skip a point of the planned argument to buy time to address the court's questions.

Conclude quickly

In your outline, you prepared a conclusion to your argument. If you have time, state your conclusion and sit down. Often, your time will expire before you reach your conclusion. In that case, you may ask the court for additional time to finish an answer to a question from the court. Complete your answer quickly (a sentence or at most two), thank the court and sit down. You should not ask for time simply to deliver your formal conclusion. Simply stop where you are, say "thank you," and sit down. As former Solicitor General Stern explained, you will rarely have time to present your conclusion. If you do, "there is no reason not to end with a short persuasive bang, which probably should be prepared in advance. But you shouldn't really expect to get to it, or be perturbed if you don't."[21]

After you've concluded your argument and thanked the court, be seated. Don't hover about in the well of the courtroom fluttering your hands and searching for an escape route. Stride confidently to your seat. If your opponent is going to argue after you, be seated at counsel table and listen politely. If both sides have concluded their arguments, be seated in the audience section or quietly leave the courtroom.

A Word About Nerves

Everyone gets nervous before an oral argument. Many first-year students approach the exercise with dread. But once it's behind them, most students are surprised at how much they enjoyed the experience. And a few butterflies are nothing to worry about because nervousness is normal. As one experienced advocate advised:

---

21. ROBERT L. STERN, APPELLATE PRACTICE IN THE UNITED STATES 433 (1981).

Nervousness at the commencement of an argument is largely unavoidable. It decreases with experience, but seldom disappears altogether, at least until the argument is underway. Writing out your first sentence and having it before you in large letters can help you get through the first few seconds. So don't be nervous about being nervous.[22]

You'll find that with practice you will be more comfortable with oral argument and will start to develop your own personal style. So don't let your initial jitters keep you from enjoying one of the highlights of advocacy.

---

22. *Id.* at 400.

Outline Template for an Oral Argument

I. Introduction

    A. Introduce yourself and your client.

    B. State the thesis of your argument.

    C. Provide a roadmap of issues.

II. Statement of facts

III. Points of argument

    A. The first issue

        1. Introduce the issue with a signpost.

        2. Discuss the strongest authority supporting your position and explain its application to your case.

        3. Explain why your opponent's argument should be rejected.

        4. Conclude briefly stating the reason the court should rule in your favor.

    B. The second issue

    Repeat steps 1–4 above.

    C. The third issue

    Repeat steps 1–4 above.

VI. Conclusion

    A. Restate the thesis of your argument.

    B. Request the specific ruling you are seeking.

    C. Thank the court.

Chapter 11

Appellate Brief

Your final project is to write an appellate brief. We'll assume that the trial court granted the defendant's motion to dismiss the complaint and entered a judgment based on this ruling. You represent the plaintiff who has decided to appeal. This chapter will first discuss special responsibilities that arise in appellate practice. It will then turn to the audience for and the form of an appellate brief.

Professional Responsibilities Arising on Appeal

Following an adverse judgment in a trial court, the disappointed attorney may be anxious to turn to more promising cases but must first discharge special duties to the unfortunate client. After entering into an attorney-client relationship, the attorney is required to "carry through to conclusion all matters undertaken for a client" unless the relationship has been terminated.[1] When a client has lost a case in a trial court, "the lawyer should advise the client of the possibility of appeal before relinquishing responsibility for the matter."[2] If the attorney does not wish to continue the representation, reasonable steps must be taken to protect the client's interests.[3] These steps include providing reasonable notice to the client, allowing time to locate substitute counsel, and turning over property and files.[4] If time to file the notice of appeal is short, the attorney should ensure that the notice is filed in time to protect the client's rights.

---

1. MODEL RULES OF PROFESSIONAL CONDUCT Rule 1.3 cmt. 3 (1997) [hereinafter MODEL RULES].
2. *Id.*
3. MODEL RULES, *supra* note 1, Rule 1.16(d).
4. *Id.*

197

Of course, this obligation to carry through on representation is constrained by the duty to avoid frivolous litigation. A disappointing outcome is not always the result of an appealable error. Before filing an appeal, counsel must carefully evaluate the possible grounds for an appeal and help the client decide whether to devote additional time, money, and energy to the case. Frivolous appeals violate the Model Rules of Professional Conduct[5] and may expose the attorney to sanctions under Fed. R. App. P. 38.

In pursuing the appeal, counsel must be scrupulously accurate in referring to the record and the applicable authorities. Misrepresentations of the law or the facts are both unethical and unpersuasive.[6] The burden is on the appellant to establish reversible error; the appellate court should only reverse a judgment where a suitable showing has been made.

Finally, as in the trial court, in appellate matters, lawyers should be courteous to opposing counsel and respectful of the court. Attorneys who attack opposing counsel in appellate briefs have been disciplined.[7] Attacks on the lower court are even worse.[8] And attacks on the appellate bench are suicidal.[9]

Purpose of an Appellate Brief

When you are the appellant, your brief must inform the court of the proceedings below, present a legal argument, and persuade the court that a reversible error was committed. An informative brief contains an accurate summary of the facts of the case and proceedings in the lower court as well as a well-reasoned analysis of the law. To demonstrate reversible error, you must establish from the record that the issue was raised and preserved in the trial court. Under the doctrine of invited error, if the attorney neglected to raise and preserve the issue below, the court of appeal will not salvage the case for

---

5. MODEL RULES, *supra* note 1, Rule 3.1.
6. MODEL RULES, *supra* note 1, Rule 3.3.
7. Donald H. Green, *Ethics in Legal Writing,* 35 FED. BAR NEWS & J. 402 (1988).
8. Allen v. Seidman, 881 F.2d 375 (7th Cir. 1989).
9. Patton v. State Department of Health and Rehabilitative Services, 597 So. 2d 302 (Fla. Dist. Ct. App. 1991); Vandenberghe v. Poole, 163 So. 2d 51 (Fla. Dist. Ct. App. 1964).

the client. Moreover, the harmless error standard provides that the court of appeal must disregard "any error or defect in the proceeding which does not affect the substantial rights of the parties."[10] Today, the brief may be your the only opportunity to persuade the court because many cases are decided without oral argument.

Audience for an Appellate Brief

Your audience on appeal is different from your audience in the trial court. In most appellate courts, law clerks or staff attorneys do much of the initial work and will probably recommend the disposition the court should make. As Diana Pratt explains, your first audience on appeal is usually a recent law school graduate; write your brief so "that this attorney readily understands the issues and how existing precedent should be applied to decide the case."[11]

The appellate court is different from the trial court in two other respects. First, unlike the trial judge who is required to view motions to dismiss with a bias in favor of the plaintiff,[12] the appellate court has a preconceived notion that the trial judge was correct and that the appellant is wrong. As Michael Tigar cautions, judges on the court of appeal "are institutionally committed to being skeptical about the appellant's version."[13] You have the burden of demonstrating reversible error to an audience which is biased against you.

Second, unlike the trial judge whom you could address as an individual with known likes, dislikes, and predilections, the appellate bench assigned to decide your case will usually be unknown to you when you write your brief. For example, more than twenty judges currently sit on the Ninth Circuit bench. When you write your brief, you have no idea which three judges will ultimately read your brief and decide your case. Your brief must be written for the entire court, not the individual judges who will actually read it.

On the other hand, one great similarity to the trial court bears emphasis. Both the trial court and the appellate court have enor-

---

10. FED. R. APP. P. 61.
11. DIANA V. PRATT, LEGAL WRITING: A SYSTEMATIC APPROACH 254–55 (2d ed. 1993).
12. Ash Creek Mining Co. v. Lujan, 969 F.2d 868 (10th Cir. 1992).
13. MICHAEL E. TIGAR, FEDERAL APPEALS 340 (2d ed. 1993).

mous workloads. For example, the twenty-eight judges on the Ninth Circuit Court of Appeal disposed of 8,593 appeals in 1994.[14] Given this workload, every judge appreciates clear, concise, and readable writing.

Form and Content of an Appellate Brief

The appellant has the burden of perfecting the appeal by filing a timely notice of appeal, preparing the record, and filing an opening brief. Although the preliminary steps are mechanical, they are critical. Pay special attention to time limits because they can be quite short. For example, in the federal system, the notice of appeal must be filed within 30 days after the entry of judgment.[15] Failure is fatal. If you miss the deadline, the appeal is barred.[16] The next step is to assemble the record. The appellant must arrange to have the transcript prepared and the docket entries and relevant documents copied. The record must be transmitted to and filed in the court of appeal within the time limits provided by the court's rules. The court will dismiss an appeal or refuse to consider an appellant's arguments if the record is defective.[17]

Once the notice of appeal is filed and the record is assembled, the next task is drafting the opening brief. Rule 28 of the Federal Rules of Appellate Procedure requires the opening brief to include: (a) a table of contents; (b) a table of authorities; (c) a statement of the subject matter and appellate jurisdiction; (d) a statement of the issues; (e) a statement of the case; (f) a summary of the argument; (g) an argument; and (h) a short conclusion. Local rules may supplement the requirements of Rule 28. We'll turn now to consider each section of the brief and a few typical local rules. An outline template and sample appellate brief are included at the end of this chapter.

---

14. 9TH CIR. CT. APP., 1994 ANNUAL REPORT 56 (1995).
15. FED. R. APP. P. 4.
16. Browder v. Director, Department of Corrections, 434 U.S. 257 (1978).
17. Syncom Capital Corp. v. Wade, 924 F.2d 167 (9th Cir. 1991).

Table of contents

The table of contents must contain all the divisions and subdivisions of the brief. Ideally, for a simple appeal, it should be complete on one page. The point headings must appear in full as they appear in the brief. Remember that the appellate court is not familiar with your case, so the table of contents is your first opportunity to tell your story. The headings, read together, should acquaint the court with the legal points and their application to the facts of your case. Your goal is to provide the court with a persuasive summary of your case; a good one will be appreciated. As Judge Frank M. Coffin explained, "I like an informative table of contents, valuing it more than a statement of the issues. I like it when it is selective and prioritized, i.e., when it does not include too many issues."[18]

Table of authorities

The table of authorities must list all the authorities in proper citation form and the pages on which they appear in the brief. Divide the table into "Cases," "Statutes and Rules," and "Other Authorities." These headings should be centered. List cases alphabetically. List the statutes alphabetically according to the code cited. If you cite more than one section of a code, list the sections in numerical order. For each authority, provide a reference to every page of the brief where it is cited. Fortunately, many word processing programs allow you to assemble the table automatically.

Subject matter and appellate jurisdiction

Fed. R. App. P. 28(a)(2) requires a statement of the basis for jurisdiction of both the district court and the court of appeals. Both must be supported by the citation of statutory authority and refer to the relevant facts establishing jurisdiction. For example:

> The district court had jurisdiction of this civil action under 28 U.S.C. §§ 1331, 1332, and 1343 because the action arises under 42 U.S.C. §§ 1983 as a civil rights action for violations

---

18. Frank M. Coffin, On Appeal 120 (1993).

of the eighth amendment prohibition of cruel and unusual punishment. This appeal is from a final judgment disposing of all claims in favor of defendant which was entered on May 15, 1998. A timely notice of appeal was filed on June 10, 1998. Therefore this court has jurisdiction under 28 U.S.C. § 1291.

Issue statement

A good issue statement sharply focuses the court on the legal question to be resolved and ties it to the facts of the case. It should be short and readable. For example:

> [W]hether an owner may protect personal property in an unoccupied boarded-up farm house against trespassers and thieves by a spring gun capable of inflicting death or serious bodily injury.[19]

As this example illustrates, the issue statement follows the same approach as questions presented in office memos, proceeding from the general legal context to the specific facts of the case. And while the issue statement seems to present objective information, it is subtly persuasive. The owner was willing to kill someone to protect some stuff in an abandoned house? What if a child had been shot? The issue statement should have only one possible answer.

As you craft your issue statement, be sure to avoid: a generalized statement which ignores the facts; a fact-laden statement which obscures the legal point; and an emotional statement which undermines your credibility. Consider the following possible issue statements in the same case:

Generalized: Whether the trial court erred in dismissing the complaint.

Fact-laden: Whether the plaintiff's complaint properly alleged she suffered severe emotional distress, including headaches, sleeplessness, depression, weight loss and loss of appetite, following an argument with defendant on May 6, 1998, at the Submarine Sandwich Shoppe, at the corner of Seventh Avenue and Main Street in Missoula, Montana,

---

19. Katko v. Briney, 183 N.W. 2d 657 (Iowa 1971).

that occurred when plaintiff attempted to order a tuna salad sandwich on rye toast without pickles.

Emotional: Whether plaintiff has a right to recover for defendant's outrageous behavior which inflicted severe, unrelenting, and unbearable emotional distress on plaintiff in violation of sacred constitutional principles which our veterans have fought and died to preserve.

Better: Whether the complaint states a cause of action under the 1964 Civil Rights Act by alleging that the defendant refused to serve plaintiff in a public restaurant because she is an African-American.

Statement of the case

Rule 28(a)(4) requires that the statement of the case be divided into two sections: (1) a statement of the nature of the case, the course of proceedings, and disposition in the lower court; and (2) a statement of facts with specific references to the record.

Nature of the case, course of proceedings, and disposition below

This first section of the statement of the case should be set off by a subheading. It should be short and specific. It should also pique the court's interest and alert the court to the issues on appeal. For example:

This is a civil rights action by a prisoner who was denied necessary medical treatment in violation of the eighth amendment prohibition of cruel and unusual punishment. Specifically, despite repeated orders from outside consulting doctors that plaintiff needed eye surgery to save his vision, the defendant failed to authorize or arrange the surgery. As a result, plaintiff is now blind. The complaint was filed on January 2, 1998. On February 20, 1998, the defendant moved to dismiss under Rule 12(b)(6) of the Fed. R. Civ. P. on the grounds that the complaint failed to allege sufficient facts to state a claim for relief since it failed to set forth specific evidence showing defendant's subjective knowledge of the medical reports. Following briefing by the parties and a hearing, the trial court granted the motion and entered judgment for the defendant on March 30, 1998. A notice of appeal was filed on April 15, 1998.[20]

Statement of facts

The statement of facts should tell your story in an interesting and orderly manner. Present the facts in chronological order and use the past tense. Stick to the facts relevant to the issue on appeal. Use plain English, not legalese. Present the facts accurately but favorably to your client. Emphasize favorable facts by placement, expansion, and forceful language; minimize unfavorable facts. Adopt an objective tone. A compelling statement of facts will argue for itself. The court should see how justice will be served by ruling in your client's favor. By the end of the statement of facts, the court should be on your side. As James McElhaney explains, "The statement of facts is the most important part of the brief because it points the way to elemental justice."[21]

Under Rule 28(a)(4), your statement of facts must include references to the record on appeal. Under Rule 30(a), the appellant is required to prepare an appendix of the record containing the relevant docket entries in the proceedings below and any relevant portions of the pleadings or other documents on which the parties rely. In this case, the appendix would include the complaint, the order granting the defendant's motion to dismiss, and the judgment of dismissal. Some circuits have adopted somewhat different requirements for the record on appeal.[22] But whatever form the record takes, the statement of facts must specifically refer to it. Detailed and specific references are required both by rules of court and by principles of persuasion. The court will find your case more credible if you demonstrate that every statement is supported by the record.

Summary of argument

Under Rule 28(a)(5), the appellant shall include a summary of argument containing "a succinct, clear, and accurate statement of the

---

20. This statement would be supported by references to the record.

21. James W. McElhaney, *The Art of Persuasive Legal Writing*, A.B.A. J., Jan. 1996, at 78.

22. For example, the Ninth Circuit requires excerpts of record rather than appendices. 9th Cir. R. 30-1.

arguments made in the body of the brief." The Rule further provides that the summary should not merely repeat the argument
headings.

According to Michael Tigar, the summary presents a unique opportunity to provide an overview of the entire case and "to single
out the most important aspect of each argument and telegraph it to
the judge."[23] The summary should cite and summarize the leading
cases determined by your answer to the following question: "What
'leading cases' would I want the judges to single out and read on
their first trip through this brief?"[24] In discussing the leading cases,
the summary should present them in the context of the facts of the
case and demonstrate how the application of the law to the facts
compels a favorable ruling.

You might wish to turn now to the summary of argument in the
sample brief included at the end of this chapter. As you'll see, the
summary reflects the organization of the argument which is divided
into three parts. The entire argument section of the brief is about
eight pages long; the summary is about one page long. The summary provides citations and brief explanations of the most important cases and demonstrates how they support a favorable ruling
when applied to the case on appeal.

Argument

Like the points and authorities in the trial court, the argument
section of the appellate brief consists of point headings and narrative argument.

Point headings

Each heading should state succinctly a point of your argument.
The headings should present your argument so that the court will
be compelled to rule in your favor if the points stated in your headings are well taken.[25] The headings should be complete sentences
tying the law to the facts of your case. Keep in mind that the head-

---

23. TIGAR, *supra* note 13, at 344–345.
24. *Id.* at 345.
25. Lowery v. Robinson, 238 Cal. App. 2d 36, 42, 47 Cal. Rptr. 495, 499
(1965).

ings, read together, should summarize your argument when they are presented in the table of contents. Your headings should be five lines or less.

Example: The trial court properly sustained the demurrer to the defamation action: School Board Candidate Larsen's opinion about the teachers' strike is protected by the First Amendment.

Not: The demurrer

Not: The demurrer was properly sustained.

Not: The trial court properly sustained the demurrer on First Amendment grounds.

Not: The complaint failed to state a cause of action for defamation.

The example ties the legal issue to the facts of the case. The others are "blind headnotes" which fail to show the application of an abstract legal principle to the case on appeal. Remember, the points should summarize your argument in terms of both the facts and the law.

Many appellate advocates subdivide their arguments into subheadings to provide a detailed outline for the court. For example, the previous example could be subdivided as follows:

I. The trial court properly sustained the demurrer to the defamation action: School Board Candidate Larsen's opinion about the teachers' strike is protected by the First Amendment.

A. In a defamation action, a demurrer is properly sustained where the complaint discloses on its face that the statements at issue are protected by the First Amendment.

B. The First Amendment protects statements of opinion about public officials pertaining to matters of public interest.

C. As a matter of law, Larsen's statement that School Board Member Fisher supported the striking school teachers was a statement of opinion about a public official pertaining to a matter of public interest.

D. Because Larsen's statement is protected opinion as a matter of law under the First Amendment, the trial court properly sustained Larsen's demurrer.

In outlining your argument, consider creating subheadings for your major point headings. Experiment with a detailed approach and a broad approach to determine which you think is most helpful and persuasive.

Even though you lost in the court below, avoid couching your headings in negative and defensive language. Strive for a positive approach:

Don't write: The trial court erred in granting the motion because the plaintiff's action was not barred by the statute of limitations.

Write: The plaintiff's action was timely because it was filed within the first six months of the one-year period allowed by the statute of limitations.

Finally, pay attention to the location of your headings on the page. A heading should never appear at the bottom of a page. At least three lines of text should follow each point heading on the page. If less than three lines follow the heading, move it to the top of the next page.

Narrative argument

In drafting the narrative argument, concentrate on the organization and the application of law to fact. Remember that your brief should stand on its own and demonstrate that the trial court committed reversible error.

Organization

Rule 28(a)(6) requires the argument to include "for each issue a concise statement of the applicable standard of review; this statement may appear in the discussion of each issue or under a separate heading placed before the discussion of the issues." The standard of review refers to the degree of deference the appellate court should give to the trial court's decision. For example, in ruling on pretrial discovery motions, the court of appeal gives the trial court wide latitude. The court will only reverse these rulings where the appellant demonstrates that the trial court abused its broad discretion. On the other hand, a dismissal for failure to state a claim will be reviewed strictly on appeal. The court will reverse a judgment following a motion to dismiss if the court has any doubt about the plaintiff's ability to state a claim. As you can see, the standard of review is a threshold issue which must be squarely addressed at the beginning of your argument. For example:

> An appellate court reviews a district court's denial of summary judgment based on qualified immunity *de novo. ActUp!/ Portland v. Bagley*, 988 F.2d 868, 871 (9th Cir. 1993). On review, an appellate court determines while, "viewing the evidence in the light most favorable to the nonmoving party, whether there are any genuine issues of material fact and whether the district court correctly applied the relevant substantive law." *Hamilton v. Endell*, 981 F.2d 1062, 1065 (9th Cir. 1992).

After you've established the standard of review, turn to the substantive arguments. Discuss the relevant authorities logically and persuasively. Each section of your brief should have an introduction providing an overview of the point. Emphasize the arguments in your favor and minimize the arguments against you by following the principles of primacy and recency. Begin with the strongest authority supporting the point and apply it to the facts of your case. Then anticipate and minimize the unwelcome authorities by sandwiching them in the middle of your discussion and explaining why they should be rejected. Finally, close on a strong point and synthesize the analysis with a conclusion stating the reason you should prevail.

Application of law to facts

Too frequently attorneys (and students) extract an abstract rule from a case without presenting the facts, procedure, or rationale of the case. When you present a case you should include the facts of the cited case to establish that it applies to your case. Remember that if the facts are different, the result may be different. Also include the procedural context to establish the standard for review. For example, on summary judgment, conflicting inferences are resolved in favor of the party opposing summary judgment. Conversely, following trial, inferences drawn by the trier of fact are presumed to be true. Thus, evidence sufficient to withstand a summary judgment may not be sufficient to justify a reversal following trial. Simply put, the procedural context often determines the outcome of a case. A persuasive presentation also includes the rationale of the case, explaining the court's reasoning and the policies supporting the decision. In short, a good brief includes the facts, procedure, holding, and rationale of all major cases.

Another common error is to state the law and the error asserted without demonstrating the application of the law to the facts of the case on appeal. For example, if the appellant is arguing that a civil rights action was improperly dismissed, a dissertation on constitutional law is insufficient. The appellant must also pinpoint the allegations of the complaint that establish the violation. Explain how each authority applies to your case. Don't leave it to the court to draw the conclusions. How is your case like the cited authority? How is it different? Should the authority be followed or distinguished? Why? Show the court how the policies supporting the cited authority apply to your case. As one commentator observed, attorneys who fail to explain how authorities apply to the case before the court risk two evils: "[First] the court may simply ignore the citation. Alternatively, the judges or their clerks may review all the cited authority, but fail to rely on it in the manner envisioned by the citing attorney. A short statement of the citing attorney's thinking prevents either evil."[26]

In applying the law to your case, don't shy away from unwelcome authorities; meet them head on. Addressing adverse authorities is required both as a matter of professional responsibility and persuasiveness. Show the court that you have considered all the relevant precedents and can distinguish those that would seem to support your opponent's position. Show the court that your opponent's cases are factually distinguishable, that your case falls within an exception to the rule in your opponent's cases, that more recent rulings undermine your opponent's cases, or, when necessary, that they are just flat wrong. Don't ignore your opponent's authorities and don't devote too much space to them or you will give them undue emphasis. Carefully think through the arguments you can make against the unwelcome authorities and state those arguments concisely.

Common sense suggests a few exceptions to the requirement of fully presenting and applying every case you cite. First, if you are citing a case solely for a well-recognized rule of procedural law or

---

26. Stephen Easton, *Losing Your Appeal*, FED. LAW., Nov.–Dec. 1995, at 32.

general background, your discussion may be more limited. Second, where several cases make the same point, you may present one case fully and then present the others by giving a parenthetical explanation of the facts and holdings. For example:

> See also *Brown v. Lucy*, 95 F.3d 342 (9th Cir. 1994) (court of appeal upheld a judgment of dismissal for failure to state a cause of action for intentional infliction of emotional distress finding the conduct alleged was not sufficiently extreme and outrageous where the only allegations were that the defendant repeatedly moved a football just before plaintiff attempted to punt); *Calvin v. Hobbes*, 104 F.3d 945 (9th Cir. 1995) (court of appeal upheld a judgment of dismissal for failure to state a cause of action for intentional infliction of emotional distress finding the conduct alleged was not sufficiently extreme and outrageous where the only allegations were that the defendant repeatedly jumped out from behind a door and roared at plaintiff as he arrived home from school).

Be selective in citing authority; string citations are not very helpful. One exception to this rule may arise when your point is to show that the weight of authority supports your argument. String citations may be effective to establish the crushing weight of authority in your favor. Usually, however, one killer case that is dead on point will be more persuasive than a series of unanalyzed citations.

Finally, use quotations sparingly. Don't just quote a statute and let the court figure out whether it helps or hurts your client. When you quote a statute, edit it carefully so that only relevant language is included. If you paraphrase a statute, make sure your version is accurate. Show how the statute applies to the facts of your case. Quote sparingly from cases and be sure to explain the relevance of the quotation to your analysis. Well-edited quotations will enhance the credibility of your brief; long quotations will bore the court. The citation for quoted material should appear in the body of your brief, not in a footnote, because some judges see footnotes as an attempt to evade page and spacing restrictions. Provide a pinpoint citation to the page on which the quoted material appears.

Conclusion

Rule 28(a)(7) requires "[a] short conclusion stating the precise relief sought." Don't rehash the entire brief and don't raise new arguments. If your brief has been divided into several sections, you may wish to pull it all together in a few sentences. If you have a tasteful yet memorable way to conclude your argument, use it. Often a simple and formal conclusion is best, stating that you seek reversal of the judgment and providing the reason the court should reverse.

Local rules requirements

Formal requirements

Under the Federal Rules of Civil Procedure, the circuit courts of appeal may adopt supplemental local rules. These rules frequently impose additional formal requirements for briefs. For example, local rules may impose page limits, word limits, margin requirements, and font sizes.[27] They may also specify the number of copies to be filed,[28] and the color of the cover that is required.[29] As you can see, these rules can be detailed and demanding.

To illustrate, the Ninth Circuit has adopted Circuit Rule 32 to supplement the federal requirements for the form of a brief. Circuit Rule 32 provides in part:

(b) **Typeface.** Either a proportionately spaced typeface of 14 points or more, or a monospaced typeface of no more than 10.5 characters per inch may be used in a brief.

(c) **Paper Size, Margins and Line Spacing.** A brief must be on 8 ½ by 11 inch paper. The side margins must be at least 1 inch, and the top and bottom margins must be at least 1 ¼ inch. The text must be double spaced, but quotations more than two lines long may be indented and single spaced, and headings and footnotes may be single spaced.

(d) **Text Style.** Text shall be in roman, non-script text. Case names, headings and signals may be underlined in italics or in bold.

(e) **Calculation of Length.** (1) Proportionately spaced briefs. A principal brief must not exceed 14,000 words and a reply brief must not exceed 7,000 words. No brief may have an average of more than 280 words per page, including footnotes and quotations.

* * * *

---

27. 9TH CIR. R. 32.
28. 9TH CIR. R. 31-1.
29. 9TH CIR. R. 32.

(4) Certificate of Compliance: The brief must be accompanied by a certification of compliance which states the brief's line spacing and states either:

> (i) the brief is proportionately spaced, together with the typeface, point size and word count; or

> (ii) the brief uses monospaced typeface, together with the number of characters per inch, and word count, or the number of counted pages, (1) or (2)(I) above.

* * * *

(h) Form of briefs and the appendix.

* * * *

[T]he cover of the brief of the appellant should be blue; that of the appellee, red; that of an intervenor or amicus curiae, green; that of any reply brief, gray.

The detail of Circuit Rule 32 is typical of local rules imposing formal requirements. For this reason, in practice you should be sure to consult the local rules well in advance of your filing deadline so that you will have time to comply. It is dangerous to rely on the federal rules. For example, while the Federal Rule imposes a 50 page limit for opening briefs, the Ninth Circuit imposes a 40 page limit for monotyped briefs,[30] requires wide margins, double-spacing, and a blue cover for opening briefs.[31] If you wait until the last minute to consult the local rules, you will frantically search for blue paper while slashing 10 pages from your brief.

The page limits imposed by the courts underscore the need to be selective in identifying the issues for appeal and to develop a concise writing style. As James McElhaney reports, "There are some judges who delight in reading only up to the page limit they have imposed by local rule and then stopping. At least one appellate judge on the Eastern Seaboard actually tears off the offending pages so he will be unable to read any further, if for some reason he actually finds the brief interesting."[32] In addition to page limits, courts are increasingly specifying font sizes, minimum margins, and word-count restrictions to counteract clever word processing tricks to

---

30. 9TH CIR. R. 32(c).
31. 9TH CIR. R. 32(h).
32. McElhaney, *supra* note 21, at 74.

evade the page limits.[33] If you want the court to read your argument, you must comply with these restrictions.

Content requirements

In addition to local rules prescribing the form of briefs, some circuits have adopted rules imposing additional content requirements. For instance, in addition to the requirements of Fed. R. Civ. P. 28, the Ninth Circuit requires:

- *Statement regarding attorney fees.* If a party will seek attorney's fees for the appeal, the brief must identify authority for a fee award. 9th Cir. R. 28-2.3.

- *Statement regarding bail status.* The opening brief in a criminal appeal must state the bail status of the defendant. 9th Cir. R. 28-2.4.

- *Statement of reviewability.* As to each issue, the appellant shall state where in the record on appeal the issue was raised and ruled on. Moreover, if the appellant complains of a ruling to which a party must have objected at trial, the brief must state where in the record the objection and ruling are set forth. 9th Cir. R. 28-2.5.

- *Statement of related cases.* The appellant must identify any known related cases pending in the court. 9th Cir. R. 28-2.6.

As you can see, completing an appellate brief requires strict attention to detailed formal requirements. While these requirements may seem exceedingly technical or even trivial, the consequences of ignoring them are dire. As simply stated by the Ninth Circuit, a brief that violates the local rules "may be stricken by the Court."[34] Some courts enforce local rules aggressively, imposing sanctions and discipline for violations.[35] Although local rules are arcane and annoying, they are valuable because they tell us exactly what the court wants. Without local rules, we might innocently commit some appellate blunder that would distract and disgruntle the court. The local rules tell us how to keep our readers happy.

---

33. 9TH CIR. R. 28-3.1.
34. 9TH CIR. R. 28-1(a).
35. Starnes v. Smith, 37 F.3d 1455 (10th Cir. 1994); In Interest of I.H., 614 So. 2d 662 (Fla. Dist. Ct. App. 1993); Elliott v. Elliott, 648 So. 2d 135 (Fla. Dist. Ct. App. 1994).

Outline Template for an Appellate Brief

I.   Table of contents

II. Table of authorities

III. Statement of subject matter and appellate jurisdiction

IV. Issue statement

V.   Statement of the case

    A. Nature of the case, course of proceedings, and disposition below

    B. Statement of facts

VI. Summary of argument

VII. Standard of review

VIII. Argument

    1. Point heading for the first point: state the conclusion the court should reach tying the legal issue to the facts of your case.

       a. Introductory paragraph providing an overview of the argument.

       b. Present the strongest authority for your position.

       c. Apply that authority to the facts of your case.

       d. Present the next strongest authority for your position.

       e. Apply that authority to the facts of your case.

       f. Present the most dangerous unwelcome authority.

       g. Distinguish the unwelcome authority.

       h. Present and distinguish any other unwelcome authorities.

       i. Present an authority supporting the distinction you are drawing.

       j. Concluding paragraph synthesizing the analysis.

    2. Point heading for the second point: state the conclusion the court should reach tying the legal issue to the facts of your case.

       Repeat steps a–j above.

IX. Conclusion

    State precisely the relief you are seeking and the reason it should be granted.

Sample Appellate Brief

IN THE UNITED STATES COURT OF APPEALS
FOR THE NINTH CIRCUIT

NO. 50-15281

GREGORY JONES, ROBERT SMITH,
KEITH BROWN, and THOMAS BROWN,

Plaintiffs/Appellants,

v.

UNITED STATES OF AMERICA,

Defendant/Appellee.

ON APPEAL FROM THE UNITED STATES DISTRICT COURT
FOR THE NORTHERN DISTRICT OF COLUMBIA
THE HONORABLE JACOB MARLEY, DISTRICT JUDGE

APPELLANTS' OPENING BRIEF

Robin Brennan
MASON & VAN OWEN
111 Main Street, Suite 707
Centerville, CA 98736
(505) 987-4563

Table of Contents

Table of Authorities

Cases

Statutes and Rules

Subject Matter and Appellate Jurisdiction

Plaintiffs filed this personal injury action under the Federal Tort Claims Act, 28 U.S.C. § 2671 et seq. AA 1-5.[1] Under 28 U.S.C. § 1346(b), the district court properly exercised its federal question jurisdiction. Plaintiffs appeal from a final judgment which the district court entered on March 25, 1998, disposing of all claims in favor of defendant. AA 17. Plaintiffs filed a timely notice of appeal on April 15, 1998. Therefore this court has jurisdiction under 28 U.S.C. § 1291.

Issue Presented for Review

Plaintiffs were land-based workers who were injured by toxic chemicals while removing asbestos on the USS Enterprise which was in dry-dock. They were not engaged in work traditionally performed by seamen, were not exposed to maritime risks, and were not injured by maritime hazards. The issues presented by this appeal are:

1. Whether the trial court erred in dismissing the action on the grounds that it is barred by the admiralty statute of limitations even though the incident did not threaten to disrupt maritime commerce.

2. Whether the trial court erred in dismissing the action on the grounds that it is barred by the admiralty statute of limitations even though the incident did not involve a traditional maritime activity.

Statement of the Case

A. Nature of the Case, Course of Proceedings, and Disposition Below

On December 17, 1997, Plaintiffs filed this action under the Federal Tort Claims Act to recover for injuries they suffered from toxic exposure on the USS Enterprise. AA 1-5. In response, Defendant moved to dismiss under Rule 12(b)(6) of the Fed. R. Civ. P. claiming that the case was barred by the admiralty statute of limitations. AA 6-15. Following briefing and argument by both sides, the district court granted Defendant's motion and entered a judgment disposing of all claims in favor of Defendant on March 25, 1998. AA 16-17.

---

1. In this brief, the abbreviation AA refers to the Appendix on Appeal.

1

B. Statement of Facts

In September, 1996, Gregory Jones, Robert Smith, Keith Brown and Thomas Brown were members of the Insulators and Asbestos Workers Union, Local 16, who were working for Western MacArthur Company (Western MacArthur), a land-based asbestos removal subcontractor. They were removing asbestos on the USS Enterprise while the ship was in dry-dock. AA 2. Seamen never performed the work covered under this asbestos-removal subcontract; Defendant always subcontracts out this work to land-based workers. AA 3.

The subcontract required the removal of asbestos insulation from the pipes in air conditioning compartment number 2 of the Enterprise. AA 3. To prepare for this asbestos removal, Defendant removed freon from the compressor and stored it drums in compartment 2. AA 3. In accordance with safety procedures, Defendant sealed the compartment to keep asbestos fibers from escaping. AA 3.

Defendant knew that it was dangerous to store freon in a confined space and that drums should not be stored in an asbestos removal area because of the hazard. AA 3. Because of the health hazard, government regulations required Defendant to post a conspicuous warning sign in the freon storage area. AA 3. Yet, despite knowing of this hazard to the asbestos workers, Defendant neglected to post the required warning on compartment 2. AA 3.

In addition to failing to warn of the hazard, Defendant negligently stored the toxic freon in improperly sealed containers. Specifically, in violation of safety regulations, two of the drums had their caps loosely sealed and one drum had no cap at all. AA 4. As a result of Defendant's negligence, freon vapor accumulated in compartment 2 on September 26, 1996. AA 4.

On the morning of September 26, 1996, the four Plaintiffs entered compartment 2 to begin their asbestos removal work. Within a minute or two of entering the compartment, the men began gasping for air and felt like they were suffocating. They became dizzy and nauseous. After two to five minutes, they managed to escape. AA 4. After their exposure, a local, land-based ambulance was summoned and the workers were treated at the emergency room of a local hospital. AA 4.

All of the men have suffered recurring neurological and physical injuries from this toxic exposure. AA 4. They have been unable to work and have incurred substantial medical and related expenses.

2

AA 4. By this action, they seek compensation for these damages and injuries. AA 5.

Summary of Argument

1. Plaintiffs brought this personal injury action under the FTCA which provides that the United States is liable to the same extent as a private individual. 28 U.S.C.A. § 2674. The complaint alleges that Defendant negligently stored toxic chemicals where Plaintiffs were hired to remove asbestos on Defendant's property. When Plaintiffs attempted to perform their work, they were overcome with toxic fumes and became incapacitated. They have suffered permanent personal injuries. Defendant concedes that if the FTCA applies, the action was timely filed.

2. The admiralty statute of limitations does not bar this action because the Plaintiffs' toxic exposure on a dry-docked vessel did not threaten to disrupt maritime commerce. Admiralty jurisdiction only attaches where the incident at issue has "a potentially disruptive impact on maritime commerce." *Jerome B. Grubart, Inc. v. Great Lakes Dredge & Dock Co.*, 513 U.S. 527, 534 (1995). In *Grubart*, this test was satisfied where the incident damaged an underwater structure and led to the closure of the Chicago River for over a month, ceasing all river traffic, including both commuter ferries and commercial barges. *Id.* at 539. In contrast to the *Grubart* case, in the present case the brief exposure of four land-based workers to toxic chemicals posed no threat to disrupt maritime commerce. Since the incident posed no threat to maritime commerce, admiralty jurisdiction does not apply.

3. The admiralty statute of limitations does not bar this action because the incident did not involve a traditional maritime activity. Admiralty jurisdiction only attaches where the parties engage in traditional maritime activities. *Executive Jet Aviation, Inc. v. City of Cleveland*, 409 U.S. 249 (1972); *Foremost Insurance Co. v. Richardson*, 457 U.S. 688 (1982). This Court has repeatedly held that asbestos removal, the work being performed by Plaintiffs, is not a traditional maritime activity. *Myhran v. Johns-Manville Corp.*, 741 F.2d 1119 (9th Cir. 1984); *Martinez v. Pacific Industrial Service Corporation*, 904 F.2d 521 (9th Cir. 1990). Since the traditional maritime activity requirement is not satisfied, admiralty jurisdiction does not apply.

Standard of Review

A judgment following a motion to dismiss is final and subject to immediate appellate review. *King v. Williams Industries, Inc.*, 724 F.2d 240, 243 (14th Cir. 1983). In reviewing a dismissal for failure to state a claim, the court of appeal must accept all well-pleaded allegations as true and resolve all factual disputes in favor of the plaintiff. *Id.* The court must reverse the dismissal unless it appears beyond doubt that the plaintiff can prove no set of facts supporting the claim. *Id.*

Argument

I

UNDER THE FEDERAL TORT CLAIMS ACT, PLAINTIFFS TIMELY FILED THIS ACTION TO RECOVER FOR PERSONAL INJURIES SUFFERED WHILE REMOVING ASBESTOS ON GOVERNMENT PROPERTY

The Federal Tort Claims Act (FTCA) governs tort actions against the United States, providing that the government is "liable in the same manner and to the same extent as a private individual." 28 U.S.C.A. § 2674. See also 28 U.S.C.A. § 1346(b). Under the FTCA, a person injured through the negligence of the United States may bring an action in the United States District Court. 28 U.S.C.A. §§ 1346(b), 2671 et seq.

The present action is a straight-forward tort action against the United States. Plaintiffs seek recovery for the injuries they suffered as a result of Defendant's negligent conduct in failing to provide a safe workplace, improperly storing toxic chemicals, failing to warn workers of known dangers, and subsequently destroying the poisons which prevented proper diagnosis and treatment of the injuries from toxic exposure. The action is therefore properly filed under the FTCA.

Moreover, the action is timely under the FTCA. As alleged in the complaint, on August 26, 1997, Plaintiffs filed claims with the United States Navy. AA 4. The United States Navy failed to finally dispose of these claim within six months after their submission. Indeed, to date Defendant has never denied Plaintiffs' claims. *Id.* Since the statutory period has expired, Plaintiffs are entitled to deem their claims denied and to proceed with this civil action. 28 U.S.C.A. § 2675(a). In fact, Defendant agrees that this action is timely under the FTCA. AA 8.

II
ADMIRALTY JURISDICTION DOES NOT ATTACH BECAUSE REMOVING ASBESTOS DOES NOT CREATE A MARITIME HAZARD AND IS NOT A MARITIME ACTIVITY

Defendant moved to dismiss the action on the grounds that it was barred by the admiralty statute of limitations. As the United States Supreme Court has most recently explained, the party seeking to invoke admiralty jurisdiction must show that the incident at issue has a connection with maritime activity. *Jerome B. Grubart, Inc. v. Great Lakes Dredge & Dock Co.*, 513 U.S. 527, 534 (1995). To find this connection, the court must first conclude that the type of incident involved has a "potentially disruptive impact on maritime commerce." *Id.* at 538–539. If so, the court must then find that the activity giving rise to the incident has a substantial relationship to a traditional maritime activity. *Id.* at 539. Defendant failed to meet either of these requirements. Because Defendant has failed to establish any basis for admiralty jurisdiction, Plaintiffs' action is not barred by the admiralty statute of limitations.

    A. Admiralty jurisdiction does not attach because Plaintiffs' injuries suffered during asbestos removal on a dry-docked vessel posed no threat to maritime commerce.

To invoke maritime jurisdiction, Defendant must establish a maritime connection by showing that "the incident involved was of a sort with the potential to disrupt maritime commerce." *Jerome B. Grubart, Inc. v. Great Lakes Dredge & Dock Co.*, 513 U.S. 527, 538 (1995). As the following discussion will show, the Defendant failed to meet this threshold maritime connection requirement.

In *Grubart*, the United States Supreme Court reaffirmed and clarified the admiralty connection requirement. There, a dredging company weakened an underground tunnel by negligently driving piles into the riverbed from a barge on the Chicago River. The weakened tunnel collapsed and the river flowed through the tunnel to buildings along the Chicago Loop. The flood victims sued in state court for damages. The dredging company sued in federal court seeking the protection of a statutory liability limit which applies in admiralty jurisdiction. The issue before the Court was whether admiralty jurisdiction applied to claims that the dredging company's negligent pile driving in the navigable waters of the Chicago River caused the flood damage.

5

The Court found that admiralty jurisdiction governed the action because the incident had a sufficient maritime connection. As the Court explained, the connection test turns on whether the "general features" of the incident were "likely to disrupt commercial activity." *Id.* at 538. Applying that approach to the facts before it, the Court concluded that the incident had a "potentially disruptive effect on maritime commerce" because the damage to the structure below the riverbed closed the river for more than a month, ceasing river traffic including both passenger ferries and commercial barges. *Id.* at 539. The Court pointed to numerous other cases applying admiralty jurisdiction where damaged underground structures threatened to disrupt and indeed disrupted commercial activity on navigable waters. *Id.*

The facts of the present case should be contrasted to those in *Grubart*. Here, four land-based workers were briefly exposed to toxic fumes from air-conditioning chemicals stored in a few barrels in a sealed room on a dry-docked vessel. After their exposure, a local ambulance was summoned and the workers were treated at the emergency room of a local hospital. This incident posed no threat to maritime commerce and caused no disruption of commercial activity. Thus, the incident involved in this case fails to meet the *Grubart* maritime connection requirement.

In reaffirming the maritime connection requirement, the *Grubart* Court relied on *Sisson v. Ruby*, 497 U.S. 358 (1990). In *Sisson*, a fire started on a docked pleasure craft and then spread to neighboring boats and the marina. The owners of the marina and other vessels sued the owner of the boat where the fire had started. The defendant sought to invoke admiralty jurisdiction to limit liability. The Seventh Circuit concluded that admiralty jurisdiction did not attach although it recognized that the fire threatened the disruption of maritime commerce. The Supreme Court agreed to review the case and reversed the decision.

To determine whether admiralty jurisdiction attached, Justice Marshall focused on the hazard to maritime commerce, tracing this theme through the most recent admiralty decisions and the historical purposes underlying admiralty jurisdiction. *Id.* at 2895–2896, citing *Executive Jet Aviation, Inc. v. City of Cleveland*, 409 U.S. 249 (1972) (an aircraft sinking in the water could create a hazard for the navigation of commercial vessels) and *Foremost Ins. Co. v. Richardson*, 457 U.S. 668 (1982) (a collision at the mouth of the St.

Lawrence Seaway could disrupt commercial traffic). While declining to hold that navigation was the sole activity to confer admiralty jurisdiction, the Court stressed that "[t]he fundamental interest giving rise to maritime jurisdiction is 'the protection of maritime commerce.'" *Sisson* at 367.

In determining whether the *Sisson* accident implicated maritime commerce, the Court observed that a fire on a vessel moored at a marina on a navigable waterway could spread to other vessels or make the marina inaccessible. As the Court stated, "Indeed, fire is one of the most significant hazards facing commercial vessels." *Id.* at 362. This hazard had in fact materialized in the *Sisson* case since the fire had spread to the marina and to other vessels moored nearby. As the *Sisson* Court explained, "a fire on a vessel docked at a marina on navigable waters... plainly satisfies the requirement of potential disruption to commercial maritime activity." *Id.* at 362.

The *Sisson* case provides helpful guidance in the present action. To determine whether the injuries resulted from a traditional maritime activity, we must focus on whether the incident satisfies "the requirement of potential disruption to commercial maritime activity." *Id.* at 362. Here land-based asbestos workers ripped out asbestos on the Enterprise while it was in a graving dry-dock for major renovations. Defendant failed to provide Plaintiffs a safe workplace for asbestos removal and failed to warn them about the toxic chemicals negligently stored in the workplace. Maritime commerce was never threatened by this localized exposure of land-based asbestos workers to toxins on a dry-docked ship. Under *Sisson*, since the activity posed no threat to navigation or to maritime commerce, admiralty jurisdiction does not attach.

In short, the United States Supreme Court has recently reaffirmed the requirement of establishing a maritime connection to invoke admiralty jurisdiction. In this case, Defendant failed to meet this requirement since the incident which injured Plaintiffs posed no threat to disrupt maritime commerce. Since admiralty jurisdiction does not apply, the action is not barred by the admiralty statute of limitations.

B. Admiralty jurisdiction does not attach because asbestos removal is not a traditional maritime activity.

In addition to failing to show a threat to maritime commerce, Defendant also failed to meet the second prong of the connection test which requires that the incident involve a traditional maritime activity. Indeed, this Court has repeatedly and consistently held that admiralty jurisdiction does not attach to actions by asbestos-removal workers injured while working on dry-docked vessels because asbestos removal is not a traditional maritime activity. *Myhran v. Johns-Manville Corp.*, 741 F.2d 1119 (9th Cir. 1984); *Martinez v. Pacific Industrial Service Corporation*, 904 F.2d 521 (9th Cir. 1990).

The starting point for analysis is the most recent Supreme Court decision explaining the maritime activity test, *Jerome B. Grubart, Inc. v. Great Lakes Dredge & Dock Co.*, 513 U.S. 527, 538 (1995). According to the Court, the question is "whether the tortfeasor's activity...on navigable waters is so closely related to activity traditionally subject to admiralty law that the reasons for applying special admiralty rules would apply." *Id.* at 539–540. Activities which satisfy this test include navigating boats, storing them at a marina on navigable waters, repairing a vessel on a navigable waterway, but not flying an airplane over the water. *Id.* at 540. The Court emphasized that the test requires that "at least one alleged tortfeasor was engaging in activity substantially related to traditional maritime activity." *Id.* at 541.

This maritime activity test has been applied by this Court to the exact activity at issue in this case—asbestos removal. *Myhran v. Johns-Manville Corp.*, 741 F.2d 1119 (9th Cir. 1984). In *Myhran*, as in this action, a U.S. Navy ship was being renovated and repaired in dry dock. The *Myhran* court considered whether injuries suffered by land-based workers while making asbestos repairs on a ship were subject to admiralty jurisdiction. Specifically, Myhran was a pipefitter whose job required him to remove insulation materials before working on pipes. *Id.* at 1120. As this Court explained, although admiralty jurisdiction historically depended solely on the locality of the wrong, the United States Supreme Court has rejected the locality test and now requires a showing that the tort claim has a sufficient nexus to traditional maritime activities. *Id.* at 1121.

The *Myhran* court then analyzed whether asbestos removal satisfied the maritime activity test, noting that "the inquiry...must be based upon the work actually performed by the injured worker." *Id.* at 1122. This Court pursued the inquiry by applying the four factors developed in *Owens-Illinois, Inc. v. United States District Court*, 698 F.2d 967 (9th Cir. 1983).

The first factor is the history and purpose of admiralty law. The *Myhran* court ruled that asbestos exposure during ship repairs did

8

not require the application of federal substantive law or the expertise of a court in admiralty as to navigation or water-based commerce. *Myhran* at 1122. The same is true in this action. Here, as in *Myhran*, Plaintiffs' chemical exposure during asbestos repairs has nothing to do with navigation or water-based commerce which are the traditional concerns of admiralty law. Moreover, neither the *Myhran* case nor the present action create the need for uniform standards tied to maritime concerns. Whether the workers are on a ship or in a building, safe working conditions for asbestos removal have no relationship to maritime activities and no implications for navigation and commerce.

Second, the *Myhran* court considered the plaintiff's occupational function and role. The court acknowledged that admiralty law extends to personal injury claims by seamen and others doing seamen's work but pointed out that the plaintiff was not a seaman and was not performing work traditionally done by seamen. The court cited with approval the *Owens-Illinois* case stating that "installing and cleaning up around the installation of asbestos is not a maritime role." *Myhran* at 1122. The same is true in the present action. Here, as in *Myhran*, the Plaintiffs were not seamen and were not performing seamen's work. Rather, Plaintiffs were performing asbestos work which is not a maritime role.

Third, the *Myhran* court considered the vehicles and instrumentalities involved in the plaintiff's activity. The *Myhran* court again relied on the *Owens-Illinois* case and quoted with approval the following observation: "While ships were obviously involved here, the tools and safety equipment (or lack thereof) present in the installation and clean-up of asbestos — unlike the navigational equipment and safety devices of a vessel — possess few maritime attributes." *Myhran* at 1122, quoting *Owens-Illinois*, 698 F.2d at 971. The observation is apt in the present case. The tools and safety equipment Plaintiffs used to rip out asbestos lack any maritime attributes. Plaintiffs use the same tools and safety equipment to rip out asbestos on ships in dry-dock that they use in buildings on dry land. AA 4.

The final factor considered was whether the asbestos exposure bore any inherent relationship to a maritime activity. The *Myhran* court noted that asbestos exposure was not a traditional maritime hazard and that thousands of land-based workers suffered the same injury. The same is true in the present case. Here, as in *Myhran*,

Plaintiffs were exposed to toxic chemicals from an air-conditioning unit, including freon, which are not exclusively or traditionally a maritime hazard.

In short, the *Myhran* court concluded from its four-factor analysis that the plaintiff's chemical exposure while removing asbestos was not subject to admiralty law since the maritime activity requirement was not satisfied. The same analysis demonstrates that Plaintiffs' toxic exposure while removing asbestos does not bear a significant relationship to traditional maritime activities and is therefore not subject to admiralty law.

The wisdom of the *Myhran* analysis is reflected by the numerous decisions of other circuit courts concluding that asbestos removal is not a maritime activity. Indeed, in addition to the Ninth Circuit, the First, Second, Third, Fourth, Fifth, Sixth, and Eleventh Circuits have all concluded that injuries suffered by land-based asbestos workers bear no significant relationship to traditional maritime activity. *Drake v. Raymark*, 772 F.2d 1007, 1016 (1st Cir. 1985); *Keene Corp. v. United States*, 700 F.2d 836 (2d Cir. 1983), *cert. denied*, 464 U.S. 864 (1983); *Eagle-Picher Ind. v. United States*, 846 F.2d 888, 896 (3d Cir. 1988), *cert. denied*, 488 U.S. 965 (1989); *Burnette v. Nicolet, Inc.*, 818 F.2d 1098, 1101–1102 (4th Cir. 1986); *Oman v. Johns-Manville Corp.*, 764 F.2d 224, 230 (4th Cir. 1985), *cert. denied*, 474 U.S. 970 (1985); *Woessner v. Johns-Manville Sales Corp.*, 757 F.2d 634, 646 (5th Cir. 1985); *Petersen v. Chesapeake and Ohio Ry. Co*, 784 F.2d 732, 736 (6th Cir. 1986); *Harville v. Johns-Manville Prod. Corp.*, 731 F.2d 775, 783–787 (11th Cir. 1984).

Defendant attempts to gloss over the *Myhran* Court's ruling by labeling Plaintiffs as "ship repair workers" and from that label concluding that "all parties have direct involvement with traditional maritime activity." AA 18. This conclusion is wrong for two reasons: (1) as a matter of fact, Plaintiffs were asbestos removal workers, not ship repair workers; and (2) as a matter of law, asbestos removal—unlike ship repair—is not a traditional maritime activity.

First, the complaint alleges that Plaintiffs were land-based asbestos removal workers, not ship repair workers. Plaintiffs were all members of the Insulators and Asbestos Workers Union, Local 16. AA 2. Seamen never performed the work required by this asbestos removal subcontract. AA 3. Plaintiffs used the same tools and performed the same tasks in ripping out the asbestos on the Enterprise as on jobs on dry land. AA 4.

Second, the law distinguishes asbestos removal from ship repair for purposes of admiralty jurisdiction. *Martinez v. Pacific Industrial Service Corporation*, 904 F.2d 521 (9th Cir. 1990). In *Martinez*, a worker sued for injuries he sustained while cleaning a boiler tube. Focusing on traditional maritime activities, this Court explained that Martinez performed work that was both routinely and essentially necessary to the operation of the vessel as part of the rhythm of maintaining the ship as a functioning vehicle. *Id.* at 524–525. This Court stressed that the product (a pump) which caused the injury was used with a manual which was specially prepared for the Navy. *Id.* According to the Court, Martinez's "work bore directly on the function of a vessel and had an intimate connection with maritime commerce." *Id.* at 525. The *Martinez* Court contrasted the work performed by Martinez with the work of asbestos workers: "Unlike the asbestos-installer or the pipefitter removing asbestos, what Martinez did was work traditionally linked with the sea." *Id.* at 524.

In short, Defendant attempts to blur the distinction this Court has carefully delineated between workers who perform tasks intimately connected with the functioning of the vessel and land-based workers who perform tasks which have no traditional maritime nexus. The first group is limited to maritime specialists who perform work traditionally performed by seamen which are connected with maritime commerce. *Martinez v. Pacific Industrial Service Corporation*, 904 F.2d 521 (9th Cir. 1990). The second group includes land-based asbestos workers, including Plaintiffs in this action. *Myhran v. Johns-Manville Corp.*, 741 F.2d 1119 (9th Cir. 1984). This Court's careful distinction should be reaffirmed because asbestos removal is not a traditional maritime activity, does not bear on maritime commerce, and therefore does not justify the invocation of admiralty jurisdiction. *Myhran v. Johns-Manville Corp.*, 741 F.2d 1119 (9th Cir. 1984); *Owens-Illinois, Inc. v. United States District Court*, 698 F.2d 967 (9th Cir. 1983).

In short, this Court has repeatedly and consistently held that admiralty jurisdiction does not attach where land-based asbestos removal workers seek damages for personal injuries because their work fails the traditional maritime activity test. For this reason, the District Court erred in holding that admiralty jurisdiction attaches to the present action.

Conclusion

To invoke admiralty jurisdiction, Defendant must establish that the incident at issue posed a threat to maritime commerce and that it involved a traditional maritime activity. Neither test has been satisfied. First, maritime commerce was not threatened by the isolated exposure of four land-based workers to leaky chemical barrels in a sealed room on a dry-docked vessel. Second, asbestos removal is not a traditional maritime activity. Since admiralty jurisdiction does not apply to this action, the judgment should be reversed and the case remanded for a trial under the Federal Tort Claims Act, 28 U.S.C.A. §§ 1346(b), 2671 et seq.

Dated: March 25, 1998   Respectfully submitted,
                             MASON & VAN OWEN

_____

Robin Brennan
Counsel for Plaintiffs/Appellants

12

Chapter 12

Rewritten Appellate Brief

Your final assignment is to revise, edit, and polish your appellate brief. As you have learned, the revision process begins by reviewing the substance and large-scale organization of the document. The second step is to review each paragraph. The third step is to edit the draft both to improve readability and to polish the tone and style. This chapter discusses two more plain English lessons and provides a few more suggestions for persuasive writing. Finally, proofread your brief carefully.

Rewrite Your Brief

Reconsider the content

In the Book of Genesis, God created the world in 400 words, and the Declaration of Independence launched the American Revolution in 1321 words.[1] These spare writings get to the point and stick to it. Your brief should do the same. As experts have observed, "Winning briefs are puny things — not comprehensive, but focused. A judge can carry one home in a coat pocket."[2] Judges find the quality of a brief to be inversely proportionate to its length and urge lawyers to present their strongest case in a couple of pages.[3] The trick is to select your best arguments and forsake all others.[4] Marginal argu-

---

1. Marson v. Jones & Laughlin Steel Corp., 87 F.R.D. 151, 152 n. 1 (E.D. Wis. 1980).

2. Mark Herrman & Katherine B. Jenks, *Great Briefs and Winning Briefs*, 19 LITIG. 56 (1993).

3. Carla F. Black, Esq., STUDENT LAW. , Apr. 1991, at 36.

4. Herrman & Jenks, *supra* note 2, at 57.

ments waste space, distract the court, and undermine your credibility. As you review your brief, consider whether you have exercised discipline and judgment by eliminating weak arguments and focusing on the winners.

After pruning your arguments, review chapter 11, and check the content of each section of your brief. Have you included all the required sections and satisfied the appellate rules? Does the table of contents persuasively summarize your argument? Does the table of authorities properly cite every authority and list every page on which it appears? Have you explained the basis of subject matter and appellate jurisdiction? Does the issue statement frame the primary legal issue(s) in terms of the facts of your case? Does the statement of the case include: (1) the nature of the case, course of proceedings, and disposition below; and (2) an orderly statement of facts? Does the argument summary acquaint the reader with the major arguments and the key supporting authorities? Do your point headings provide the structure of your argument? Do they tie the law to the facts and compel conclusion in your favor? Have you included all the relevant authorities? Have you thoroughly presented them (facts, procedure, holding, and rationale)? Have you applied them to our case? Have you anticipated your opponent's arguments and refuted them? Are you persuaded by your analysis? Have you included a brief conclusion stating the precise relief sought?

Revise the large-scale organization

Once you're satisfied with the content of your brief, consider its large-scale organization. While appellate rules impose many formal constraints, you have flexibility within the argument section. Outline the argument by highlighting the topic sentences. Does each section of the argument have an introduction and a conclusion? Have you used placement to emphasize your strongest authorities? Is the structure of your argument logical and persuasive?

Review each paragraph

After the large-scale revision, check each paragraph. Does every sentence develop the paragraph's topic? Is each paragraph a readable length? Break up the long ones and combine the choppy ones. Have you provided transitions between paragraphs?

Edit Your Brief

This week, you'll study two new lessons from *Plain English for Lawyers*.[5] The first teaches how to avoid distracting language quirks. The second explains why lawyers distrust punctuation, why you should learn to punctuate carefully, and how to do so. Finally, we'll consider a few more suggestions for persuasive writing.

Avoid language quirks

In Chapter 8 of *Plain English for Lawyers*, Richard Wydick teaches us to avoid several common language quirks. Two of these quirks are particularly distracting: elegant variation and sexist language. Elegant variation is the practice of using a synonym instead of repeating a word. But the reader is never sure whether the synonym is selected to indicate a distinction or just for fun. For example, instead of repeating the word "contract" the writer provides variety by using the words "agreement," "understanding," and "covenant." But the reader is confused. Are we talking about one contract or three different documents? A simple rule solves this problem: If you mean the same thing, use the same word. While elegant variation may baffle your reader, sexist language will infuriate her. Avoiding sexist language takes some thought, but can be done without resorting to the cumbersome pairing of "he and she" at every turn. Wydick provides many useful suggestions.

Another language quirk is the use of "as such" to vaguely connect ideas without regard to their specific relationship. This usage is both confusing and wrong. As one commentator explains: "*As such* should always refer to an antecedent noun (either a person or a thing), and it means either 'as being the person or thing previously referred to,' or 'in that capacity,' or 'in or by themselves.' "[6] For example:

> The Academic Senate, as such, is responsible for establishing educational policy for the University.

> The corporation, as such, is vicariously liable for the acts of its employees within the course and scope of employment.

---

5. Richard C. Wydick, Plain English for Lawyers (4th ed. 1998).
6. *The Punctuated Lawyer*, Fed. Law. , Mar.–Apr. 1995, at 44.

Punctuate carefully

Punctuation affects both readability and meaning. Wydick provides a concise guide in Chapter 9 of *Plain English for Lawyers* which shows you how to handle those mischievous commas and puzzling semicolons. Study it before rewriting your brief. As you rewrite your brief, pay special attention to commas and apostrophes. Be sure you check for contractions. While contractions can give letters and informal documents a conversational tone, they should only be used in formal court documents when included in a direct quotation.

Be persuasive

We now turn to three new suggestions for improving the persuasiveness of your brief: (1) be diplomatic in criticizing judges; (2) qualify only when necessary; and (3) use figures of speech cautiously.

Criticize judges diplomatically

In your first draft, you may call the trial court judge all kinds of nasty names. When you rewrite it, get over your anger and use your head. The judge reading your appellate brief may have just returned from a camping trip with the judge you are attacking. Your attack on a friend will turn the court against you. The same rule of diplomacy applies when your are distinguishing decisions that hurt your case. If you rely on a case written by a well-respected and universally-beloved judge, you may wish to use a judge's name to enhance your credibility. But the safer practice is to focus on the law, not the judge.

Qualify only when necessary

Often to be accurate you must make qualified statements. But unnecessary qualifiers and equivocations weaken your arguments. Make absolute statements whenever you can. Similarly, state your point of law as the law, not as an argument or a contention. For example, assume you represent a landlord in an action brought by a tenant who was attacked in her apartment. This is the first crime that ever occurred on the premises. From your research, you've concluded that all cases imposing liability on landlords have relied on a prior crime on the premises to establish the foreseeability of future crimes.

Don't write: It would seem to appear that the courts have never imposed liability on a landlord absent prior crimes on the premises.

Don't write: It is our contention that the courts have never imposed liability on a landlord absent prior crimes on the premises.

Don't write: It can be argued that the courts have never imposed liability on a landlord absent prior crimes on the premises.

Write: The courts have always required a prior crime on the premises before imposing liability on the landlord.

Write: A landlord has never been held liable for an intruder's crimes absent prior crimes on the premises.

Use figures of speech cautiously

Colorful figures of speech can make your writing fresh and lively. Great legal writers are often remembered for their apt use of similes, metaphors, and other figures of speech. For example, when Oliver Wendall Holmes explained the fundamental difference between intentional and unintentional conduct, he wrote: "Even a dog distinguishes between being stumbled over and being kicked."[7] And Abraham Lincoln summed up voter responsibility by stating:

> It is the people's business. The election is in their hands. If they turn their backs to the fire and get scorched in the rear, they'll find they have got to sit on the blister.[8]

Literature is one source of figures of speech. A good book of quotations will often provide a memorable way to express an elusive thought. The quotation need not be from legal sources. After all, we've all learned valuable lessons from Winnie the Pooh. Myths, fables, fairy tales, and poetry are all possibilities. For the beginner, however, the safest source is probably legal literature; excellent books of legal quotations are available. Be very selective. Make sure any quotation you include is concise, that its relevance is immedi-

---

7. HENRY WEIHOFEN, LEGAL WRITING STYLE 116 (2d ed. 1980).
8. *Id.* at 118.

ately clear, and that it makes the point better than you ever could. After all, over-used or inapt quotations will irritate your busy reader. Indeed, because quotations use up precious space and may annoy the court, some appellate specialists advise you to avoid them altogether.[9]

If you can't find an apt quotation, perhaps you can come up with your own fresh comparisons as Wydick does in *Plain English for Lawyers*. One of my favorites is the comparison of semicolons to poisonous mushrooms: "Some writers put semicolons and wild mushrooms in the same category: some are nice, and some are not, and since it is hard to tell the difference, they should all be avoided."[10]

Just as Wydick uses analogies to teach punctuation, trial lawyers use them to persuade juries. For example, one lawyer represented several families who lived near an ammonia factory plagued with frequent leaks. Because the factory had no monitor and no alarm, night time gas leaks continued to flood the neighborhood until someone telephoned the factory manager, who then drove over to shut off the leak. In closing argument, the lawyer reminded the jury of the days when canaries were released into coal mines to detect poison gas. Since canaries were expendable, they were an effective and cheap warning system. The lawyer argued that the ammonia company used its neighbors like the coal miners used canaries. In explaining their record punitive damages award, several jurors repeated the canary analogy.

But be careful. Trite expressions, mixed metaphors, and awkward comparisons are boring, confusing, and annoying. As Henry Weihofen explained: "There are dangers in using figures of speech. They must be used with discrimination and restraint."[11] Hmmm . . . like wild mushrooms.

---

9. Michael H. Rubin, *Better Appellate Brief Writing*, *In Brief*, Great (Or At Least Really Effective) Legal Writing for Litigators and Appellate Law., 1996 A.B.A. Sec. Litig. 25.
10. Wydick, *supra* note 5, at 95.
11. Weihofen, *supra* note 7, at 119.

Proofread Your Brief

It's 4:30 p.m. on Thursday afternoon. The judge had a root canal in the morning and spent most of the afternoon in criminal motion hearings. With a groan, the judge turns to the stack of nearly 100 briefs to read that month and selects your brief.[12] It looks pretty good; it has the right color cover, it's double-spaced, it's in 14 point type, it has wide margins, and it's within the page limits. The judge starts reading. The table of contents lays out the structure of the argument and summarizes a few carefully selected issues by tying the key legal points to the facts of the case. The judge thinks, "This isn't too bad. Maybe I can slog through it without nodding off." The judge checks for jurisdiction, is satisfied, and moves on to the issue statement: Whether the defendant was illegal arrested based on an uncorroborated tip from an paid police informant. The judge winces at "illegal arrested" and scowls at "an paid informant." Although these errors would have eluded the most sophisticated spell-checking program, the judge spots them immediately. Reading an error-laden brief is like listening to someone with bad hiccups — pretty soon the reader starts timing the hiccup intervals instead of listening to what the speaker is trying to say. Proofread.

---

12. According the Hon. Harry Pregerson, each judge on the Ninth Circuit hears 20–30 cases per month. In addition to these 60–90 briefs, the judges read excerpts of records, case authorities, and parts of reporters' transcripts, as well as civil and criminal motions. Hon. Harry Pregerson, *The Seven Sins of Appellate Brief Writing and Other Transgressions*, 34 UCLA L. Rev. 431, 433–434 (1986). Judge Frank M. Coffin estimated that federal circuit court judges read 1,000–2,000 pages of briefs and listen to 25–30 arguments in the same week. Hon. Frank M. Coffin, *Our Appellate Advocacy*, The Docket 1, Summer 1987. State court justices are equally burdened. According to one commentator, state supreme courts may hear 10 arguments and read 30 to 40 briefs in a single week. At 30–50 pages per brief, that comes to 900–2000 pages per week. Mark Rust, *Mistakes to Avoid on Appeal*, A.B.A. J., Sept. 1988, at 78.

Rewriting Checklist for an Appellate Brief

I. Rewriting

    A. Reconsider the content:

        1. Have you included all the sections required by the appellate rules?

        2. Does your table of contents persuasively summarize your arguments?

        3. Does your table of authorities properly cite every authority and list every page where it appears?

        4. Have you provided the basis for subject matter and appellate jurisdiction?

        5. Does your issue statement focus on the precise legal issue on appeal in terms of the facts of your case?

        6. Does your statement of the case include the nature of the case, course of proceedings, and disposition below?

        7. Does your statement of the case include a statement of facts which is clear, complete, and interesting?

        8. Does your summary of the argument cite key authorities and explain their application to your case?

        9. Do your point headings provide a roadmap of your argument tying the legal points to the facts of your case?

        10. Does your argument address the standard of review for each issue?

        11. Have you included all necessary authorities, both welcome and unwelcome?

        12. Have you thoroughly and persuasively presented them including the facts, procedure, holding, and rationale of each case?

        13. Have you applied the authorities to your problem?

        14. Have you considered policy arguments?

        15. Have you anticipated counter-arguments and rebutted them?

        16. Have you synthesized your analysis?

B. Revise the large-scale organization:

1. Have you included introductory paragraphs to each section of the argument?

2. Can you outline your brief using topic sentences?

3. Is the organization persuasive?

   a. Did you open with your strongest argument and most persuasive authority?

   b. Did you sandwich weak points and unwelcome authorities in the middle?

   c. Did you end with a strong argument?

4. Have you provided conclusions to each section of the argument?

C. Review each paragraph:

1. Does each paragraph have a topic sentence?

2. Do the other sentences develop the topic?

3. Have you checked paragraph length?

4. Have you provided transitions?

II. Editing

A. Edit each sentence:

1. Have you written short sentences?

2. Have you omitted surplus words?

3. Have you used base verbs?

4. Have you preferred the active voice?

5. Have you adopted conventional legal usage?

6. Have you arranged your words with care?

7. Have you chosen your words with care?

8. Have you avoided language quirks?

9. Have you punctuated your brief carefully?

B. Use quotations sparingly:

1. Have you avoided block quotations?

2. Have you edited quotations carefully?

C. Use persuasive writing techniques:
1. Have you been respectful?
2. Have you been subtle?
3. Have you been positive?
4. Have you avoided clichés?
5. Have you arranged your words for emphasis?
6. Have you used concrete words to emphasize and abstract words to minimize?
7. Have you used parallelism?
8. Have you been diplomatic in criticizing judges?
9. Have you qualified only when necessary?
10. Have you used figures of speech cautiously?

III. Proofreading
A. Have you checked for grammatical errors?
B. Have you checked for spelling and punctuation errors?
C. Have you checked for proper citation form?